THE
Common Sense
Guide
TO
Mental Health
Care

THE
Common Sense
Guide
TO
Mental Health
Care

CHRISTINE AMMER

with

NATHAN T. SIDLEY, M.D.

The Lewis Publishing Company
Lexington, Massachusetts
Brattleboro, Vermont

First Edition

This book was manufactured in the United States of America. It is designed by Irving Perkins Associates and published by The Lewis Publishing Company, Fessenden Road, Brattleboro, Vermont 05301.

Library of Congress Cataloging in Publication Data

Ammer, Christine.
   The common sense guide to mental health care.
   Includes index.
   1. Mental health services.   2. Psychotherapy.
3. Mental illness.   I. Sidley, Nathan T., 1929-II. Title.
RA790.A56 1982   362.2   82-14850
ISBN 0–86616–020–5
ISBN 0–86616–019–1 (pbk.)

Contents

Therapy Works — Transactional Analysis
(T.A.) — Encounter Groups and Marathons —
"Eclectic" Therapy

What Are Psychoactive Drugs? — Antianxiety
Drugs (Tranquilizers) — Antidepressants —
Antimanic Drugs — Antipsychotic Drugs —
Drugs for Hyperactivity — Antialcoholism Drugs

"Shock" Therapy — Electroconvulsive Therapy
(ECT) — Nutritional Therapy — Other Physical
Therapies — Surgery

The History of Asylums — Who Should Be
Hospitalized? — Kinds of Inpatient Facility —
Crisis Intervention/Brief Treatment —
Intermediate Treatment/Two to Nine Weeks —
Milieu Therapy — Private Mental Hospital vs.
General Hospital — The State or County Mental
Hospital — Veterans Administration (VA)
Hospitals — Residential Facilities for Children —
Nursing Homes — How to Pick A Hospital —
Leaving the Hospital: Aftercare — Partial
Hospitalization — Residential Aftercare

Goals of Treatment — The Therapy Contract —
What About Group Therapy? — Is Your
Therapy Working? — Resistance — When Is
Therapy Finished? — Evaluating Somatic
Therapies — ECT — Evaluating A Hospital —
Evaluating Children's Programs

PREFACE

In recent years more and more people have become involved with mental health services of one kind or another, ranging from special education in the school classroom to support groups of various kinds offered by clinics, churches, or other organizations, from counseling for short-term temporary problems to hospitalization for more serious illness. They may find themselves involved both directly, when they or their relatives or friends seek treatment, and indirectly, as a matter of public interest. Mental health care is one of the largest health expenditures in both federal and state budgets. In addition to personal and humanitarian concerns, therefore, it has become an important issue, politically, economically, judicially, and financially.

As consumers and citizens we can only behave intelligently and safely when we understand the issues and the alternatives. Even in a time of personal crisis there often are choices we can and should make in our own best interest. Yet where mental health services are concerned, a number of factors conspire against us as consumers. First, there is lingering public prejudice against mental health problems, leading to fear and shame that we will be considered "crazy" or "unstable" or even worse, which may keep us from asking necessary and perfectly legitimate questions. Second, traditional methods of psychiatry call for giving very little information to patients lest it interfere with the healing process, and to some extent the reluctance to disclose basic facts and opinions persists among many practitioners. Third, knowledge about the human mind is not yet (and probably never will be) a "hard" science, and therefore practitioners frequently disagree concerning just what is wrong with an individual and what treatment is appropriate. This does not mean such a person cannot be helped— far from it, many can be and are—but it can make the process of finding treatment bewildering and cumbersome. And finally, mental health practitioners, like other professionals, are apt to favor the methods and disciplines they know best, and to overlook or disdain others that may be equally effective.

For all these reasons we saw the need for an accurate, up-to-date, straightforward guide to mental health care. We begin, therefore, at the very beginning, by defining mental illness and describing how to get help

in an emergency. We go on to describe the signs of mental illness, the symptoms of the most common disorders, and how to get a professional evaluation. We suggest means of finding treatment, describe the qualifications of the many kinds of mental health practitioner—psychiatrists, analysts, counselors, social workers, etc.—and ways of choosing a therapist. We describe the most important of the many kinds of psychotherapy and how they work, how they differ, and which kinds are appropriate for which problems. We describe the various physical treatments—tranquilizers and other medication, shock treatment, vitamins. We describe hospitalization, the various kinds of facilities and what to look for in a hospital. We suggest ways you can evaluate treatment, how to tell whether or not it is effective, and the family's role. We devote chapters to insurance coverage and other financial concerns, to means of preventing mental illness, to its legal implications, and to the most recent research in the field, most of which is funded by our tax money.

Our emphasis throughout is on the consumer's viewpoint. You can only get good answers if you know what to ask, and how to evaluate the information you are given. We hope our guidelines make it easier to find one's way.

Profound gratitude is due to the many experts and friends who gave unstintingly of their time to answer questions and make invaluable suggestions, criticisms, and corrections. Among those who merit special thanks are Karen Ann Ammer, Research Assistant, Mental Health Policy Research Program, Woodrow Wilson School of Public and International Affairs, Princeton University; Cynthia P. Anderson, ACSW; Theodore Anderson, M.D., former Medical Director, Stoney Brook Counseling Center, and Assistant Clinical Professor of Psychiatry, Boston University Medical School; Maureen Burke-Green, R.N., Director, Arlington Branch, Mystic Valley Partial Hospitalization Program; Mary Fischelis, R.N., Psychiatric Nursing Coordinator, Emerson Hospital; Anne O. Freed, MSW, Director, Counseling Services, Family Service Association of Greater Boston, and Adjunct Professor of Social Work, Boston University School of Social Work; Marvin Goldfarb, Director, Home Care Services, Minuteman Home Care Corporation; Jon E. Gudeman, M.D., Center Director, Massachusetts Mental Health Center, and Associate Professor of Psychiatry, Harvard University Medical School; John G. Gunderson, M.D., Director of Psychotherapy, McLean Hospital, and Associate Professor of Psychiatry, Harvard University Medical School; James Harburger, M.D., Chief of Psychiatry, Cambridge Branch, Harvard Community Health Plan; Ber-

nie Jenkins, Director, Mental Health Association of Central Middlesex; Norine Johnson, Ph.D., Director, Psychology Department, Kennedy Memorial Hospital for Children; Rosemary Johnston, MSW, Director, CONTACT-Boston; Peter J. Lang, Ph.D., Research Professor of Clinical Psychology, University of Florida; Nancy Langman-Dorwart, R.N., Director of Consultation and Education, Mystic Valley Comprehensive Community Mental Health Center; Robert E. Larson, Jr., Executive Director, CONTACT Teleministries, U.S.A.; the Reverend Polly Laughland-Guild, Follen Community Church; John F. Morrall, M.D., Chief, Psychiatric Services, V.A. Outpatient Clinic, Boston; Anne Newton, National Council on Crime and Delinquency; Penelope Penland, Ph.D., clinical psychologist; Michael Singer, Ph.D., clinical psychologist, Eliot Community Mental Health Center; Fay Snider, MSW, Co-Director, Institute of Family Life and Learning; John J. Spillane, M.D., Assistant Director of Admissions and Evaluation Services, McLean Hospital; Joan Stewart, Center for Mental Health and Psychiatric Services, American Hospital Association; Harold N. Weiner, Family Service Association of America; Jerome Weinstein, Director, Divorce Resource and Mediation Center. This book has been vastly improved through their assistance; its errors and shortcomings are wholly the authors' responsibility.

Christine Ammer and
Nathan T. Sidley, M.D.

CHAPTER 1

Buying Mental Health Care

Health care is a commodity. We buy medical care in order to treat an illness or injury, to prevent an illness from becoming worse, or to maintain good health by making sure no undetected condition will undermine it. All but the last are true for mental health care, too. Most of us do not have regular mental health checkups comparable to regular physicals, but we probably should, and perhaps one day this will be common practice.

In the meantime, all of us are indirect buyers of mental health care. Millions of tax dollars are spent on it each year. In addition, an estimated thirty-four million Americans are direct consumers of mental health care, mostly in the form of one or another kind of psychotherapy.

Unlike other forms of health care, which rely heavily on products and equipment, mental health care is mainly a service industry. The bulk of expenditures is for services rendered by individual practitioners. With millions of dollars being spent, there should be lots of services provided, and in fact there are. The trouble is that they are hard to find and even harder to evaluate. Furthermore, just when we need mental health care services the most—when we are in emotional distress, sometimes in desperate straits—we are likely to be too distraught to make sensible decisions and choices.

Mental health care often has been described as a maze; even professionals frequently lose their way in it. There are no hard and fast rules for what service is most suitable for a particular client, or what treatment is most effective for a particular disorder. The stan-

dards for providers are murky, too. Literally anyone can hang out
a shingle saying "Counselor" or "Therapist" and undertake treatment, regardless of training or experience or competence. We would
not think of entrusting the care of our bodies to just anyone, and
we certainly should not do so with our minds.

The indications for buying mental health services are not very
clear-cut. It is a lot easier to distinguish between a small cut and a
large, festering wound than to tell if an emotional problem is mild
and self-limited or potentially serious and in need of professional
treatment.

Then, even if we decide we need treatment and can locate a
licensed professional to provide it, how do we know it's the best or
even the right treatment?

In order to find appropriate treatment for our problems and to
get our money's worth from the treatment, we need to know more.
We need to know when to seek help, what kinds of service are
available, how to find one appropriate for the particular problem
at hand, how much the service will cost, how to evaluate whether
or not a treatment is satisfactory. And, given the particular nature
of mental illness, we need to know our legal rights, too.

Mental illness is a frightening concept for most of us. That is all
the more reason to find some rational ways of deciding what might
be wrong and figuring out what to do about it.

NINE CASES

*Betty A., 47, has a medicine cabinet full of pills. At least once
a month she calls her family doctor, complaining of stomach
upsets, sleeplessness, backache, and a host of other ailments.
Her doctor rarely can find a physical cause for her symptoms
but each time suggests that she try some new medication. It
usually doesn't help for long.*

*John B., 25, lost his job last week after getting in a fist fight with
a fellow worker. It is the fourth time in less than a year that his
violent behavior has gotten him in trouble. This time the other
man, whose jaw he broke, is planning to sue him.*

Jane C., 68, has been grief-stricken since her husband died eighteen months ago. She weeps constantly, and lately she has been having more and more trouble remembering things. Last week she couldn't find her car after parking it at the shopping center; yesterday she went visiting and left her dinner on the stove, causing a small fire in her kitchen.

William D., 36, has quit his job, moved out of his family's suburban home to a high-rise apartment in the city, and is about to buy an expensive cabin cruiser. However, he hasn't enough in the bank to meet the payments on the family car, let alone buy any luxury items.

Kathy E., 17, refuses to eat, claiming she is far too fat. She has lost twenty-five pounds in the past two months and was, if anything, quite slender to start with.

Wanda F., 28, a housewife with three young children, is afraid to leave her house. One evening four months ago she went shopping for groceries while her husband took care of the children, and she found herself standing paralyzed in an aisle of the store, panic-stricken and unable to move. A neighbor who saw her helped her get home. Since then she has been seized with fear every time she plans to go out, and now she cannot even take her small children for a walk.

Donald G., 19, an A student in high school, dropped out of college during his freshman year and now spends all his time in his room at home, refusing to leave except for meals. He scarcely speaks to his family and has seen none of his former friends. His mother sometimes hears him talking behind his closed door, even though she knows he is alone and there is no telephone in the room.

Harry and Mary H., a couple in their thirties, quarrel constantly. They have two children, and Harry has two other children from two previous marriages. He has walked out on Mary several

*times, vowing he would not return. Their sex life has dwindled
to zero, and their older child, Mark, has begun to have terrible
temper tantrums and nightmares.*

*Stephen I., 10, is not doing well in his third-grade class, even
though he is repeating the grade. He has been allowed out for
recess only once all year, his teacher making him stay in because
of his disruptive and destructive behavior. He is sent to the
principal's office several times a week. The school now wants
to suspend him.*

These situations have a number of features in common:

- They are not unusual. Chances are you know one or more individuals who resemble one or more of these persons.
- A person is behaving markedly differently from those about him,
  or quite differently from his or her previous pattern. Donald was
  an excellent student in high school and functioned well enough
  to be admitted to college; Harry and Mary loved each other
  enough to marry and have two children; Jane had never "lost"
  her car before or started a fire.
- The person in question is suffering. Betty is in physical discomfort
  or pain much of the time; John suffers the humiliations of being
  fired and facing a lawsuit; Kathy hates her appearance; Stephen
  is miserable about constantly being punished.
- Those close to the person also are suffering. William's family may
  lose their car if he cannot meet payments, Stephen's and Kathy's
  parents are frantic with worry, Donald's mother doesn't know
  what to do about him.
- Financial cost is incurred, both directly and in lost productive
  capacity. The unemployment of John and William (and the consequent loss of purchasing power), the cost of a teacher's time in
  dealing with Stephen's problems, the postponement of income
  that Donald will earn after he completes his education, medical
  bills incurred by Betty and by Kathy's parents—all drain financial
  resources.
- Each of these situations represents a common mental illness.

WHAT IS MENTAL ILLNESS?

What actually is mental illness? It is *any one or more* of the following conditions persisting over a long period of time and to a marked degree, so that it adversely affects one's life:

1. An inability to learn or work, which cannot be explained by intellectual, sensory, or health factors.
2. An inability to build or maintain satisfactory personal relationships with family members, friends, and teachers or employers.
3. Inappropriate kinds of behavior or feelings under normal circumstances.
4. A general pervasive mood of unhappiness.
5. A tendency to develop physical symptoms or fears associated with personal or school or work problems.

Note, however, that all of us experience some of these conditions now and then. When we do, we are apt to say we are having a "problem." A so-called problem is regarded as a mental illness when it lasts long enough and is severe enough to interfere significantly with one's life.

Who Is Mentally Ill?

It can be anyone—your neighbor, your friend, your relative, you yourself. A mentally ill person doesn't necessarily look or act ill, at least not all the time. There are no barriers whatever. Age, education, income—none is a factor. Mental illness can affect two-year-olds and octogenarians, adults who are grade-school dropouts and those with advanced degrees, poor and rich, women and men.

In 1981 it was estimated that at least one of every seven Americans suffers from some form of mental disorder, ranging from mild to severe. Even with so many victims, there is substantial fear of and prejudice against mental patients.

THE STIGMA OF MENTAL ILLNESS

Few of us mind saying we don't feel well if something is physically wrong, but mental illness is not something we readily admit to.

Indeed, we avoid the very term. At best we regard mental illness as embarrassing; at worst it is shameful.

Like most prejudices, that against mental illness arises from misconception and myth. Some common ones are:

- Mental patients (or former patients) may become violent.
  THE TRUTH is that some severely ill individuals do behave violently and aggressively, but their proportion among mental patients is quite small. Most mentally ill persons are quiet and withdrawn.
- Mental illness is hereditary, and marrying into a family with mental illness makes it likely that your children will go crazy.
  THE TRUTH is that certain forms of mental illness do seem to have a genetic component, but we know very little about the mechanism of inherited mental disorders. When a parent has a mental illness, the children may or may not develop a mental illness; usually they do not.
- Mentally ill persons act crazy.
  THE TRUTH is that some do and many others don't. Many are able to function well enough so that their illness is not noticeable except to family members and close friends, and sometimes not even to them.
- Mental illness is incurable, and a person who has ever been treated for an emotional disturbance can never again be wholly trusted.
  THE TRUTH is that many mental illnesses can be cured, in the sense that the person never again has a serious mental disorder. Mental illness does not necessarily recur. In fact, about half of those ill enough to require hospitalization recover sufficiently so that they never again require any treatment (in or out of a hospital).

Prejudice makes us reluctant to describe ourselves or a friend or relative as "mentally ill." Instead we use such euphemisms as "troubled," "emotionally disturbed," "distressed," "having personal problems," or "needing help." These expressions, along with cruder terms such as "lunatic," "insane," "crazy," "mad," "nuts," and "nervous breakdown," all mean much the same thing: that a person has some kind of mental disorder, which may be mild or severe, short-lived or long-term.

A far worse result of prejudice is that it keeps some individuals from seeking treatment. Afraid to admit to a handicap, they do nothing about it, although many would greatly benefit from treatment.

Mental Illness Is Hard to Live With

When a person is physically ill we are inclined to make allowances, even when the illness causes us annoyance or difficulty of some kind, or when the patient acts grouchy or unpleasant. It is harder to remember that the mentally ill person, too, is suffering, and is just as much in need of understanding and support.

Mental illness often manifests itself in unpleasant ways. Among them are extreme lassitude and weariness ("I just can't seem to do it/make up my mind/get going; I just don't care"); belligerence and quarrelsomeness, with the ill person seeming always ready to pick a fight; exaggerated worry and anxiety over trifles; suspiciousness and mistrust ("Everyone is picking on me; they're out to get me"); extreme selfishness and self-absorption ("What's in it for me?"); and poor emotional control, with violent outbursts out of proportion to the cause and often at inappropriate times. Such behavior inevitably irritates others.

Consequently well-meaning relatives and friends may be tempted to scold or badger the ill person to change his or her behavior. But telling a mentally ill person to "snap out of it" or "shape up" is rarely helpful and may, by putting additional pressure on him or her, make matters worse. The behavior is part of the illness. Though a troubled person often can act normally for brief periods, over the long term he/she can no more change behavior at will than a man with pneumonia can clear his lungs on command. A depressed woman might smile when told to but she cannot change her underlying mood, no matter how hard she tries.

CAUSES OF MENTAL ILLNESS

Some mental impairments actually are physical illnesses, that is, they result from a demonstrable organic cause. This cause may lie in the brain itself or in some other part of the body. Brain tumors, endocrine disorders, cerebral vascular accident (stroke), multiple sclerosis, Huntington's chorea, vitamin B_{12} deficiency, and head injury are but some of the problems that can give rise to *organic mental illness*, with symptoms exactly like those of the *functional mental illnesses* for which no physical cause can be found. In some organic disorders removal of the underlying cause—correction of a hormone deficiency or removal of a tumor—eliminates the symptoms completely. For others no cure has yet been found.

Some organic brain disorders are genetic (inherited) in origin, others are environmental, and still others involve both genetic and environmental factors. Some inherited defects affect the brain only under particular environmental conditions. For example, phenylketonuria, an inherited deficiency of a particular enzyme, requires certain environmental conditions—specifically, the consumption of food containing an essential amino acid that the body cannot break down without this enzyme—to bring on brain damage. Other genetic defects affect the brain immediately, as in Down's syndrome, usually caused by the presence of an extra chromosome. Still others appear only late in life, among them Huntington's chorea.

Environmental causes of brain damage take many forms. Mental retardation and cerebral palsy often result from abnormalities in the fetal environment (as a baby develops in the womb) or that occur during the process of birth. A mother's exposure during pregnancy to drugs, alcohol, or other toxins, or to certain infections, such as rubella (German measles), may cause abnormal brain development in her baby. After birth, bacterial and viral infections, toxic chemicals both within and outside the body, and injury or disease that compromise the brain's blood supply all can lead to mental disorders.

During the past few decades there has been increasing evidence suggesting that certain of the most serious functional mental illnesses also have organic causes. Schizophrenia, manic-depressive disease, and major depression all tend to run in families, pointing to the possibility of a genetic component. Also, these very severe disorders are likely to respond to drugs, indicating that they may involve a biochemical derangement of some kind. Some experts believe that eventually all of the functional mental disorders will be found to have organic causes, or at least that certain individuals will be found to have a specific inborn predisposition to develop a mental illness. Others believe that most mental illnesses are primarily the product of learned behavior.

THE LANGUAGE OF MENTAL HEALTH CARE

More important to our understanding is the fact that, whatever their causes, mental illnesses express themselves in behavior, in how people think, act, and feel. Mental health professionals often say that when people behave appropriately they *adapt* well to circumstances; when they do not, their behavior is *maladaptive.* For example, feeling terror in the face of danger or grieving over the death of a loved one is a normal response. Feeling fear when there is no real danger or continuing to grieve unabatedly for many months after a loss is maladaptive.

Despite gaps in knowledge, mental health professionals have developed a terminology used to distinguish among different kinds of mental illness. The terms and the system of classification they represent are constantly changing as more is learned, but some continue to be in common use. The most severe disorders are referred to as *psychoses,* and their acute manifestations as *psychotic episodes.* They involve severe disturbances of thought, communication, memory, and emotion, in which a person may have trouble distinguishing fantasy from reality. They include schizophrenia, manic-depressive diseases, and acute (major) depression. Less crippling but just as distressing are *neuroses,* or *neurotic disorders,** characterized by unrealistic, inappropriate thoughts, feelings, or actions. While a

*DSM III, the most recent (1980) Diagnostic and Statistical Manual of the American Psychiatric Association, no longer uses "neurosis," but describes these disorders by their symptoms. However, the terms are still in common usage.

person undergoing a psychotic episode may not even realize that something is seriously wrong, the neurotic usually is troubled but unable to do anything about it. Other common classes of disorder are *substance addiction,* which includes drug addiction and alcoholism; *psychosomatic* or *somatoform disorders,* in which mental problems take the form of physical symptoms; and *personality* or *character disorders,* which include immature and irresponsible behavior that can lead to crimes of various kinds. (Specific disorders and their symptoms are discussed more fully in Chapter 4.)

Although much remains to be learned about the causes of their illness, many mentally ill persons can be successfully treated. First, however, one must be aware of the need for treatment. Before we go on to discuss how you can tell if something is wrong (Chapter 3), we must deal with those occasions when you know something serious is wrong and immediate help is needed—the psychiatric crisis or emergency.

CHAPTER 2

Help! Psychiatric Emergencies

Most mental illnesses, like physical illnesses, are not very dramatic. Just as there is a far greater incidence of common colds and stomach upsets than there is of pneumonia and heart attacks, so there are far more garden-variety emotional problems than psychiatric emergencies.

Sometimes, however, it is obvious that something must be done, and done fast. This situation is called an *emergency* or *crisis*.

Any acute psychiatric disorder can *become* an emergency, but the most serious are those that involve violence or the threat of violence. Violent behavior, or the threat of it, should *never* be overlooked.

WHO IS IN CRISIS?

The following are instances where immediate professional attention and counseling are required:

1. A person threatening him- or herself with death or injury.
2. A person threatening someone else with death or injury.
3. A person making a violent outburst against another person or against someone's property.
4. A victim of physical violence, whether inflicted by a family member or an outsider.
5. A victim of sexual assault.
6. A person behaving in a bizarre, incoherent, or disorganized manner—under the influence of drugs or alcohol.

11

7. A person undergoing an acute anxiety attack (see Chapter 4).

What should you do? If an individual is in immediate danger of personal harm or is threatening to commit suicide or hurt themselves badly, you must intervene at once and call for help.

Whom Do You Call?

If a person is threatening to injure someone else or someone's property, or is a victim of violent assault, call the *police.* The police usually cannot offer treatment of any kind, but they can temporarily restrain a violent person and they can supply transport to a hospital emergency room. For victims of violence, such as rape or child abuse, some police departments offer special services, including counseling. Calling the police may also provide the fastest help for a person clearly unable to take responsibility for his or her own safety—an individual running wildly into the street, ignoring on-coming traffic, or going outside half-naked in below-zero weather, or engaging in similar bizarre and potentially harmful behavior.

Suppose, however, that the person who needs help is neither in immediate physical danger nor presenting an immediate threat to others. Then whom do you call?

If there is time to seek advice concerning local resources, call your *family doctor,* or a private *mental health practitioner* you know (psychologist, psychiatrist, social worker), or the *clergy* (preferably your own pastor or rabbi). Any of these is apt to have experience with similar problems and be familiar with local hospitals, clinics, and other services. If none is available or able to make a recommendation, call any of the following:

1. The emergency ward of your local psychiatric hospital. They are well equipped to advise you.
2. The emergency service of your community mental health center. (If you don't know the name, look in the phone book white pages or yellow pages under Mental Health Center.) All such centers have a 24-hour telephone emergency line and can either offer help themselves or advise you where to call or go.

3. The emergency room of a nearby general hospital. (If you don't know the name, look in the phone book under Hospital.) If the hospital does not offer psychiatric emergency service itself, it can refer you to the nearest hospital that does. However, before you take yourself or someone else there, be sure to phone first so that the person is expected. Also, it is wise to ask how long a wait might be expected; if it's several hours, you may want to try to find another facility. Although procedures vary from hospital to hospital, a patient in psychiatric crisis is usually seen and evaluated by a psychiatrist, who either is part of the emergency room staff or, more often, simply on call. Since many emergency rooms do not have a psychiatrist or other mental health professional on duty round the clock, a wait of some time (minutes to hours) is to be expected.

4. A telephone hot line. Many areas have such services to provide advice if you are in crisis or you are helping someone else. Hot lines, manned twenty-four hours a day by volunteers, are likely to be listed in the phone book white pages under such listings as Contact, Crisis, Emergency, Help, Hotline, Suicide. If the problem is specifically drug- or alcohol-related, look in the phone book under Drug(s) or Alcohol(ics). If the crisis is related to Pregnancy or Rape, you may find help under either of these headings. If a young child has been injured by an adult, look under Child Abuse.

A hot line may refer you to a crisis center, usually one of the facilities listed above (hospital-connected). Such a center may offer overnight or brief hospitalization, usually in the emergency ward, with little or no red tape involved in being admitted or released.

If the person you are trying to help resists your assistance or refuses to go for help, you must use your own best judgment. If he/she is, in your opinion, a danger to self or others, you may have to call the police. If you believe there is a possible threat of such danger, you may want to point it out to a close relative of the person. If you yourself are a close relative, you may wish to consult other family members.

None of these decisions is easy, and there can be no hard and fast rules. If you are not sure what to do, or what your obligation is, you may want to seek advice from one of the professional sources listed above.

UNTIL HELP ARRIVES

What should you do in the meantime? Whatever the underlying cause of an outbreak of violent behavior, the person is usually prompted to act out of either rage or fear, which in turn comes from his/her sense of either extreme frustration or extreme help-lessness. It is unwise for you to aggravate these feelings by showing anger or contempt. Rather, remain as calm as possible and indicate your desire to help. If the person is endangering his/her own life, try to engage him or her in conversation, in talking rather than acting, until help can be summoned. If you yourself are being threat-ened or are in danger, leave as best you can, using your own judg-ment as to the safest way.

AND AFTERWARD

How does an emergency come about? An individual either has less and less ability to cope with life's ordinary stresses or is faced with an unusual stress so severe that he/she cannot handle it. Sometimes a relatively well-adjusted person is faced with an overwhelming disaster—the sudden accidental death of a loved one, for example— and requires temporary help in order to adjust to the tragedy. In other cases a crisis has no obvious cause; this usually means that a person has been ill for some time and the illness has progressed to the point where it must be treated. In effect the crisis is a call for help.

What happens afterward? That depends on the nature of the emergency, which often can be understood better by identifying the precipitating stress. If it was a catastrophe, such as one's house burning down with several family members killed or injured, coun-seling and other treatment may be needed until the person has adjusted well enough to function. If the crisis was brought on by an underlying mental illness that has become more severe, longer-term treatment may be required. Often, however, *crisis intervention* or *short-term treatment* (see Chapter 13), taking a week or less, may be all that is needed.

CHAPTER 3

Do You Need Help?
How Can You Tell?

How can you tell when you or someone you know needs help? How can you tell when symptoms are short-term and self-limiting—when, in effect, you have the psychiatric equivalent of a common cold that requires no special treatment other than rest and plenty of fluids and patience—or when you are on the verge of pneumonia and should be getting treatment?

You know this is not an emergency, yet you believe something may be wrong, and you are not really sure if there is, or what you should do.

Recently a famous psychiatric hospital ran an ad in a local paper. It was seeking volunteers to test the treatment of depression with a new drug. The ad called for individuals who felt depressed (or sad) and who had experienced at least five of the following eight symptoms:

- Sleeping too little or too much.
- Eating too little or too much.
- Agitation or being slowed down.
- Loss of interest or pleasure.
- Self-reproach or guilt.
- Difficulty thinking, concentrating, or making decisions.
- Fatigue or loss of energy.
- Feeling that life is not worth living.

We don't know how many responded, but it is probably safe to say that nine out of every ten persons over the age of fifteen have on occasion felt sad and experienced some—if not all—of these symptoms. Does that mean they are mentally ill? Does it mean they need treatment of some kind?

Not necessarily. One problem with many psychiatric symptoms is their subjective nature. How much sleep is too much? Or too little? In extreme instances, sleep can be monitored. But what about "loss of interest" or "pleasure"? Just what constitutes difficulty in making decisions?

Consider these two cases:

Dean R., 55, has changed his career five times in the past twenty years. His attic and garage are littered with the remains of discarded hobbies—elaborate photographic equipment, woodworking tools, ham radio equipment. Each year or two he takes up another hobby, or another occupation, but he soon becomes bored.

Is Dean's loss of interest or pleasure pathologic? does it represent "fatigue" or "loss of energy"? or "difficulty in making decisions"? Is he in fact suffering from depression?

Arthur S., 37, is now studying for a doctorate in computer science. He already has master's degrees in history and physics, and a doctorate in electrical engineering. Funded by scholarships and student aid, he has never held a job, not even a part-time position in any of his fields of study. Every time he completes his studies in one field he switches to another.

Is Arthur's status as a perpetual student symptomatic of mental illness? Or is he simply the eternal scholar in search of truth and knowledge?

IF YOU THINK YOU HAVE A PROBLEM, YOU MAY BE RIGHT

Suppose both Dean and Arthur decide to answer the hospital's advertisement. Is that significant? Yes, it may well be. When a person thinks something is seriously wrong, that feeling cannot be discounted. Most people do in fact know themselves fairly well, and they can discern changes in their mental functioning. A person looking for help usually does feel he or she is not functioning as well as before, or as well as possible, and that the situation has persisted long enough so it probably will not get better by itself.

Remember, also, that in general the sooner you seek treatment, the better the prospects for improvement. Just as a small infection is easier to cure than a massive one, so a minor mental disorder is more likely to respond to treatment than a major psychotic episode. If you feel persistently anxious without cause, or if you are too frightened to go out, it is time to get help now, not when you are so upset that hiding in a closet is the only comfortable alternative. Similarly, if you are grief-stricken or sad to the point of not caring what happens, get help now; don't wait until you are driven to try suicide.

EARLY WARNING SIGNS

Any of the following feelings or behavior that persists over a period of weeks or months and begins to interfere with other aspects of day-to-day living could be a signal that something is wrong:

- Sadness, either over a specific event (a death, job loss, marriage breakup) or for no reason.
- Hopelessness, demoralization, the sense that your life is out of control.
- Violent and erratic shifts of mood.
- Inability to concentrate or make decisions.
- Fear and anger because everything and everyone is against you.
- Trouble getting along with other people, in and out of the family; severe marital problems.
- Severe sleep disturbances (insomnia, nightmares).
- Sexual problems.
- Extreme fear of certain things or situations (dogs, airplanes, heights, crowds).

- Compulsive self-destructive behavior (overeating, drinking, gambling, drug abuse).
- Frequent physical complaints for which no medical cause can be found.

If you experience these symptoms or notice them in a relative or friend, it's worth getting (or suggesting that your friend seek) a professional opinion.

Bear in mind, however, that a perfectly competent mental health professional may not be able to tell for sure what is wrong. To a large extent, the diagnosis and prognosis of a mental illness—deciding what is wrong with someone and how (or if) the disorder will respond to treatment—are very much a matter of guesswork. Furthermore, some mental illnesses (sometimes even very severe ones, like acute depression) appear to cure themselves, running their course much as a common cold does.

Unlike a mild upper respiratory infection, however, a mental illness can cause considerable damage, and even death, before it subsides, and it is very difficult to predict which depressed person will get better and which will end up a suicide. Chances are that any mental illness severe enough to be noticed by family members or friends, or enough to make your life unsatisfying for a prolonged period, should at least be evaluated by an experienced professional.

GET A MEDICAL CHECKUP

Before you conclude that your problems are signs of mental illness, get a thorough medical checkup. It doesn't happen all that often, but every health practitioner knows at least one horror story about a patient who was treated for months for anxiety or hysteria or some other mental condition and then was found to have a brain tumor or other organic disease that was responsible for the bizarre symptoms. Most responsible practitioners are alert to this possibility and will recommend a medical workup for any patient whose symptoms are suspicious. But even the most conscientious can sometimes overlook this possibility, so to be on the safe side make an appointment for a thorough checkup with your family doctor or, if you have none, with a hospital outpatient clinic or similar facility. Be sure to report your "mental" symptoms to whoever performs the examination, so that he or she will not fail to order any special procedures, such as an electroencephalogram to measure brain-wave activity, that may be needed to rule out organic disease. Other special tests that may be required include a spinal tap, skull x-ray, blood tests, brain scan, and CAT scan (computerized body x-ray).

A WORD OF CAUTION

Suppose, now, that you or your relative or friend has been told that the physician can find no physical causes for concern or a need for treatment. Does this mean it is time to seek psychiatric help? Maybe.

Before we continue with a description of symptoms of the more common mental illnesses, a word of warning is in order. As every medical and nursing student soon discovers, when you are con-fronted with a list of symptoms it is very easy to imagine yourself suffering from any number of them. Consider these, for example: weakness, fatigue, increased pigmentation, weight loss. Many if not most medical students, given their rigorous schedule of classes and clinical studies, feel very tired, occasionally weak, and lose weight as a result of lack of sleep and irregular meals. If they also notice that they are getting more freckles (increased pigmentation), should they conclude that they have the beginnings of Addison's disease, a very serious endocrine disorder whose early symptoms were just described?

The same is even more true for readers of mental symptoms, which most often are subjective feelings rather than measurable, observable phenomena. Do not, therefore, be too quick to conclude that your teen-age daughter is clinically depressed or that you are "losing your mind." Diagnosis is not easy for expert practitioners. You yourself cannot become a diagnostic expert just by reading a book.

CHAPTER 4

What Could be Wrong?
Symptoms of Mental Illnesses

Unlike physical illness, which your doctor has now ruled out for you or your relative, mental disorders are rarely characterized by signs, but, rather, by symptoms. A *sign*, medically speaking, is objective evidence of disease that can be verified, such as a skin rash, rapid pulse, or high blood pressure. A *symptom* is subjective evidence that cannot necessarily be verified, such as a headache, insomnia, or nausea.

Symptoms and signs are what a physician uses to make a diagnosis. Though it is much harder to make a diagnosis when all the evidence (or much of it) is subjective, it can be done, but with necessarily less certainty. Groups of symptoms occurring together, called *syndromes*, usually are considered evidence of particular disorders.

The remainder of this chapter describes the most common mental illnesses and their symptoms: anxiety and phobias; obsessive-compulsive disorder; depression; suicide; manic-depressive disease; schizophrenia; somatoform (psychosomatic) disorders; eating disorders; alcoholism and drug abuse; personality disorders; disorders of old age (senile dementia). Mental disorders of children are discussed in Chapter 5.

ANXIETY

One of the most common psychiatric problems is anxiety, a feeling that all of us experience now and then. Apprehension and tenseness can be normal responses to anticipating a frightening situation, such as making an important speech or taking a crucial examination, just as fear is a normal response to the threat of danger. Whether or not anxiety is justified depends on when it occurs, how long it lasts, and how disabling it is.

To be acutely frightened when one's house catches on fire or the car's brakes fail to respond is perfectly reasonable. To continue to fear fire, to be frightened by the sound of sirens, to imagine one is smelling smoke—all these reactions may take place after undergoing such a terrifying experience. But to fear fire obsessively when one has never had a bad experience with it, or to react with increasing panic for many months afterward—these are not appropriate emotional reactions.

We usually use the word "fear" to describe a response to a realistic danger and "anxiety" or "panic" to describe the same response when it has no apparent objective cause. The feeling is the same, however—a sense of profound apprehension and dread:

Wanda F . . . found herself standing paralyzed in an aisle of the store, panic-stricken and unable to move. A neighbor who saw her helped her get home.

An episode of intense panic such as this is called an *anxiety attack*. Such attacks are often accompanied by physical symptoms, among them:

- Trembling.
- Faintness.
- Sweating.
- Hot and cold flashes.
- Tingling in the hands and/or feet.
- Dizziness.
- Palpitations (rapid heartbeat).
- Chest pain or constriction.
- Difficult or labored breathing.
- Choking or smothering sensation.

In addition, one may experience a sense of unreality, or the fear of impending calamity or death.

A person who experiences *at least four* of these symptoms *and* a sense of overwhelming panic is said to be having a full-fledged anxiety attack. (Actually, picking four symptoms as a requirement for such an episode is somewhat arbitrary. A person with three symptoms of disabling severity might be more disturbed than one with five in a milder form. Nevertheless, requiring four represents an attempt to establish some common ground for diagnosis, and it is useful provided one does not regard it as a hard-and-fast rule.)

Recurrent Anxiety and Phobias

An anxiety attack ordinarily lasts from a few minutes to an hour or so, usually depending on how quickly the feared object or situation can be avoided.

Occasionally such attacks represent an isolated instance. More often, however, they recur, sometimes with increasing frequency. An anxiety attack itself is so frightening and unpleasant that it often provokes the fear of another such attack; in effect one becomes anxious about being anxious. That leads a person to fear and avoid the triggering circumstance—going into a crowded place or small enclosure or high place, or whatever the locale of the previous attack. This kind of fear—the fear of something that actually is neither dangerous nor frightening to most people—is called a *phobia.*

Wanda's form of anxiety is called *agoraphobia,* literally meaning "fear of the market place." *Phobia* comes from the Greek word *phobos,* the name of the god who inspired terror and panic. Agoraphobia need not literally involve a market, as Wanda's case does; it can be any open or crowded public place (such as an airline terminal), or a classroom, theater, or church, and in some cases, any place outside one's own home.

Agoraphobia is the most common of the phobias. It affects women twice as often as it affects men. Other kinds of phobia connected with anxiety attacks are *claustrophobia,* fear of being enclosed in a small space such as an elevator or airplane; *acrophobia,* fear of heights (balconies, tall bridges, mountain roads); *animal phobias,* especially fear of wasps, spiders, snakes, rats, mice, cats, dogs, or birds; and *social phobias,* the fear of appearing ridiculous in public, especially while eating or drinking (in a restaurant), or writing (lest one's hand shake), or walking past a line of people (as in a restaurant, bus, or subway).

Chronic Anxiety

Another form of anxiety is more chronic in nature, not so much marked by attacks of panic but persisting over a longer time. It is sometimes called *free-floating anxiety* or *generalized anxiety.* It, too, is characterized by a sense of dread and anticipation of some terrible misfortune, and it also tends to be accompanied by other symptoms, some of them physical:

- Difficulty concentrating.
- Irritability, feeling "on edge."
- Impatience.
- Trouble sleeping.
- Motor tension (shakiness, jitteriness, trembling, eye twitch or other twitches, fidgeting).
- Sweating.
- Heart pounding.
- Dry mouth.
- Clammy hands.
- Tingling in hands and/or feet.
- Flushing or pallor.
- Dizziness, lightheadedness.
- Diarrhea.
- Lump in throat.
- Frequent urination.
- Rapid pulse.
- Rapid breathing.

If a generalized feeling of dread and *at least four* of these symptoms persist for *a month or longer,* you may be suffering from generalized anxiety and might do well to seek help in coping with it.

Rule Out Physical Causes

With either specific phobias or generalized, free-floating anxiety, the sooner a person seeks help for the symptoms, the better the outlook for relief. In all such cases, however, it is especially important to rule out certain physical disorders before beginning any treatment, since some forms of organic brain disease, hyperthyroidism (overactivity of the thyroid gland), hypoglycemia (low blood sugar), overdoses of or intolerance to stimulants such as caffeine and amphetamine, or withdrawal from certain drugs such as the barbiturates all can give rise to anxiety reactions that appear identical to those caused by psychological factors alone.

Treating Anxiety

Anxiety disorders of all kinds have been successfully treated in a number of ways. Some of the physical symptoms, such as stomach upset, will respond to appropriate medication, while psychoactive drugs—both tranquilizers and antidepressants—may relieve the feelings of intense terror. However, many practitioners believe that some form of psychotherapy is necessary to treat anxiety successfully. Behavior therapies often succeed in helping persons with specific phobias (fear of dogs, heights, flying, etc.) and other anxiety disorders (see Chapter 13 for a fuller account of behavior therapy).

OBSESSIVE-COMPULSIVE DISORDER

Closely related to the anxiety disorders but often more obvious to relatives, friends, and even casual observers are the obsessive-compulsive disorders. An *obsession* is a nagging fear, doubt, or idea that a person cannot put out of his/her mind, no matter how much he/she wants to.

Marjorie A., 57, a housewife with a high-school education, is tormented with the idea that her floors are poisonous. A dozen years ago she found ants on her kitchen floor and used a strong insecticide to get rid of them. Since then she has become convinced that the kitchen floor—and in fact every floor in her house—is poisonous and will kill her if she comes in direct contact with it. She never goes barefoot, and even is afraid to touch the soles of her feet lest they somehow have become infected, too.

A *compulsion* is a repetitive, stereotyped form of behavior that a person feels compelled to perform. Washing one's hands many times a day, even when they are obviously not dirty, is one common form of compulsive behavior. Another is lining objects up in a particular order—for example, rearranging the things on top of one's desk in a certain ritual way—and checking frequently to make sure that the order has not been disturbed. Refraining from this behavior results in unbearable anxiety, and sometimes a person arranges his/her entire life around the compulsive behavior.

Actually, many otherwise normal individuals appear to think obsessively or behave compulsively in one or another area of their lives and do no harm, either to themselves or to others. The "workaholic" is a compulsive achiever who can do very well in life. It is when an obsession or compulsion becomes a source of profound stress to the individual, or when it interferes with normal functioning—when a person cannot be away from soap and water for more than half an hour at a time because of "needed" hand-washing—that treatment is indicated.

DEPRESSION

Often less obvious to the casual acquaintance or friend than either anxiety or phobia but one of the most common of all mental disorders is depression. Formerly called *melancholia,* depression has perhaps the widest range of any mental illness. It may be so mild and chronic that it can scarcely be identified at all, or so profound that a person is barely able to function. It also is potentially fatal: many individuals who commit suicide suffered from depression. Between these extremes, every imaginable gradation exists.

The overall general impression made by depression usually is slowed down functions and diminished reactions (psychiatrists call it "flattened affect"). We all have "highs" and "lows" in our lives; the depressed person seems to have a perpetual "low." When that "low" interferes significantly with day-to-day living, it constitutes a *clinical depression,* one that requires treatment.

Reactive Depression

Some depressions are *endogenous,* that is, they appear to have no particular triggering cause but seemingly arise "from within." Others are said to be *reactive,* that is, they have a definite beginning, often a loss over which the person grieves, or some other profound emotional stress or trauma.

> *Jane C. has been grief-stricken since her husband died eighteen months ago . . . weeps constantly, and lately has been having more and more trouble remembering things.*

The death of one's spouse or child tops the list of devastating events that can trigger depression. Others are divorce or separation, a serious physical illness such as cancer, a disabling accident, job loss and unemployment, and bankruptcy or other disastrous financial problems. It is natural to grieve over a serious loss, but when the sense of emptiness continues over a period of time and becomes complicated with feelings of worthlessness and despair, so that normal functioning does not resume, a clinical depression has developed.

Acute Depression

How can you tell when you or someone you know is suffering from a *major* or *acute depression?* The dominant mood is prolonged loss of interest in or pleasure from practically all of one's usual activities, accompanied by feelings of sadness, hopelessness, being "down in the dumps," and irritability, all of which persist for a considerable time. Further, the following symptoms are likely to occur:

- Marked change in appetite, leading to either significant weight loss or weight gain.
- Stomach upsets, especially constipation.
- Sleeping disturbances: either sleeping too much (hypersomnia) or too little (insomnia); early morning wakening (two hours before the normal time) is especially common.
- Physical agitation and restlessness *or* an overall physical slow-down.
- Greatly decreased interest in sex; in men, inability to sustain an erection often occurs.
- Loss of energy, constant fatigue.
- Diminished ability to concentrate and difficulty in making simple decisions.
- Feelings of worthlessness, self-reproach, and/or excessive guilt.
- Recurrent thoughts of death or wishing to be dead.

Anyone who experiences profound sadness along with any four of these other symptoms almost daily for at least two weeks, and without a logical triggering cause such as the recent death of a loved one, is probably undergoing a major depressive episode.

Endogenous depression sometimes recurs cyclically, for example, several months of depression followed by a period of relative normalcy, followed again by some months of depression, etc.

Chronic Depression

A less severe depression, sometimes called *disthymic disorder* or *depressive neurosis,* differs from a major depression largely in degree. Generally the symptoms are troublesome for a long period of time—off and on over two years (one year in the case of children and adolescents)—but not quite disabling enough to be called a major depressive episode. They may be more or less constant, or they may be separated by periods of normal mood lasting a few days to a few weeks (but never more than a few months at a time). The depressive periods themselves may be characterized by the following symptoms:

- Loss of interest in pleasurable activities and inability to respond positively to pleasurable events.
- Tearfulness and weeping.
- Feelings of worthlessness.
- Brooding about the past, feeling pessimistic about the present and future.
- Diminished sexual interest and function.
- Social withdrawal.
- Chronic fatigue, little energy.
- Sleep disturbances, either sleeping too much or too little.
- Inability to concentrate and difficulty in making decisions.
- Irritability, excessive anger over trifles.
- Thoughts of death or suicide.

The presence of at least three of these symptoms and prolonged sadness indicate the possibility of a milder but still clinical depression, which may require treatment.

Who Becomes Depressed?

How common is clinical depression? Estimates range anywhere from 5 to 30 percent of the total population. In 1980 the National Mental Health Association estimated that at any one time more than two million Americans suffer from severe depression and an additional twenty-one million are mildly or moderately depressed.

Almost anyone, from a small child to a very old person, can be affected. In fact, there is a high and fast-rising incidence of depression among teenagers and young adults. High-school counselors and college infirmaries frequently see students with problems that turn out to be, at least in some degree, depression. Part of the reason is, no doubt, that adolescence and early adulthood are times of considerable stress and change, as young people strive to find their identity and separate from their parents.

Depression apparently occurs in women anywhere from three to five times more often than in men, but it is not certain whether this finding is due to the fact that our culture permits women to express feelings, especially negative feelings, more openly and to ask for help more readily, or whether there really is a sex-linked difference. In any event, two to three times as many women seek professional help for depression. There seems to be a familial component as well, that is, depression runs in families. Whether or not there is an inherited biochemical factor in all kinds of depression is not known, but it is strongly suspected at least in some kinds of depression.

SUICIDE

The principal danger of untreated depression is suicide. It is believed that a high proportion—some say as many as 15 percent—of depressed persons eventually succeed in ending their lives. (This figure applies to manic-depressive disorder and depression combined; manic-depressive disorder is discussed further on in this chapter.) Oddly enough, a depressed person usually tends to commit suicide during a period of seeming improvement. The reason, it is believed, is that when a major depression is at its severest, inertia prevents a person from acting; with some improvement he/she is still depressed but now has enough energy to plan for death.

Suicide is the second leading cause of death (accidents rank first) among adolescents and young adults in the United States (ages 15 through 24). The rate has tripled since 1970. The risk of a depressed person's committing suicide is thought to be at least fifty times that of someone who is not depressed. Moreover, statistics for suicide are believed to be underestimates of the real figures because many cases go unreported.

What are the warning signs of suicide?

1. Suicide threats; *none should be ignored.*
2. Statements revealing a desire to die.
3. One or more previous suicide attempts.
4. Sudden change in behavior (withdrawal, moodiness, apathy).
5. Depression, especially feelings of utter hopelessness.
6. Final arrangements, such as giving away personal possessions or indicating who is to inherit what.

Suicide or the threat of it is a genuine emergency. It should *never* be ignored, even if you find yourself in the position of "betraying a confidence" by getting direct help for someone who is suicidal but refuses to seek counseling. Many people who are considering suicide have given up hope and do not believe anyone *can* help them. Often this is not true.

Treatment of Depression

Depression responds far better to various kinds of treatment than some other severe mental disorders. Further, both a severe reactive depression and the milder clinical depressions sometimes are self-limiting and cure themselves spontaneously. When this happens, the depression simply runs its course, usually within four to twelve months. Severe endogenous depressions, on the other hand, rarely go away by themselves, but they often respond to antidepressant drugs and/or to electroconvulsive therapy (ECT). Antidepressants, which have been in use since the 1950's, are among the most effective drugs in the psychiatrist's black bag, but they often take a number of weeks to work, during which some patients become so discouraged that they stop taking them and get worse (or become desperate and commit suicide). In some cases, however, they may not work. (See Chapters 15 and 16 for more information about antidepressants and also electroconvulsive therapy, or ECT, for depression.)

Unfortunately, however, depression sometimes is disguised. Even though a person's mood and behavior may have changed markedly, it is one or another physical symptom—palpitations, chest pain, back pain, trouble swallowing, trouble breathing, stomach upset, fatigue, dizziness, headache, insomnia—that drives a person to the doctor. Troubled by such symptoms, patients often do not bother to mention the mood changes that might warn the practitioner. Unless the primary-care physician is exceptionally alert, treatment for depression may be long delayed while the other complaints are treated with sleeping pills, antacids, pain-killers, and similar remedies that are useless against depression.

Occasionally depression does have a physical cause. A clinical depression in children or adults may be secondary to a physical illness. Viral infections such as influenza (flu or grippe) and mono-nucleosis, ulcers, rheumatoid arthritis, and alcoholism all are closely associated with depression. Depression also can be a side effect of medication taken for other conditions, such as some anti-biotics and blood pressure medications; cortisone and related anti-inflammatory agents used for arthritis; digitalis, used in heart dis-ease; estrogens and progesterones, hormones used in oral contra-ceptives (birth control pills); and tranquilizers, sometimes given when depression is mistaken for anxiety or some other mental dis-order.

MANIC-DEPRESSIVE DISORDER (BIPOLAR DEPRESSION)

An estimated one-third to one-half of all persons suffering from clinical depression are believed to have manic-depressive disease or bipolar depression (the rest have *unipolar depression*), which tends to develop in early adulthood or later. This form of depression often occurs in several family members, so a genetic factor is strongly suspected, that is, one is probably born with a predisposition to develop the condition.

In effect, manic-depressive disease is a mood disorder character-ized by very extreme "ups" and "downs," the former called *mania,* or *manic episodes,* and the latter *depression,* or *depressive episodes.* Out of control, the manic patient may decide to run for President of the United States, go on a shopping spree, make an impulsive (and usually foolish) business investment, or otherwise behave with extreme recklessness.

> *William quit his job, moved out of his family's suburban home to a high-rise apartment in the city, and is about to buy an expensive cabin cruiser. However, he hasn't enough in the bank to meet the payments on the family car, let alone buy any luxury items.*

William's behavior is manic. It will probably be followed by a pro-found depression in which he feels he is no good to himself or anyone else and becomes too despondent to act at all. Like any profound depression, it can end in suicide.

The manic phase of this disorder is usually considered a psychosis, involving a severe distortion of the patient's perceptions. Behavior may become so bizarre that it resembles an acute schizophrenic episode (see below). However, while schizophrenia tends primarily to disrupt thought processes, manic-depressive disease is primarily a disorder of mood (although its alternating ups and downs may secondarily affect a person's thinking). Schizophrenia often strikes during adolescence, whereas manic-depressive disease usually begins in early adulthood or later.

Manic-depressives often behave quite normally between episodes, and are able to hold jobs and function in a family setting. The more difficult phase of the illness is the manic, but in about 80 percent of cases it can be almost completely controlled by means of lithium carbonate, a powerful drug that also appears to lessen the subsequent depression. The depressive phase of the illness sometimes responds well to antidepressants. Although unipolar depression (without mania) is very common, mania rarely occurs alone, without a preceding or subsequent depression.

How can you tell if you or someone you know is undergoing a manic episode? The predominant symptom is an extended period during which the person's mood is markedly elevated and expansive, with sudden shifts to irritability and anger. Further, the following symptoms are likely to be present:

- Increased activity (of any kind) and/or physical restlessness.
- Decreased need for rest and sleep.
- Flight of ideas, that is, jumping rapidly from one thought or topic of conversation to another.
- Talking a great deal and talking very fast.
- An inflated ego, the idea (usually false) that the person can accomplish anything and everything.
- Increased distractibility, that is, the person's attention is easily drawn to unimportant details.
- Involvement in potentially self-destructive or risky behavior: spending sprees, sexual indiscretions, wild business investment, reckless driving, etc.

A predominantly elated mood accompanied by three or more of the above-named symptoms points to the strong possibility of manic-depressive disease.

SCHIZOPHRENIA

One of the most severe mental illnesses is schizoprenia, a disorder that affects one's thought processes, feelings, and ability to relate to other people. The schizophrenic literally cannot think straight; he or she has distorted perceptions and often confuses fantasy and reality. Further, his/her feelings may be completely dulled, so there is either little reaction, or inappropriate reaction to painful or pleasurable experiences—laughing as a response to hearing that someone has died, weeping at good news, and so on. Finally, social relations are at a minimum, since the schizophrenic tends to withdraw from most contact with others. Typically he/she feels lonely and misunderstood, and has very little self-esteem. Faced with quite disordered thoughts and feelings, the schizophrenic withdraws into a private world where the distinction between real and imagined disappears. One characteristic symptom of schizophrenia is auditory hallucinations, that is, hearing sounds and voices that actually do not exist.

> *Donald, 19 . . . spends all his time in his room . . . scarcely speaks to his family and has seen none of his former friends. His mother sometimes hears him talking behind his closed door, even though she knows he is alone and there is no telephone in the room.*

Typically schizophrenia begins in late adolescence or young adulthood, especially in the late teens and early twenties, and nearly always before the age of forty-five. It affects men and women with equal frequency. Until the discovery of antipsychotic drugs, schizophrenia was regarded as both incurable and untreatable; it simply got worse and worse, until the patient, by then often in the back ward of a mental hospital, stopped functioning altogether. Such patients would spend their days sitting in a corner and rocking, unable to speak or wash or use the toilet. Today the outlook for most schizophrenics is more hopeful.

How can you tell if someone is schizophrenic? During a schizophrenic episode the person is usually markedly peculiar; schizophrenia gives rise to behavior that is closest to what most people call "crazy."

It often is marked by delusions and hallucinations. A *delusion* is a false belief held in the face of either no evidence or strong evidence to the contrary, for example, that you really are Jesus Christ or that the television newscaster is sending you secret messages in code every evening. A *hallucination* is a false sensory stimulus, for example, hearing nonexistent voices or feeling nonexistent insects crawling up your legs.

In schizophrenia the following symptoms may occur:

- Strange delusions without any basis in reality, such as that one's actions and/or thoughts are controlled by some means such as a computer hooked up to the brain.
- Auditory hallucinations in which "voices" are either arguing with each other or a voice is commenting on the person's actions or telling him/her what to do.
- Delusions of grandeur, such as the idea that one is not really oneself but Napoleon or Jesus Christ.
- Persecution delusions, such as believing that people on the bus are staring at you because they are planning to kill you.
- Incoherent speech, or speech that does not make sense, accompanied by expressions of inappropriate feelings (laughing at bad news, crying at good), or by any delusions (false beliefs) or hallucinations, or by catatonic behavior (holding one body position for hours at a time).

If any one of these symptoms persists for a period of six months, and the person is functioning less well than usual at work, school, in personal grooming, or social relations, he or she could be suffering from some form of schizophrenia.

Schizophrenics in remission have described how it feels to have this disease. The feelings are miserable and terrifying. One has a sense of being unreal, a sense of separation from one's body and behavior (of being an outsider watching oneself), as well as a sense of alienation from others. (This feeling is sometimes called *depersonalization.*)

Formerly called *dementia praecox* ("precocious madness"), schizophrenia is not a single disorder but a complex of diseases. Often one or another of the symptoms—paranoia (delusions of persecution), incoherent speech and inappropriate affect (feelings), or catatonic behavior—is the principal symptom seen. Also, the course of the illness is variable. In some cases it becomes chronic, and in others, usually only those undergoing effective treatment, it goes into remission. Generally speaking, the later in life the onset of the disease, the better the outlook for improvement.

Some authorities differentiate between two basic forms of schizophrenia, *process* or *chronic schizophrenia,* with a gradual onset, and *reactive* or *acute schizophrenia,* which develops suddenly in response to some great stress. The latter usually responds better to treatment.

Three disorders have names similar to schizophrenia but are believed to be distinctly different from it: (1) *schizophreniform disorder,* which is similar to schizophrenia in every way except that it lasts a much shorter time (anywhere from two weeks to six months); (2) *schizoid personality disorder,* in which a person is emotionally cold and aloof, has no warm or tender feelings for anyone at all, is indifferent to praise, criticisms, or the feelings of others, but otherwise has no eccentricities of speech, behavior, or thought; and (3) *schizotypal personality disorder* (also called *borderline disorder* or *nonpsychotic schizophrenia*), in which a person never actually becomes psychotic but shows many of the peculiarities of the schizophrenic (odd speech, magical thinking, self-referential thinking, suspiciousness, social isolation, poor rapport with others, undue sensitivity to real or imagined criticism, and depersonalization).

Schizophrenia affects almost 1 percent of the world's population. Studies of identical twins and of children of schizophrenic parents who were raised in foster homes indicate that there almost certainly is a genetic factor in the disease. Further, the fact that antipsychotic drugs have considerable effect on schizophrenic patients is a strong indication that the disease involves a biochemical derangement.

Warning Signs of Schizophrenia

Sometimes the active psychotic phase of the disease is preceded by a somewhat less extreme set of symptoms, which may include:

- Social isolation or withdrawal, usually followed by personality changes, such as frequently becoming angry, suspicious, and/or evasive.
- Deteriorating performance at work or at school.
- Deteriorating personal hygiene and grooming, such as neglecting to bathe, change one's clothes, comb one's hair, etc.
- Overactive, frenzied behavior and inability to concentrate.
- Reversing night and day behavior, lying in bed all day and being active all night.
- Depression, sometimes difficult to distinguish from a severe clinical depression or manic-depressive disease (see above).
- Blunt or flattened affect (little emotional reaction to events that normally arouse emotion), or an inappropriate emotional reaction.
- A constantly hollow, unhappy tone.
- Peculiar behavior, such as hoarding garbage, stealing food, talking to oneself out loud in public, etc.
- Auditory hallucinations (hearing voices that aren't there).

These may be early signs of schizophrenia, or they may occur when an acute episode is subsiding.

Treatment of Schizophrenia

Acute schizophrenic patients usually need to be hospitalized, particularly during a first episode, so that complete tests and evaluation can be performed and an appropriate schedule of medication established. Despite the severity of the disorder, it should be remembered that highly creative and intelligent individuals have suffered from it—the writer Virginia Woolf and the painter Vincent Van Gogh are believed to have been schizophrenics—and that with new medication and research the outlook is fast improving. Approximately 90 percent of patients recover enough after three to twelve weeks of hospitalization to be discharged. Continuing medication can shorten subsequent episodes, make them milder, and may even abort an attack. Full recovery is uncommon, however, and usually occurs only in the first two years. After five years of illness complete recovery is rare.

PHYSICAL SYMPTOMS: REAL AND/OR IMAGINED

The relationship of body and mind is exceedingly complex and still is not understood. We know which nerves transmit the painful impulses of a burned finger to the brain, but we do not understand how anxiety can cause a headache or diarrhea, or how depression can cause constipation.

Certain serious chronic physical illnesses—diabetes, rheumatoid arthritis, and high blood pressure are among them—are affected by how a person feels. At times of stress such an illness worsens, and at calm, relaxed times it improves. Such illnesses are sometimes called *psychosomatic* or *psychophysiological,* but in 1980 the American Psychiatric Association changed its nomenclature to "psychological factors affecting physical condition" in recognition of the fact that we still don't know how they operate.

Moreover, a person can be feeling extreme pain—crippling lower back pain, for example—without any detectable organic cause whatever. One of Sigmund Freud's most famous cases showed that one can actually imagine oneself to be partially paralyzed, a condition called *conversion hysteria* or *conversion disorder* because here mental symptoms have in effect been converted into physical ones.

An entire category of mental illnesses—the so-called *somatoform disorders*—involve physical pain of one kind or another that has no discernible organic cause.

Betty A., 47, has a medicine cabinet full of pills. At least once a month she calls her family doctor, complaining of stomach upsets, sleeplessness, backache, and a host of other ailments. Her doctor rarely can find a physical cause for her symptoms. . . .

Betty suffers from so-called *somatization disorder,* one of the two principal forms of somatoform disorder. It tends to affect women more often than men, it usually begins before the age of thirty, and it drives the woman to seek frequent medical attention. In some cases a woman goes from doctor to doctor hoping to find relief; she may even undergo surgery for a nonexistent ulcer or tumor or some other major medical procedure.

Typically such a person appears, to the physician who treats her, as a demanding and complaining pest, with a long history of physical symptoms, unsuccessful treatment, and unhappy relations with physicians. Indeed such patients may so anger practitioners that they prefer to avoid them altogether, and therefore they tend to ignore their very real distress. At the worst extreme, such a patient is in danger of having the early signs of a serious physical illness, such as cancer, overlooked until it is too advanced to treat successfully, simply because she has cried "Wolf" for so long that no one pays attention any more.

The second form of common somatoform disorder affects men and women equally but tends to begin later, in middle age. Here the principal symptom is the mistaken belief that one is suffering from a serious disease, although a thorough physical examination does not reveal any evidence of it. No matter how much the doctor— or doctors—reassures the individual that his heart, for example, is in perfectly good working order, he continues to experience various disturbances of heartbeat (too rapid or irregular) or chest pain and lives in mortal fear of an impending fatal heart attack. This form of the disorder is called *hypochondriasis* or *hypochondriacal disorder.*

How can you tell if your mother-in-law, whom you're not very fond of anyway, is really ill or if she suffers from imaginary symptoms? You can suspect the latter if she has been carefully checked by a reputable physician who can find nothing wrong, yet continues to complain of at least a *dozen or more* of the following symptoms,* in addition to maintaining that she is (and has always been) in very poor health:

- Trouble swallowing, hearing, seeing (double or blurred vision), speaking (voice loss), remembering, or walking; trouble urinating; fainting or passing out; seizures or convulsions; muscle weakness, numbness, or paralysis.
- Stomach upsets (stomachache, nausea, vomiting, bloating, intolerance to various foods, diarrhea).
- Menstrual problems (pain, irregularity, excessive bleeding).
- Difficult pregnancy (severe vomiting throughout or sufficiently severe at any time to require hospitalization).
- Sexual problems (lack of interest in sex, lack of pleasure, pain during intercourse).
- Chest pain (pain, shortness of breath, palpitations, dizziness).
- Pain (in the back, joints, extremities, on urinating, elsewhere).

The hypochondriac has been a figure of fun and a source of annoyance for centuries. The seventeenth-century playwright Molière poked expert fun at him in his *The Imaginary Invalid.* Because hypochondriacs are so persistent about their complaints, one tends to lose patience with them fairly quickly. It is hard to remember that their suffering is nonetheless genuine.

EATING DISORDERS

A truly dangerous physical condition believed to be almost wholly mental in origin is anorexia nervosa.

> *Kathy J., 17, refuses to eat, claiming she is far too fat. She has lost twenty-five pounds in the past two months and was, if anything, quite slender to start with.*

DSM-III, the American Psychiatric Association's latest *Diagnostic and Statistical Manual* (1980), says at least fourteen symptoms for women and twelve for men.

Kathy may well be among the 15 percent of young women with this condition who actually starve to death. Like other anorexics, she believes she must lose more weight even when she has already lost as much as 25 percent of her total body weight.

Anorexia afflicts mainly young women in their late teens to early twenties. They not only restrict their eating drastically but may encourage further weight loss by taking strong laxatives and enemas and inducing vomiting after they eat. A related syndrome, called *bulimia* or *bulimarexia,* consists of alternate eating binges followed by self-inflicted purging and drastic dieting. Girls with either of these disorders tend to be secretive about their diets, binges, and purges.

How can you tell if your friend or your daughter is endangering her health in this way? In this age group, anyone who shows massive weight loss and a marked change in eating habits may be suspected and should be checked by the family physician or pediatrician without much delay. The sooner the condition is discovered, the better the outlook, both physically and mentally. Sometimes, however, the patient may be very resistant to advice, psychotherapy, medication, and other means used to reverse the symptoms, and may require hospitalization for a time.

Obesity

One of the most common of all eating disorders in America today is obesity, which is defined as weighing 25 percent more than one should (according to fairly standard guidelines put out by insurance companies and medical societies). Obesity is caused by compulsive overeating. In some instances it begins in early childhood; in most it begins in adulthood. It is not really known what leads a person to eat far more than his or her body needs, so that the excess is stored as fat, but it is a dangerous condition, putting one at risk for a variety of serious and potentially life-threatening disorders such as diabetes, hypertension (high blood pressure), cerebral vascular accident (stroke), heart disease, gall bladder disease, osteoarthritis and other orthopedic problems, and some kinds of cancer. Although the American Psychiatric Association does not include obesity in its list of mental disorders, there is little doubt that most obese persons would much prefer a normal weight and the great majority are unable to achieve this desire. Insight therapy (Chapter 12) may help discover why they overeat and how to adjust their habits, but it usually takes a very long time. Various kinds of behavior therapy and supportive self-help groups also have been used to treat obesity, employing a variety of techniques to alter the client's eating habits. Unfortunately many of those treated lose a great deal of weight for a time but then revert to overeating and gain it back.

ALCOHOL AND DRUG ABUSE

Alcoholism and drug dependency also represent physical problems that are caused, at least in part, by psychologic factors. Here the basic unhappiness or insecurity that leads a person to begin drinking or taking drugs in order to change how they feel is responsible, but only in part. Some individuals, it is now believed, have an inborn biochemical makeup that makes them become readily addicted to substances that, while not totally harmless for others, do not necessarily lead to addiction. We all know persons who can drink a bottle of wine a day, or consume six ounces of whiskey a day, yet can easily control their alcohol intake at will. They can literally take it or leave it. The alcohol is not really good for them—at best it is a form of junk food, or "empty calories"—but under most normal circumstances it does them no significant harm. For those predisposed to alcoholism, however, one drink almost invariably leads to another, and for some a relatively small amount causes intoxication. Such individuals seem to develop a need for alcohol, and it becomes extremely difficult to control.

Like individuals with eating disorders, alcoholics often conceal their drinking habits. They also try to convince themselves that they are not "problem drinkers." How can you tell if you drink too much? Ask yourself the following questions:*

• Has someone close to you sometimes expressed concern about your drinking?

*Developed by the National Institute on Alcohol Abuse and Alcoholism

- When faced with a problem, do you often (or always) turn to alcohol for relief?
- Are you sometimes unable to meet home or work responsibilities because of drinking?
- Have you ever required medical attention of any kind as a result of drinking?
- Have you ever experienced a blackout—a total loss of memory while still awake—when drinking?
- Have you ever come in conflict with the law in connection with your drinking?
- Have you often failed to keep the promises you made to yourself about controlling or cutting out your drinking?

If you have answered yes to even *one* of these questions, your drinking is probably affecting your life in some major ways and you should do something about it now, before it gets worse.

How can you tell if a relative or friend is becoming (or has already become) dependent on alcohol?

- Is he or she immediately ready to pour a drink when faced with a problem?
- Does he or she regularly get drunk?
- Is there a record of work missed because of drinking, or regular attendance at work but with an ill-disguised odor of liquor on the breath?
- Has the person's license been suspended for driving while drunk?
- Has the person gotten in trouble with the authorities for no "logical" reason?
- Has the person been involved in several unexplainable accidents?
- Has the person's home life become difficult because of excessive drinking or arguments resulting from drinking?

When one or more of these signs is present, it shows that a person's drinking pattern may be either already out of control or heading in that direction. Many primary-care physicians (family doctors, general practitioners, internists) seem to have a blind spot regarding alcoholism in their patients. The results of one survey of

Alcoholics Anonymous members indicated that half had tried to discuss their drinking problem with someone who told them they couldn't possibly be alcoholics, and in one-fourth of these cases the "someone" was a physician. Even psychiatrists sometimes overlook the possibility that a patient's problems are secondary to alcohol abuse, which today is believed to affect at least ten million Americans and is considered one of the largest health problems in the country.

Treatment of Alcoholism

Alcoholism can be treated, and a variety of facilities and professionals can provide treatment. The severe alcoholic person must first recover from acute intoxication and withdrawal, a process called *detoxification.* It usually takes place in a medical facility, either on an inpatient or an outpatient basis, because of the severe physical reactions that detoxification can entail. During detoxification the patient is given medication to insure safety and reduce discomfort, and is put on a nutritious diet supplemented with high-strength vitamins. At the same time, any related health problems are treated, among them gastritis, malnutrition, dehydration, and cirrhosis of the liver. Most treatment programs also offer individual, along with group and/or family therapy with therapists specifically experienced with alcoholics.

Inpatient care is offered by public and private hospitals, special detoxification centers, residential care facilities, and some alcoholism clinics, and is considered necessary for individuals suffering from acute intoxication or serious related medical problems. For individuals with early symptoms of alcoholism, outpatient treatment, usually provided by a local alcoholism treatment clinic and including medical treatment, psychotherapy, and vocational guidance, may be sufficient. After or concurrent with treatment, the self-help program of Alcoholics Anonymous (see Chapter 11) can help prevent relapse.

Alcohol treatment programs differ greatly in environment, method, and level of services. To find the appropriate treatment for you or your relative, contact one of the following agencies, most of which can be found through your telephone book: National Council on Alcoholism affili te in your area; Alcoholics Anonymous; your community alcoholism or mental health clinic; the social services or human resources department of your city or county; your county medical society; the health office or "troubled employee" program in your company. (See also the resources for alcoholism listed in the Appendix.)

PERSONALITY DISORDERS

Personality disorders (also called *character disorders*) differ from other forms of mental illness in that their predominant feature is a distorted and destructive mode of behavior toward other people. It may take the form of extreme suspiciousness and mistrust.

Mildred J., 28, suspects that others are out to get her, and will do her a bad turn. She is convinced they want to make her look ridiculous, so she is quick to feel slighted and take offense at what, to anyone else, would be a harmless remark or gesture.

Mildred's disorder is called *paranoid personality disorder,* or *paranoia,* which means the feeling of being persecuted ("persecution complex" was an older term for it). It is not so severe as the paranoia sometimes present in schizophrenia, in that Mildred is not psychotic and is perfectly able to distinguish reality from fantasy. But it is self-destructive, in that she is always expecting the worst from others and hence goes through life with "a chip on the shoulder."

In another form a person may find it virtually impossible to state his or her opinions, wishes, or demands directly, and instead treats the world with passive resistance.

James K., 22, is seemingly amiable and easygoing. If his family agrees to go to a movie after supper, he eats his meal very slowly, forcing everyone to wait for him and miss the beginning of the film. Or he may agree to do an errand on his way home from work but repeatedly "forgets" to do it. If he dislikes someone at work, he never says so directly but may begin to avoid the person, or even stay home from work.

James can express his negative feelings only indirectly, by refusing to act at all. His illness is called *passive-aggressive personality disorder* and markedly impairs his relations with family, friends, and colleagues. In fact, he has no real friends.

Perhaps the most obviously destructive form of personality disorder is the kind called *antisocial personality disorder.*

John B., 25, lost his job last week after getting in a fist fight with a fellow worker. It is the fourth time in less than a year that his violent behavior has gotten him in trouble. This time the other man, whose jaw he broke, is planning to sue him.

The antisocial person is constantly violating the rights of others, and frequently ends up in trouble with the law. Often such a person first has trouble in childhood or early adolescence with school truancy, lying, theft, running away, and impulsive behavior. In adult life he or she generally has a poor work history, with frequent job changes, and an unhappy marriage. Punishment—even jail—does not change the behavior; learning from bitter experience simply does not occur. Occasionally such antisocial behavior ends of its own accord, usually in the late thirties. More often it does not. Conventional therapies do not seem to help much, but in recent years some practitioners have reported success with behavior therapy or behavior modification methods (see Chapter 13).

We tend to focus on the harm such individuals do to others, yet in the long run their behavior is harmful to themselves, too. It is their families, perhaps, that suffer most. The individuals themselves often have blunted feelings and do not seem to suffer as profoundly as most of us do in deeply moving situations.

MENTAL PROBLEMS OF OLD AGE

Jane, the 68-year-old widow we have described before, most certainly exemplifies a case of grieving that has turned into depression.

But is it only depression that makes her forget to turn off the stove or lose her car? Could her mental condition be the result of aging?

Elderly persons who suffer from lapses of memory, especially forgetting recent events, who become disoriented as to time and place, and who lose their ability to do simple arithmetic may be suffering from a mental illness called *senile dementia*. Approximately 4.5 percent of the elderly in the United States—about one million persons in 1981—are so affected. An estimated half of them suffer from a deterioration of the brain called Alzheimer's disease or pre-senile dementia, for which no cure has yet been found. This disorder is characterized by lesions of nerves in the brain and by the deficiency of an enzyme, choline acetyltransferase, which is essential to the manufacture of the neurotransmitter acetylcholine. Alzheimer's disease begins at the age of sixty or earlier and involves progressive deterioration. The patient usually dies within ten years of its onset.

Another physical cause of senile dementia is a series of small cerebral vascular accidents (CVA's, or strokes), in which clots form in the small arteries of the brain, thereby reducing its supply of blood and oxygen. Unlike a more massive CVA, these "mini-strokes" do not incapacitate the victim all at once but gradually reduce brain function. Approximately one-fourth of all cases of senile dementia are thought to result from such strokes. Even though neither of these physical causes of mental illness is at present curable, self-help and family support programs can do a great deal for their victims, often preventing or postponing institutionalization.

The diagnosis of senile dementia is not always clear-cut. Various other diseases can mimic the symptoms, which include:

- Disoriented as to time, especially concerning when events in one's own life occurred.
- Disoriented as to place, mistaking one place for some other, familiar place.
- Disoriented as to identity of others, such as mistaking a doctor for one's own son.
- Impaired memory, particularly relating to recent events (remote memory usually remains good).

- Hallucinations, usually visual.
- Delusions concerning ordinary, everyday people and events.
- Confusion, usually alternating with lucid periods, and with the confusion worse at night.

The elderly especially can react to medication in peculiar ways, and some symptoms of senile dementia can be caused by a toxic reaction to drugs they commonly use, such as sleep medications, or diuretics for high blood pressure and heart disease. Some of the physical disorders to which the elderly are especially prone can also cause mental symptoms—conditions such as diseases of the heart, lungs, kidneys, or liver, nutritional deficiency, sight or hearing loss, and hypothermia (below-normal body temperature, a common problem in the very old). In these cases treatment of the primary physical condition can relieve the mental symptoms.

Depression: The Vicious Circle

Dementia in its early stages also tends to be marked by depression. Losing one's memory is good cause for sadness. But which comes first? Profound depression can give rise to memory loss, which may be partly or wholly reversed by means of antidepressants and other treatment. In Jane's case, we do not know if her depression affected her memory or if her natural grief turned into depression because of organic brain changes. Even more complicated are cases where a patient has received electroconvulsive treatment (ECT) for depression (see Chapter 16), since a common side effect of such treatment is impaired memory of recent events. Loss of memory can in turn cause depression—in effect, a vicious circle.

In its early stages, senile dementia is especially difficult to diagnose. If suspected, a careful medical workup is in order. It should include:

1. A detailed medical and personal history, taken either from the patient or from a knowledgeable family member or friend; it should include an inventory of all medications currently being taken.

2. A comprehensive physical examination, including blood, urine, thyroid, and neurological tests, vision and hearing evaluation, and, if the former uncover no possible cause of symptoms, a brain scan (computerized brain X-ray).
3. Psychologic and intellectual tests especially designed to detect organic brain disease.

If you suspect that your elderly relative is suffering from senile dementia, try to get him or her evaluated by a physician who specializes in the care of the elderly—a gerontologist or geriatric psychiatrist. If your own doctor cannot direct you, you may be able to locate such a person through your local or state council on elderly affairs, a reputable nursing home, or your local home-care corporation. There is also a national organization for exchanging information and advice among families of Alzheimer's victims, the Alzheimer's Disease and Related Disorders Association, 292 Madison Avenue, New York, NY 10017.

This discussion of the symptoms of the most common mental illnesses can give you some clues about what you or your relative or friend may be suffering from. In the end, however, the most important reasons for seeking professional help remain very basic:

1. One is in danger or presents a danger to others—a true emergency.
2. One cannot function normally at work or in school and/or in relations with other people.
3. One is suffering pain.

The next step is to get a professional assessment (see Chapter 6). First, however, we will review those mental disorders that affect children.

CHAPTER 5
Mental Illness in Children

An estimated twelve million American children and adolescents experience some measure of mental health problems, and of these some two million suffer severe mental disability and related handicaps. For many years mental illness in children went unrecognized unless the symptoms were extremely severe. The recognition of a mental disorder rather than willful disobedience in instances of children who could not sit still or pay attention is relatively recent and by no means universal.

> *Stephen I., 10, is not doing well in his third-grade class . . . . He has been allowed out for recess only once all year, his teacher making him stay in because of his disruptive and destructive behavior.*

Punishment or suspension from school are not likely to help this ten-year-old, yet it can be hard to differentiate between a child who needs stricter discipline and one who needs treatment. Moreover, parents are often reluctant to acknowledge that their child may have an emotional problem or a mental illness. The stigma is strong, and they may feel it casts blame on them.

Even if parents do admit—or are forced to admit—that something is wrong with their child, it may be difficult to determine just what is the matter. Young children do not readily express their thoughts and feelings in words. They are more likely to show such symptoms as aggressive behavior toward other children, sleep disturbances, eating disturbances, and the like.

ANXIETY AND PHOBIAS

Anxiety disorders in children often take the form of such habits as nail-biting, thumb-sucking, head-banging, rocking, or hair-pulling. Anxiety may also express itself in physical disorders, especially stomach upsets and respiratory difficulties, as well as sleep disturbances. Overanxious children tend to be fearful of new people and new situations, and are excessively wary of body injury. Sometimes their anxiety can create learning problems resembling those of children with learning disabilities (see below).

A common form of anxiety disorder in children is *separation anxiety,* that is, excessive clinging to and reluctance to leave the parents or others to whom the child is closely attached. In school-age children this may take the form of *school phobia,* that is, persistent fearfulness about leaving home to go to school. On school days such a child often complains of (and experiences) physical symptoms—stomachache, headache, nausea. While it is natural for children to feel apprehensive when they first start nursery school, kindergarten, and first grade, and in some cases their early school experiences may need to be postponed on this account, generally such fearfulness subsides after a relatively short time. In some youngsters, however, it may persist to the point where school attendance can no longer be avoided and something must be done. Similarly, a child with separation anxiety may become unduly anxious about possible harm befalling his/her parents, or about being abandoned by the parents, or some similar calamity for which there is no basis in reality.

In other youngsters, acute anxiety may express itself in night terrors, repeated episodes of abrupt waking and panic, or in eating disorders such as pica (habitually eating paper, clay, or other non-foods), refusal to eat, or overeating.

Adolescents may develop bulimia or anorexia nervosa (see under eating disorders in Chapter 4).

DEPRESSION

Depression in children may take the same form as in adults—a persistent feeling of sadness and low self-esteem, with feelings of being worthless and rejected ("I'm no good," "I can't do anything right," "No one likes me"). A temporary mood disturbance of this kind is not unnatural, but if it persists and the child begins to withdraw from siblings and friends, and there has been no external event (illness, hospitalization, loss) that can account for it, the child may need treatment for depression. Like adults, depressed children often complain of physical ailments, particularly stomachache, headache, sleep problems, and fatigue. In a young child depression is sometimes expressed in temper tantrums, aggressive behavior, or nightmares.

Depression is common in adolescence, a period normally characterized by wide mood swings. Teenagers seem to experience frequent "highs" and "lows," but a persistent low that remains unaltered by pleasurable events may indicate a need for help. As was pointed out in Chapter 4, suicide is the second leading cause of death among adolescents and young adults, so no teenager's persistent sadness or comments such as "I wish I were dead" should be overlooked. Older children also occasionally express their underlying sadness in a violent way, in truancy, vandalism, or running away from home.

ANTISOCIAL BEHAVIOR

Lying, stealing, setting fires or other acts of vandalism, getting in trouble with the police—these problems are more likely to attract prompt attention than depression. To some extent, some of these forms of behavior are normal among very young children, who "lie" because they are not able to distinguish between truth and falsehood or "steal" because they fail to understand the concept of property rights. Further, most young children occasionally have trouble controlling their aggressive impulses. But when aggressive behavior physically harms other children, or when there are frequent complaints from other parents, teachers, and neighbors, something is amiss, and professional advice may be needed. (See also the section on juvenile delinquency in Chapter 22.)

CHILDHOOD PSYCHOSIS

There is some disagreement as to whether or not children actually get schizophrenia. Some authorities maintain that childhood psychosis or schizophrenia—and they tend to use the terms interchangeably—is an appropriate label for any very severe emotional disturbance found in babies as early as three to four months of age and as late as adolescence, characterized by markedly bizarre behavior.

Childhood psychosis is in any event quite rare—less than one child in 1,000 is so diagnosed—and in most cases the child's behavior is so different from that of other children that the parents nearly always sense that something serious is wrong. A characteristic symptom is persistent social isolation, that is, lack of friends, no interest in making friends, no pleasure from peer interaction, and general avoidance of contact with other children in play, sports, or other activities.

Autism

One of the most tragic and, fortunately, very rare disorders of young children is autism. It afflicts approximately one child in 3,000, and affects boys three to four times more often than girls. Its cause is not known. Some authorities still believe it is parent-induced, a view widely held in the 1950s and 1960s, but more recent thinking leans toward an organic cause.

Autism usually begins before the age of two and one-half, and its foremost symptom is an inability to relate to people and to social situations in a normal way. The autistic child acts aloof and inaccessible; he does not smile at his mother or raise his arms to be picked up. He usually does not develop normal speech, although he will cry—sometimes almost constantly—and make noises. If picked up and held, the autistic child often holds his body rigid, seemingly resisting affectionate human contact.

In addition to such aloof behavior, autistic children may show one or more of the following symptoms:

- Severe speech and language disturbance, ranging from not talking at all to bizarre speech patterns (such as echoing aloud everything he hears).
- Preoccupation with particular objects, such as playing with a single toy all day long, day after day.
- Resistance to environmental change of any kind—different food, rearranged furniture, changes in schedule, etc.
- Unusual repetitive body movements, such as head-banging, rocking, hand-flapping, and the like.
- Failure to react appropriately or consistently to external stimuli; for example, jumping at a soft sound and not responding at all to a loud noise, or not reacting to being burned by a match.
- Acute and excessive anxiety without apparent cause.
- Lack of a sense of identity, shown in self-injurious behavior (pulling out own hair, biting self, etc.), or reversing personal pronouns ("You want milk" instead of "I want milk").

Autism may be primary (occur in the absence of other disorders) and often appears in a family where the other children are normal. It may also be secondary to recognized disturbances, such as brain damage, metabolic disorders, or other organic problems. Superficially the autistic child may resemble a severely retarded child, but in fact physical development is usually normal, and in some areas there is marked intelligence. Some autistic children who scarcely speak can read very well and can repeat complex sentences that have been read to them. On the other hand, they tend to have limited understanding of what they repeat or attach unusual meanings to the words.

The outlook for autistic children is not very hopeful. Even with devoted care, 85 to 90 percent eventually end up in institutions, where they remain for life. Those who can develop speech and social relations to levels sufficient to function independently still seem very eccentric to strangers and/or very immature for their years.

Over the past few decades there has been great progress in developing a range of teaching techniques that can and do help severely disturbed children develop appropriate behavior, gain mastery over their abilities, and lead more productive lives. Information about the facilities in your area is available from the National Society for Autistic Children, Suite 1017, 1234 Massachusetts Avenue NW, Washington, DC 20005.

OTHER DEVELOPMENTAL PROBLEMS

One symptom that often prompts parents to seek professional advice is a child's failure to begin speaking. This symptom, of course, can point not only to autism but to deafness, mental retardation, or some other organic problem, or it may mean nothing at all—some children simply develop certain skills far more slowly than others. When, then, should a parent seek advice about a child's slow development? Here are some cautionary signs:

In infancy—
- Slow motor development—not crawling by seven months, not walking by sixteen months.
- Failure to form social attachments—not smiling at three to four months, not acknowledging the parents as special by six months, not showing separation anxiety (crying when they leave) at eight or nine months.
- Slowness to understand language and to talk—not speaking a single word at twelve months, not responding to own name or to voices, not using many words by eighteen months.
- Unusual sensitivities and irritability.
- Problems in eating and sleeping.
- Failure to show normal physical growth.
- Failure to show normal feelings of pleasure and pain.

During toddler years—
- Hyperactivity.
- Unusual aggressiveness.
- Failure to advance language skills.

During preschool and early school years
• Trouble in learning, especially in reading.
• Unusual fears and preoccupations.
• Trouble in paying attention.

What should parents do? The first person to turn to is the family doctor or the child's pediatrician. If the doctor seems uninterested in the problem, or if both physician and parents feel the need for further advice, a child psychiatrist or a psychologist who specializes in child development should be consulted, in order to perform a *developmental evaluation.*

Diagnosing autism or other severely disturbed behavior or mental retardation in a young child is often complicated by the presence of specific sensory or motor defects (for example, impaired hearing may delay learning to speak), of a condition such as cerebral palsy that delays motor development, or of mental retardation, alone or in conjunction with emotional disturbance. Often the symptoms overlap and several problems exist at the same time. Brain-injured and epileptic children have psychiatric disturbances far more frequently than physically normal children, and also far more frequently than children with physical disorders not involving the central nervous system. Psychiatric disorders are especially common among youngsters with temporal lobe epilepsy. Sorting out these difficulties, both physical and psychological, requires expert help.

HYPERACTIVITY AND LEARNING DISABILITIES

There is a similar overlap of symptoms with hyperactivity, learning disabilities, and mental retardation. Frequently it is very hard to tell if a child has organic brain damage of some kind that impairs learning, or if emotional problems are responsible, or if an organic handicap has given rise to (secondary) emotional problems. Stephen, the third-grader whose behavior disrupts the class, is a typical example. Is he hyperactive? Is he retarded? Does he have emotional problems? If more than one is true, which came first?

An estimated 10 percent of all schoolchildren have learning problems caused by mental retardation, emotional problems, or brain dysfunction. Hyperactivity, the condition in which a child can't pay attention long enough to learn anything, is part of the "learning disabilities syndrome." About 40 percent of all learning-disabled youngsters are hyperactive. In the 1950s this condition was called "minimal brain damage" because its symptoms are so similar to those of known brain damage, even though no evidence of organic damage can be found in these children. Later came "minimal brain dysfunction (MBD)," another label now in disfavor. More recent names for hyperactivity are *hyperkinetic reaction* and *attentional deficit disorder*. About four out of five hyperactive youngsters are boys, and a high proportion are first-born children; the reasons for these findings are not known.

Who Is Hyperactive?

How can you tell the difference between a normal but very lively child and a hyperactive one? In addition to their seemingly constant jumpiness, such children usually show *all* of the following symptoms:

- Impulsive behavior—they are quick to react, and act on impulse, without thought of the consequences.
- Distractibility—that is, short attention span; they are easily diverted from the task at hand.
- Excitability—they are easily aroused.

If all these symptoms are present, appeared before the age of seven, have persisted for at least six months, and appear in more than one setting (both home *and* school, or school *and* neighborhood), there is cause to suspect hyperactivity.

A variety of other symptoms—mental, physical, and emotional—also may be present. A physical examination usually shows no gross abnormalities, but an electroencephalogram (EEG) may show something amiss.

To evaluate such children thoroughly, a team approach is needed, involving the family physician or pediatrician, a child psychologist, psychiatrist, social worker, speech pathologist, and others trained in special education. The symptoms must be differentiated from mental retardation (impaired intellect) by means of intelligence tests; from organic disorders such as a degenerative disease of the central nervous system; and from psychiatric disorders such as primary autism or severe depression. The special education specialists then are enlisted to pinpoint the precise nature of the learning disability—for example, dyslexia (perception problems that hamper reading and writing).

The causes of hyperactivity and learning disability are not really known, but most authorities feel they have multiple causes that vary from individual to individual. Among them are brain damage (occurring before, during, or after birth), a lag in the development or maturation of some part of the central nervous system (since these disabilities sometimes are outgrown), a genetic factor (in about half of all cases other members of the family are affected by a similar problem), a biochemical cause related to the neurotransmitters or another area of brain chemistry, some other dysfunction in the brain, nutritional deficiencies, and allergies. The symptoms tend to lessen with age, but attention span and ability to concentrate often remain a problem throughout life. Also, academic failures frequently produce low self-esteem and feelings of depression, which sometimes (some authorities say in as many as one-fourth of cases) find expression in antisocial behavior.

Every Child is Different

A special word of caution is in order. To parents their own child is always different from other children—better in some respects, worse in others. Parents who want the best for their children—that is, practically all parents—may be inclined to worry too much over individual differences. The range of normal behavior is very wide, and so is the range of normal development. Differences in intellect, motor coordination, temperament, sociability, and ways of learning are to be expected. What, then, are the warning signs of a real problem?

1. The child's behavior is very different from that of his or her peers.

2. Compared to children of the same age, the child has trouble controlling impulsive behavior.
3. The child has trouble getting along with other children of the same age.
4. The child has trouble learning things that others of the same age can learn readily.
5. The child has recurring physical symptoms for which no organic cause can be found (headache, stomachache, etc.).
6. The child either is very withdrawn, retreating from social contact, or is very aggressive toward others.
7. The child's behavior difficulties occur not only at home or at school or in the neighborhood, but in at least two of these places.
8. The problem behavior has lasted for some months.
9. Efforts by family members and teachers have not helped the child.

The more symptoms that apply, and the longer-lasting the problem has been, without improvement despite efforts to help, the more important it is to seek professional advice soon. The Association for Children with Learning Disabilities, 4156 Library Road, Pittsburgh, PA 15234 (telephone: 412-341-1515) can, through its local chapters, provide information about various services available to such children.

MENTAL RETARDATION

In recent years special programs and special education have advanced considerably to help those youngsters who are mentally retarded. Retardation is defined as significantly below-average intellectual functioning along with deficits in adaptive behavior—that is, low intelligence combined with impaired ability to attain the personal independence and social responsibility expected for one's age. In young children this takes the form of lags in sensory-motor development, communication skills (speech and language), self-help skills, and socialization (interaction with others).

It is important to understand that there are *degrees* of mental retardation, and that by far the majority of retarded individuals—an estimated 89 percent of retarded youngsters and adults—fall into the category called "mildly retarded." Of the rest, approximately 6 percent are moderately retarded, 3.5 percent are severely retarded, and 1.5 percent profoundly retarded. Most mildly retarded children are able to remain at home with their families during the school years and eventually live independently as self-supporting adults. The very fact of retardation, however, subjects both these youngsters and their families to considerable emotional stress, and consequently they are advised to seek as much support as possible from special organizations and community agencies that can serve them. The National Association for Retarded Citizens (2709 Avenue E, East Arlington, TX 76011) has numerous local offices that provide information on services and programs for mentally retarded children. Local agencies can also be located through your mental health association; through Closer Look Information Center, Box 1492, Washington, DC 20012; and through the Council for Exceptional Children, 1920 Association Drive, Reston, VA 22091 (toll-free telephone: 800-336-3728).

For more about psychotherapy for children, see Chapter 13; for residential facilities for children, Chapter 17; for evaluation of children's programs, Chapter 18; the family's role, Chapter 19; and juvenile delinquency, Chapter 22.

CHAPTER 6

What's Wrong: A Professional Opinion

Once it is decided that you, your relative, or your friend will seek treatment for a problem, the next step is to find out whether or not a mental health professional agrees that treatment is indeed indicated. As pointed out before, some practitioners believe that if you *think* you need therapy you undoubtedly do, but not everyone subscribes to this school of thought. Further, what you or your friend may regard as a serious, long-term problem may, in the opinion of a professional, be insufficiently serious to require any treatment or mild enough that a short-term approach seems the best course.

A REAL-LIFE CASE

Arlene H., 54, a legal secretary, was brought to the hospital by ambulance at 2 P.M. on a hot August day. While sitting on the steps of her office building during lunch hour, she had suddenly complained of dizziness and collapsed. Although conscious by the time she was admitted, she seemed disoriented. A careful physical examination showed nothing out of the ordinary. Asked if she was taking any medication, she said she took only strong headache remedies because she had been getting headaches for the past year. Six months earlier she had seen a neurosurgeon, who had performed nerve conduction tests and found no cause for the headaches.

At the hospital, Arlene seemed strangely unconcerned, even though she had no recollection of how she got there. The attending physician could find no underlying illness but suspected she was suffering from depression and called in a psychiatrist for consultation.

The weekend intervened, and the psychiatrist who saw her two days later recorded the following statements she made (among others) during the interview:

1. I don't remember how I got here. I think it was yesterday. Today is August 12 (it was actually August 24). I do remember getting dizzy and falling on my way to the bathroom this morning, but that's happened before. Also, the coffee tastes different from how I make it.
2. I'm not a nervous person, but sometimes I'm a little "slow-motion." I've always been good at my work though, but not so much during the past two months.
3. My mother died four months ago. I took care of her for the past four years, while she was in and out of the nursing home. I haven't been able to cry for her. But I couldn't cry when my father died, either.
4. My appetite isn't good, and I don't feel well in general, but that began before my mother died.

The psychiatrist also interviewed Arlene's husband, Herb, who said:

1. My wife's changed. She's lost her vitality and pep. She never smiles any more, and I think she doesn't give a damn about anything.
2. She's changed at work, too, I think. She's not as friendly as she used to be, she doesn't get along so well with people, and she isn't doing her work as well.
3. She gets angry when I ask her about it. I think she's really depressed about her mother's death.

The psychiatrist agreed with the attending physician that this was a puzzling case and suggested starting Arlene on an anti-depressant drug and performing more tests. A spinal tap and electroencephalogram (measuring brain-wave activity) showed no abnormalities. The psychiatrist returned and spoke briefly with Arlene again, and then told her physician he did not think she was depressed. In fact, he did not find her condition typical of any functional disorder he had seen. Rather, he thought there might be an organic problem and suggested a CAT scan.

Arlene's CAT scan was performed a couple of days later. It revealed a brain tumor, which was successfully removed that same week. Two months later she was back at work, functioning normally.

Arlene was among the fortunate. Two alert practitioners realized that there might be something seriously wrong and pursued it until they found out what it was. And she was doubly fortunate in that her tumor could be removed without further damaging her brain, and her functioning fully restored.

Asked why he suspected organic disease, the psychiatrist later summed up his findings. There were four signs: progressive head-ache, falling spells, decreased intellectual function (both reported at work and evident during the interview), and a kind of apathy or indifference that seemed to him markedly different from "sadness" or "grieving."

Her experience underlines the importance of a medical checkup to ensure that mental symptoms which cannot be logically explained are not in fact being caused by organic disease.

THE EVALUATION PROCESS

After a medical checkup has ruled out this possibility, you still need a professional opinion concerning your mental problems. Formu-lating this opinion is called *evaluation* or *assessment*.

Most mental health professionals have a set procedure for eval-uating clients, which varies somewhat according to the therapist's personal beliefs and training.

COMMONLY USED PSYCHOLOGIC TESTS

Intelligence Tests	*For Ages*	*Assesses*	*Method*
Bayley Scales of Infant Development	1 to 30 months	Cognitive function and motor development	Doing developmental tasks
Cattell Infant Intelligence Scale	2 to 30 months	Cognitive function and motor development; helps early diagnosis of brain damage, mental retardation	Doing developmental tasks
Stanford-Binet Intelligence Scale, Form L–M	2 to adult (best, 3 to 8)	Intellectual functioning	Problem-solving
Wechsler Preschool and Primary Scale of Intelligence (WPPSI)	4 to 6½	Intellectual functioning	Problem-solving
Wechsler Intelligence Scale for Children (WISC)	5 to 15 (best, 7 to 13)	Intellectual functioning	Problem-solving
Wechsler Adult Intelligence Scale-Revised (WAIS-R)	16+	Intellectual functioning	Problem-solving
Personality Tests, Projective*			
Children's Apperception Test (CAT)	2 to 10	Personality conflicts	Make up story based on pictures
Thematic Apperception Test (TAT)	adults to 65	Personality conflicts	Make up story based on pictures

Personality Tests, Nonprojective	*For Ages*	*Assesses*	*Method*
Draw-A-Person (Family/House/Tree) Test	2 to adult	Personality conflicts; for drawing person, also intellectual functioning, visual/motor coordination	Draw picture on blank sheet of paper
Rorschach (Ink-blot)	3 to adult	Personality conflicts, thought processes	Tell what a series of ink blots look like to you
Minnesota Multiphasic Personality Inventory (MMPI)	15 to adult	Personality; yields scores on scales representing diagnostic categories (schizophrenia, etc.)	Decide if each of 550 statements applies to you or not
Vineland Social Maturity Test	Infancy to adult	Independent social functioning	Interview with individual or guardian
Tests for learning disabilities and/or organic brain damage			
Illinois Test of Psycholinguistic Ability (ITPA)	2 to 10	Auditory and visual perception skills/deficits	Language functioning
Frostig Developmental Test of Visual Perception	4 to 8	Visual perception	Paper and pencil test
Bender Visual Motor Gestalt Test	5 to adult	Perceptual and motor skills/deficits	Copying geometric figures
Benton Visual Retention Test	8 to adult	Visual memory	Reproduce geometric figures from memory

*Intentionally ambiguous questions designed to draw different responses from individuals, revealing personal thoughts and feelings.

Some rely on standardized tests, usually administered by psychologists who specialize in diagnostic testing. Others may rely on one or more interviews with the client, calling in other mental health professionals only if special circumstances seem to warrant it.

Anywhere from *one to three interviews* are the average time needed for an evaluation. At the end of that time the therapist should be able to explain what he/she believes to be the nature of the problem and what treatment, if any, he or she recommends.

Among the simplest tests employed are those to determine whether or not an individual's basic cognitive functions are within a normal range. These tests include questions concerning orientation as to place, time, and person (Where are we now? What is today's date and day of the week? What is your name? What is my name?), counting backward from 100 by 7s (100, 93, 86, etc.) or making change correctly, the interpretation of simple proverbs (What does "A stitch in time saves nine" mean?), and recent and remote memory (What did you eat today? Where were you born?). These questions usually are presented at an initial interview with a person who seems disoriented or otherwise out of touch with reality. More extensive tests are used to check for neurological impairment or other defects due to organic brain disease or injury, personality characteristics, and intelligence. The accompanying chart describes some of the most widely used tests in psychologic evaluation.

Sometimes evaluation must be performed in a hospital, where a person can be observed over a period of time by a variety of experts—neurologist, psychiatrist, psychologist, nurses, social workers, speech and other special therapists—who can then combine their findings. Inpatient evaluation is used most often for those who are judged to be a danger to themselves or others (they may be committed for a given period, for observation), for individuals in whom organic brain disease is suspected and who require medical tests, and for children who need medical treatment in addition to psychotherapy or who suffer from physical handicaps such as epilepsy or cerebral palsy, or who are being evaluated for educational aptitude and achievement potential (sometimes called a *core* or *team evaluation* because it involves parents and numerous professionals, such as social worker, teacher, educational psychologist, neurologist, etc.) Typically such an evaluation takes a week but, depending on individual factors, it may require more or less time.

A thorough evaluation takes into account not only psychological factors and somatic factors (physical disease) but also environmental factors. A young boy growing up in dire poverty may be slow to acquire speech simply because his parents never have time (or do not know enough) to talk to him; similarly an undernourished child may do very poorly in school. A family situation where one of the members is seriously ill or disturbed can cause intolerable stress for some of the other members, giving rise to emotional symptoms. A careful assessment should uncover and take into account the client's life situation.

After the evaluation is complete you can consider the recommendations made and decide whether or not to act on them. Remember that in most cases this is the client's own decision. The only exceptions are those cases where a person is committed (see Chapter 22 for more about these legal procedures) or is so ill, with thought processes and judgment so severely impaired, that in effect a relative must make the decision.

Further, if you're not satisfied with either the evaluation or the recommendations, get a *second opinion*. It is far better to be sure of your course of action now, before you have invested time and money in a treatment that may not be the best, or even the right one. As pointed out before, the symptoms of mental illness overlap, and diagnosis of mental illness is more an art than a science. If you are uneasy about the results of one evaluation, consult another qualified professional.

CHAPTER 7

Getting Help—
How Do You Find It?

It has now been decided, and you agree, that mental-health help of one kind or another is needed. How can you find a competent practitioner?

Even though your problem may not qualify as an emergency, you might first try the same sources to refer you to someone: your family doctor, a private mental health practitioner (a psychiatrist, a psychologist, a social worker) of your acquaintance, or the clergy (preferably your own pastor or rabbi).

YOUR DOCTOR

The old-time family physician who treated every ailment, made house calls at all hours, and knew each family member intimately is a thing of the past, but today's general practitioners, family practitioners, pediatricians, and internists all are frequently called on to provide initial care and referral for persons in emotional distress, and some undertake long-term care as well. Nearly two-thirds of all referrals to private psychiatrists are made by family doctors. Often a mental illness first appears in the form of physical symptoms (lack of sleep, stomach upset, headache, etc.) driving an individual to seek medical advice. Or, even if the distress is obviously mental in origin, one's doctor is still looked on as a trusted adviser. Further,

68

in routine physical examinations the doctor is often in a position to recognize early evidence of mental disorders, especially in children but also in adults.

In an emergency, as we have said, a physician is likely to know the nearest place for you or your relative to go, and may even be able to give some immediate treatment personally (administer a sedative, for example). As for referring you to a specific therapist, the physician may or may not be a good source.

Some doctors look down on psychotherapy, either because they believe mental problems are better handled medically, or because they feel mental illness is somehow "unreal" (at least, compared to physical illness) and can be "outgrown" or "gotten over" without treatment. When they do make referrals, they often have a strong preference for psychiatrists, who have medical backgrounds like their own, even when a psychologist, social worker, or other therapist might be just as useful and more readily available (and usually less expensive, too).

Does your doctor share these prejudices? It may be hard to find out. If your doctor does seem sympathetic and knowledgeable and you ask about a therapist, you might inquire what the results have been for patients previously referred to this person—in other words, ask if he/she has sent other patients to this therapist. If so, how well have they done? Some referrals from physicians work out very well, and the conscientious family doctor generally provides some followup, even if only in the form of asking "How are things going now?" during the next office visit.

ASKING OTHER PROFESSIONALS

If you happen to know someone in the mental health field, you may ask him or her for advice. Remember, however, that they are just as likely as a physician to recommend someone in their own specialty (psychologists tend to refer you to a psychologist, social workers to a social worker, etc.). This is not necessarily bad but it does limit your choices. Also, the professionals you consult may not always know very much about the therapists and facilities they are recommending. Some follow up on referrals; others don't.

Another source of information is the clergy. A growing number are trained in pastoral counseling (see Chapter 8) and have established contacts with mental health professionals and various facilities. They tend to keep in touch with parishioners after they have been referred elsewhere, so they know something of the results of treatment they have recommended.

Industrial physicians and personnel officers of large companies often are experienced with mental health problems and can refer employees to a therapist or clinic. They, too, are likely to have feedback concerning the outcome of treatment.

COSTS OF HELP

Even at this early stage you also must consider the costs of different kinds of help. Finances are a grim reality. Few of us budget for a mental breakdown, yet what good does it do, for example, to find a marvelous alcoholism center to dry out Aunt Bertha if it costs $200 a day and she and Uncle Jack are barely making ends meet on his unemployment compensation? Some professionals go so far as to say that the first step in seeking help should be to list one's financial assets. That is something of an exaggeration, but money can't be overlooked entirely. All the money in the world won't help your autistic son if you can't find a therapist or facility agreeing to take him on as a patient.

AGENCIES TO CONSULT

If you or whoever must pay the bills has limited financial means, one of the first things to investigate is the possibility of state or Federal programs that can aid the individual in need of help. The best way to get this information is through a community mental health center or a social agency such as a family service agency. Both have social workers on their staff who are knowledgeable about these matters.

The community mental health center is a direct-help agency for all mental health problems. What they can't handle themselves, they can refer to other professionals. A phone call should get you an appointment; if you need help fast, say so, and you may get an interview within a day or so. Some community mental health centers have walk-in clinics where you can make an appointment. (See also below.)

If there is no community mental health center near you, the nearest state mental hospital may be able to tell you about the various state-supported mental health programs for which you might be eligible. If you think you are entitled to federal help, the nearest Veterans Administration hospital can give you information on federal programs.

The state mental health association or a county mental health association are local divisions of the National Mental Health Association, an organization whose main jobs are information, referral, and advocacy. The branch nearest you is likely to know of clinics and services available in your area. Most cities and counties have NAMH branches, listed in the phone book under Mental Health Association or under the name of your city or county. Some branches publish directories of local resources; if they themselves do not, they will know if any other social agency in your area, such as United Way, does. They may or may not recommend individual practitioners; more often they will give you the names of several with offices near you.

When you consult an agency, such as a family service agency or mental health association branch, you may need both patience and persistence. It is better to describe your problem instead of simply asking about a specific kind of help or facility. Be prepared to explain your problem fully, and let the agency decide what service(s) or facility might be appropriate. For example, if you are trying to find a place to detoxify alcoholic Aunt Bertha, explain that your aunt is an alcoholic of so many years' standing who has become both drunk and disoriented and who needs medical help to dry out. The agency may then suggest the available facilities. If you ask only for an alcohol detoxification center and there happens to be none nearby, you may be told just that and will have reached a dead end.

Don't give up if the first or second (or third or fourth) agency doesn't have the information you need, or cannot offer help. Ask them whom you should call next, or, if they say they don't know, ask who they think might know.

If you live in a small town far from a big city with numerous agencies, a good start for you might be the counseling service or psychology department of a nearby college or university. They sometimes refer students who need help and are apt to know of local resources. Other sources of referral are the psychiatric service of a local hospital, local schools of psychotherapy or social work, and friends or family members who have had good experience with one or another therapist. These are mainly sources for names of practitioners in your area, but may not tell you much else about them.

The next chapter discusses the training and qualifications of various kinds of practitioner.

CHAPTER 8

Mental Health Care Providers: Individual Therapists

Suppose your problem has been narrowed down to finding a suitable therapist. Or, if you or your child or your Uncle Jack need to be hospitalized for a time, you will be dealing with one or more individual therapists on a one-to-one basis. Who are these people?

The principal mental health care providers in a hospital or other inpatient setting are psychiatrists, neurologists, clinical psychologists, psychiatric social workers, psychiatric nurses, aides (mental health workers), and occupational therapists. These individuals also may (and often do) work outside a hospital setting. Outside the hospital, psychotherapy also is performed by psychoanalysts, lay analysts, and counselors of various kinds: marriage counselors, family counselors, sex therapists, divorce counselors, rehabilitation counselors, school counselors, vocational guidance counselors, pastoral counselors.

How do these professionals differ from one another? What are their qualifications? Their backgrounds and credentials may not make them the best (or even the right) therapist for you, but at least they tell you something about them.

PSYCHIATRISTS

The psychiatrist has completed four years of medical school, one year of postgraduate training (often called *internship*), and has passed a licensing examination in his or her state. Legally this is all that is needed to practice psychiatry—that is, any licensed physician may practice it—but most psychiatrists also have spent at least three years (usually four) as a resident physician in an institution where mental illness is treated (state hospital, psychiatric service of a general hospital, private mental hospital, or mental health center). Their period of residency includes work with physical therapies (see Chapters 15 and 16) and with both individual and group psychotherapy, but it does not include psychoanalysis (see below). The quality of residency programs varies; the best are those affiliated with a medical school (the remaining one-third are less rigorous). Those who want additional special training in psychotherapy usually attend a postgraduate program at a psychotherapy institute (which may or may not be a psychoanalytic institute).

After two years of additional experience following their residency, psychiatrists may take the examinations of the Board of Psychiatry and Neurology of the American Medical Association, which leads to board certification. In the United States about one-half of the 30,000 psychiatrists practicing in 1980 were board-certified. Approximately half of those who take the board examinations fail them, but they still may (and do) practice psychiatry.

Psychiatrists can become associate members of the American Psychiatric Association (APA) after one year of practice, and full members after three years. In 1981 26,000 American psychiatrists were members (or about 86 percent of all psychiatrists); almost 90 percent of them were men. Membership indicates professional responsibility but does not signify competence in psychotherapy.

Because psychiatrists also are physicians, they may prescribe drugs and administer physical treatment such as electroconvulsive therapy (ECT). Such treatment by them is covered by any health insurance plan that includes mental health coverage. Of the other mental health professionals, only those psychoanalysts who also are physicians may prescribe drugs. Other than that, there are no Federal standards regarding who may treat what disorder or how.

The *child psychiatrist* specializes in diagnosis and treatment of children. In order to be board-certified in child psychiatry he or she must complete a five-year residency, including at least two years of supervised clinical experience with adults and two with children, and must pass a special examination in this area.

Psychiatrists practice various kinds of psychotherapy—individual, family, group—according to their interests. Some specialize in children, others treat only adults, and still others treat patients of any age. Some psychiatrists take on patients with any kind of mental disorder, including the psychoses, while others concentrate on treating less severe disorders. In a hospital (either general or mental), it is usually a psychiatrist who is in charge of directing the care of all inpatients.

Both the American Psychiatric Association and the American Medical Association, as well as the licensing boards of some states, require that psychiatrists keep up with new developments in their field by periodically taking courses, attending professional meetings where research results are shared, and the like. Of the mental health professionals in private practice, the psychiatrist's fees tend to be higher than those of psychologists and social workers. Also, because nine out of ten American psychiatrists are male, if you want a woman therapist you are less likely to find one who is a psychiatrist.

NEUROLOGISTS

A neurologist is a physician who specializes in organic disorders of the brain and nervous system. He or she has a degree in medicine, postgraduate training and experience in this field, certification as a specialist, and a state license permitting him or her to practice. Neurologists usually have received some training in psychiatry. Those who specialize in surgery are called *neurosurgeons* or *neural surgeons*. Consultation with and testing by a neurologist may be

SUMMARY OF STANDARDS FOR MENTAL HEALTH PROFESSIONALS
(Listed under Each Category in Order of Importance)

Psychiatrist:

Completed psychiatric residency, preferably in affiliation with a medical school

Member of the American Psychiatric Association

Board-certified by the American Board of Psychiatry and Neurology (in child psychiatry if the client is a child)

Graduate of psychotherapy or psychoanalytic institute

Clinical psychologist:

Master's degree in clinical psychology

State certification or license*

Ph.D., Psy.D., or Ed.D. in psychology

Member of the American Psychological Association

Diploma in clinical psychology from the American Board of Professional Psychology (ABPP, CL)

Graduate of psychotherapy or psychoanalytic institute

Psychiatric social worker:

Master's degree (MSW) with two years' supervised clinical experience in social work

Certification by state and/or Academy of Certified Social Workers (ACSW)

Graduate of psychotherapy or psychoanalytic training program

Ph.D. or DSW in social work

Psychiatric nurse:

Master's degree in psychiatric nursing (MA, MS, MN, MSN)

Certification by American Nurses Association

Graduate of psychotherapy training program

Psychoanalyst:

Ph.D. in psychology or M.D.

State license as psychologist or physician

Certification by an accredited psychoanalytic institute

*Licensing laws, passed by the various states, require competence in a particular field and restrict practice in that field to those who are licensed. Certification requirements are set by either the state or a professional organization (or both, in which case they are not necessarily the same), and attest to an individual's demonstrated skills but do not restrict practice to those who are certified. Licensing and certification for all the professions but doctors and nurses are relatively new, and therefore practitioners whose practice predates the laws may be licensed under a "grandfather clause," even though they may not meet all the present requirements (an older clinical psychologist might have only a master's degree, for example).

required for patients whose mental symptoms are suspected of being caused by an organic disease.

PSYCHOLOGISTS

The *clinical psychologist* is a psychologist who specializes in the study of abnormal human behavior in a clinical setting. He or she may have any of several degrees: master of arts (MA), master of science (MS), doctor of philosophy in psychology (Ph.D.), doctor of psychology (Psy.D.), or doctor of education (Ed.D.). The title "psychologist" is usually governed by state law and requires a Ph.D. or other doctoral degree with at least two years of supervised experience at a psychiatric hospital or clinic and the passing of an examination. Four years of graduate school and a one-year internship lead to a Ph.D. in clinical psychology or the newer, more practice-oriented degree of Psy.D.

In many states, the state psychological association, a branch of the American Psychological Association, sets standards and tests for certification of their members (who require a doctoral degree to join) as accredited psychologists. In 1981 the Association had 50,000 members in forty-two different divisions; about 23,000 of them practiced in fields related to mental health.

Psychologists are trained in graduate schools, in special clinical psychology programs, and, since 1969, in schools of professional psychology. Some clinical psychologists have a diploma from the American Board of Examiners in Professional Psychology (ABPP, CL). At present it is the only board in the United States that tests for competence in psychotherapy, and it requires passing examinations after at least five years of postdoctoral experience. Only about 10 percent of the psychologists practicing in the United States in 1980 applied for this diploma.

Since 1975 there has been a National Register of Health Service Providers in Psychology, which lists all the psychologists licensed or certified in their respective states who have a doctorate in psychology and two years' supervised experience (one of them postdoctoral) in mental health services of some kind (not necessarily psychotherapy). Psychologists who desire additional clinical training can attend a training institute in psychotherapy or psychoanalysis.

Treatment by a clinical psychologist is not necessarily covered by insurance plans that include mental health coverage. By 1981 about thirty states had adopted laws allowing psychologists to send their outpatients' bills directly to insurance companies, but in states without such laws they could not do so, nor did Medicare or Medicaid cover treatment.

Psychologists perform all kinds of psychotherapy—individual, family, group—according to their interests. They are more likely to be interested in behavior therapy (Chapter 13) than psychiatrists are, since behaviorism was originally entirely within their discipline, but this is not necessarily true of all psychologists. They also still do psychological testing, the clinical application with which they first became associated, as well as school counseling and vocational guidance. About 25,000 psychologists were practicing in the United States in 1981; about one-fourth were women. In general their fees in private practice were lower than those of psychiatrists but higher than those of social workers.

SOCIAL WORKERS

A social worker has completed four years of college and two years of postgraduate study in a school of social work, leading to a master's degree of social work (MSW). A *psychiatric* or *clinical social worker* is one who has concentrated on psychiatric casework, doing field work in a mental hospital, mental health clinic, or family service agency that provides guidance, counseling, and treatment for clients with emotional problems. Psychiatric social workers usually continue to work in one of these facilities but some go into the private practice of psychotherapy.

The psychiatric social worker in a hospital or other inpatient facility maintains contact between patients and their families, serves as part of a treatment team (along with the psychiatrist, psychologist, nurses, and aides), helps the family understand and adjust to problems created by hospitalization, and supervises the rehabilitation of the patient after discharge. In a clinic the social worker usually sees clients and their families when they first come, and helps interpret the clinic for them. Then, depending on the clinic, the social worker either acts as a liaison with the family, giving counseling and guidance while psychiatrists or other professionals treat the client, or actually conducts psychotherapy.

The National Association of Social Workers has a system of voluntary accreditation whereby members who have a master's degree in social work and two years' supervised clinical experience, and who pass an examination, are accredited as members of the Academy of Certified Social Workers (ACSW). Note, however, that not all ACSWs practice psychotherapy. About half the states license or certify social workers (certified social worker, CSW), the requirements for which tend to be similar to those for the ACSW. The National Association of Social Workers publishes a Register of Clinical Social Workers that lists those ACSW members who have had two years' postgraduate experience in clinical social work practice. Another organization, the Society of Clinical Social Work Psychotherapists, is composed of trained therapists as well as certified graduates of master's or doctoral programs in social work. The National Registry of Health Care Providers in Social Work lists persons with all the training needed for an ACSW but with special emphasis on psychotherapy. They do not need to pass an examination, however. Such listing is voluntary and some well-qualified social workers simply never apply for it.

Those social workers who want additional training in psychotherapy or psychoanalytic work may acquire it through a program that accepts students without doctorates (many psychotherapy and psychoanalytic institutes do require a doctorate). With or without this additional training, social workers in private practice perform various kinds of therapy—individual, couples, family, group.

Whether or not health insurance covers treatment by a social worker depends on where you live. In 1976 California made social workers doing outpatient therapy eligible for private insurance payments provided the therapy was recommended by a physician (not necessarily a psychiatrist), but other states have been slow to follow suit. Those who oppose such payment believe that the training and licensing of social workers varies so much that an MSW degree tells you very little about either background or competence. It is likely, however, that this objection will eventually be overcome. About two-thirds of the 100,000 social workers in the United States are women. In private practice social workers tend to charge lower fees than either psychiatrists or psychologists.

PSYCHIATRIC NURSES

The psychiatric nurse is a registered nurse (R.N.) who may or may not have special training in working with psychiatric patients. All nursing programs give some basic theoretical and practical experience in this area, usually including several months' work in a psychiatric inpatient unit. The registered nurse has completed either three years of training at the diploma level in a hospital-affiliated nursing school or a four-year college program with a nursing major, leading to a BA, BS, or BSN, and has passed state licensing examinations to become registered. There is no special license for psychiatric nursing, which therefore may be performed by any general nurse. However, a nurse may become certified as a mental health specialist by meeting certification requirements of the American Nurses Association (a master's degree in psychiatric nursing; two years' supervised clinical experience, at least one of them postgraduate; passing of a written examination; documentation for competence as a clinician). In 1981 an estimated 11,000 nurses in the United States chose to specialize in this field.

Nurses involved in mental patient care in state hospitals, general hospitals with a psychiatric service, and mental health centers often are ordinary registered nurses who receive on-the-job training in mental health care. Some hospitals also employ nurses who have graduated from two-year associate degree programs (usually offered by community colleges) or even briefer (twelve- to eighteen-month) training programs that qualify graduates to be licensed as practical nurses (LPN). These less highly trained nurses usually work under close supervision from registered nurses and other professionals. Some registered nurses take one to two years' additional graduate work to earn a master's degree in psychiatric nursing (MA, MS, MN, master of nursing, or MSN, master of science in nursing). These nurses often plan, carry out, and evaluate the nursing of psychiatric inpatients and also conduct training programs on the job for other nurses. Nurses may go on to a doctoral degree, but only a small percentage do so, and of these few do clinical work in mental health.

In the hospital or inpatient clinic, psychiatric nurses are directly involved in treatment, assisting with the administration of drugs and electroconvulsive therapy (ECT). They also may take patient histories, evaluate the current mental status of a patient, and coordinate treatment teams. Nurses also are increasingly practicing psychotherapy, principally as cotherapists in group therapy, although some may work as individual therapists under a psychiatrist's direction. Outside the hospital some psychiatric nurses have established a private practice in psychotherapy (individual, family, group, etc.).

Nurses may obtain additional training in psychotherapy or psychoanalytic training institutes that accept students without a doctorate. Although there is no state certification as such, some state nursing associations grant a certificate in psychiatric nursing for those who have met certain requirements, which may be quite demanding (a master's degree including at least three semesters of supervised clinical work, two years' postgraduate supervised experience in therapy, and a term of personal therapy). Nevertheless, in 1981 insurance coverage for mental illness did not include therapy administered by a psychiatric nurse. About 99 percent of all nurses in the United States were women, so someone looking for a male psychotherapist would do well to look among the other professions.

AIDES

The psychiatric aide, formerly called *orderly* or *attendant* and now occasionally called *mental health worker* or *mental health technician*, has in recent years assumed increased responsibility for inpatient care. Aides are found only in a private or public hospital or other inpatient facility, and their training ranges from very minimal (high school education with on-the-job training only) to fairly extensive (bachelor's or master's degree and special training). In 1980 there were an estimated 140 two-year college programs for mental health workers in the United States, although the first such program was only established in 1965. At present there is no special licensing or certification for aides, and their duties vary widely. Some act strictly as nurses' aides, doing work comparable to that of aides on medical and surgical wards in general hospitals. Others undertake some individual and group therapy, usually under supervision, and activity therapy such as art therapy, dance therapy, or music therapy; those participating in the last three usually have at least a bachelor's degree with a major in the relevant field.

OCCUPATIONAL THERAPISTS

The occupational therapist (OT) usually works in a psychiatric hospital, general hospital, or day hospital, conducting programs involving work, recreation, and creative activities. OT's evaluate patients with respect to their abilities and emotional and/or physical handicaps. They have completed either a four-year college program with specialization in occupational therapy, leading to a BS, or a master's degree program in occupational therapy, which involves at least six months' supervised clinical experience. After obtaining either of these degrees, they may become registered (OTR) by passing an examination given by the American Occupational Therapy Association.

PSYCHOANALYSTS

A psychoanalyst is any person who has been trained in and uses Freudian or Jungian methods of psychotherapy (see Chapter 12 for a fuller explanation of Freud's and Jung's theories). There are several kinds of psychoanalyst, depending on the individual's background and education: the M.D. psychiatrist, the Ph.D. psychologist, the college graduate (bachelor's or master's degree) with a major in psychology or a related field. All three continue their education with three to four years' training in a psychoanalytic institute that has state accreditation. There they usually are taught by practicing analysts in a program of class study (twenty-five to thirty courses in all), personal psychoanalysis, supervised practice (called a "control analysis"), and experience in a clinic or hospital. Upon completing this program, they are given a certificate by the institute declaring them qualified for the full-time professional practice of psychoanalysis. Some institutes accept only M.D.s, others only M.D.s or Ph.D.s, and still others candidates with less advanced degrees, such as social workers.

The majority of psychoanalysts in the United States, however, are either psychiatrists or psychologists with a doctoral degree. Most training institutes for analysts will not accept candidates under twenty-five, so it is hard to find a certified analyst under the age of thirty. Psychoanalytic training is long and expensive, as is psychoanalytic treatment.

A fourth category is the so-called *lay analyst,* who may or may not have formal training and generally has neither licensing nor certification. A lay analyst may simply be anyone who goes into practice as an "analyst."

COUNSELORS

Just as anyone may call him- or herself an "analyst" or a "psychotherapist," so anyone may hang out a shingle saying "counselor." Strictly speaking, counselors are advisers, and of course you can always take their advice or leave it. Nevertheless, someone in emotional distress who is looking for help is, like any physically ill person, very vulnerable and thus more likely to take advice—especially advice they seek and are paying for—than to ignore it. Therefore it is important that you look into the credentials of whoever is described simply as a "counselor." Those in the counseling fields recognize the importance of maintaining standards of professional conduct and competence, and they increasingly have set up regulations for themselves.

COUPLES AND FAMILY COUNSELORS

Couples, married or not, and families may be counseled by any of the professionals described so far who do individual and group therapy, that is, psychiatrists, clinical psychologists, psychiatric social workers, and psychiatric nurses. In addition, there are therapists who specialize in working with couples and families but who do not necessarily have the same credentials or training. Their professional organization is the American Association of Marriage and Family Counselors, which requires that its members have at least a master's degree in psychology, social work, or some related field, plus a year of supervised clinical internship, followed by three years of professional practice. Today many states have licensing laws for practitioners. (See also family therapy in Chapter 14.)

Sex Therapists

Since about 1960 several rather specialized forms of couples counseling have developed. One is *sex therapy,* short-term psychotherapy that addresses itself principally to problems of sexual dysfunction—the inability to enjoy sexual relations to the fullest—experienced by one or both members of a couple. Because its very nature makes sex therapy readily open to abuse by the unscrupulous and/or unqualified, a person or couple considering it should take care to find a reputable practitioner. The American Association of Sex Educators, Counselors, and Therapists certifies therapists who hold at least a master's degree, and can usually recommend experienced, qualified therapists in various localities. In addition, you should ask any sex therapist you consider using about his or her training, which should include an advanced degree in social work, psychology, or medicine. (See also the section on sex therapy in Chapter 13.)

Divorce Counselors

An even newer specialized form of family counseling is *divorce counseling and mediation,* which concentrates on the problems of couples and families who are faced with divorce. Divorce counselors address such questions as child support, alimony, property division, child custody, visitation rights, and co-parenting. They try to help separating couples reach amicable agreement on these difficult issues and seek to reduce the often bitter conflicts associated with them. The kind of counseling and therapy provided is quite flexible, ranging from counseling of individuals, couples, and couples with children, to group therapy for separating and divorced individuals, children and adolescents whose parents are being divorced, or people who are remarrying and becoming (or have become) stepparents.

To the extent that it minimizes the disruption in the lives of children of divorcing parents and helps divorcing couples adjust to this major change in their lives, divorce mediation is a form of preventive psychotherapy. (See also Chapter 21.) There is no licensing or certification for counselors in this field. Practitioners generally have a background in social work or family therapy of one kind or another and usually work with consultants in law and child psychiatry.

REHABILITATION COUNSELORS

A rehabilitation counselor helps individuals who have had a physical or mental illness return to work, or, if they must change occupations owing to disability, to be trained for and to find new work. The counselor also helps clients obtain medical and mental health services they may need, as well as education. Because their principal focus is to return a person to gainful employment, which is regarded as important for mental health as well as economic well-being, they are sometimes called *vocational rehabilitation counselors.*

Most such counselors are employed by state rehabilitation commissions, which may assign them to mental health centers or other state-funded facilities, or by hospitals and rehabilitation centers. Their training includes four years of college and a two-year specialized master's degree program that includes the study of psychology, counseling techniques, community resources, and vocational and medical rehabilitation. Some rehabilitation counselors go on to obtain a doctorate in the field; the majority of these go on to work with the mentally ill.

The National Commission on Rehabilitation Counselor Certification awards a certificate (CRC) to those counselors who have completed master's level training and have passed an examination. In 1981 rehabilitation counselors did not require a license to practice, although several states were planning to set up licensing laws.

EDUCATIONAL COUNSELORS

An *educational* or *school counselor* is usually a clinical psychologist (see above) who has either a master's degree or a doctorate (Ph.D., Ed.D., Psy.D.). They generally have special training in psychologic testing as well as in counseling youngsters in a school or college setting, which is where they are most likely to be employed. Some counselors address themselves to students' personal and family problems; others confine themselves to dealing with learning problems, educational and vocational choices, and related issues. Like other clinical psychologists, they usually must be licensed or certified in their state, or certified by the state psychological association. Those who are members of the American Psychological Association may apply for a diploma in counseling (ABPP, CO), which requires that they meet rather stringent standards. Some educational counselors work partly or entirely in private practice.

In the United States the services of educational counselors in the public schools are free. Moreover, at present public schools are required by law (Public Law 94-142, passed in 1975) to insure that every handicapped child has a free, appropriate education. Here "handicapped" means children who are mentally retarded, seriously emotionally disturbed, physically handicapped in any way (impaired sight, hearing, speech, orthopedically, etc.), or have special learning disabilities. A child whose handicaps interfere with learning is legally entitled to certain diagnostic and treatment services provided by the school. Since the passage of this law, educational counselors have become increasingly involved in helping to assess children's abilities and performance by testing, and developing an individualized educational plan (IEP) for every youngster who has been determined as having "special educational needs."

In addition, there are still counselors who specialize in advising students on educational and career choices. Often called *guidance* or *vocational counselors,* they generally work within a school system. These counselors ordinarily have a master's degree in their specialty and are trained to administer and interpret psychological tests, as well as to be familiar with the requirements of various colleges and careers. Vocational counselors rarely are certified by the state but they may apply for professional membership in the National Vocational Guidance Association, whose members are required to have basic credentials. Some are certified through their state's department of education, although this usually is limited to counselors who also are certified teachers and therefore excludes those who do not have such certification. Insofar as their work is done in public schools, it is free of charge.

PASTORAL COUNSELORS

Priests, ministers, and rabbis have traditionally advised members of their congregations. People tend to trust their pastor with personal problems of a private nature, feeling that this is a person who knows the family and will not betray a confidence. There is no social stigma on consulting one's pastor, nor is there usually a charge for doing so. And, of course, many individuals believe in the healing power of prayer. For all these reasons, a member of the clergy often is the first person to be consulted about a specific mental health problem.

Informally the clergy have been mental health practitioners for hundreds of years. Traditionally they are present at many of the great emotional occasions of life: birth, marriage, serious illness, death. For unhappy events it is part of the clergy's job to comfort individuals and families going through difficult times.

Today many pastors receive formal education in counseling as part of their training, and those who are particularly interested in this aspect of their ministry usually take additional training, some of it quite intensive. For example, one pastor who was interviewed had had more than a year of clinical pastoral education, which included a six-month period of supervised work at a large state mental hospital. Some denominations operate a centralized pastoral counseling service in places where they have enough members to warrant it. Such a center offers specific programs and services to individuals and families in the congregations it serves, including short- and long-term counseling for individuals, couples, and families; evaluation and referral for those whose needs it cannot meet; and education and consultation for pastors who wish to enhance their counseling skills.

The problems people bring to a pastor range from murder and suicide to family problems (with children, spouse, elderly parents), alcoholism, drug abuse, and all the common forms of mental illness. Of the problems brought in, the largest category are family problems. The next most important group consists of spiritual problems, relating to such matters as belief in God and life after death. An estimated 80 percent of all problems brought to them are handled by the clergy alone. Of the rest, about half are referred immediately, most often to a community mental health center, and the rest are subsequently referred to other therapists.

Most pastoral counseling is short-term, consisting of one or two sessions. Many pastors feel they cannot devote too much time to a few members of the congregation. One study indicates that the clergy spend about 6 percent of their time (two to three hours a week) doing counseling. Emergencies are referred immediately to a crisis center or hospital, and serious or long-term problems to a community mental health center or individual mental health practitioner. Unlike others who make such referrals, pastors frequently follow up such cases and may continue to see individuals who are receiving treatment elsewhere, although usually on an irregular basis.

The clergy predominantly see members of their own congregation, but if they have the time they are occasionally willing to see outsiders, and if able, will nearly always give help or advice in an emergency.

The American Association of Pastoral Counselors is a professional organization that has set standards for training and certification of individuals and institutions in the field of pastoral counseling. Members must meet certain requirements as to education, supervised clinical experience, and assessment of qualifications and professional competence by a committee of peers. There are three levels—member, fellow, and diplomate—with increasing requirements for each category. Members must hold a master of divinity degree from an accredited theological school, have completed one unit of clinical pastoral education, and have done at least 375 hours of counseling (125 of them under supervision); fellows must hold an advanced degree (master's or doctorate) in pastoral counseling and have done at least 1,375 hours of counseling, 250 of it under supervision; diplomates must, in addition to these requirements, demonstrate ability to teach and supervise others in pastoral counseling, having supervised at least five trainees for thirty hours each, one-third of that amount under supervision. In addition, the Association has set standards for pastoral counseling centers and other facilities providing training in the field. In 1981 the Association had approximately 1,500 members and an additional 300 counselors-in-training.

CHAPTER 9

How To Choose An Individual Therapist

You now know the basic qualifications behind the titles and degrees, but does that tell you how to choose a therapist? Not really. Rather, these tell you the minimum requirements—that a doctor went to an accredited medical school and is board-certified, that a social worker has at least a master's degree.

HOW *NOT* TO CHOOSE A THERAPIST

Do *not* go by whether the medical school attended is a prestigious one. Fine schools graduate incompetent therapists as well as competent ones.

Do *not* go solely by degrees, memberships, and the like.

Do *not* go by your friends, relatives, or neighbors, or at least take what they say with a grain of salt. They are not necessarily competent in judging whether or not a therapist is good.

Do *not* go by your county medical society. It is not a referral agency and can tell you little or nothing other than the names of licensed physicians in your area who practice psychiatry (most will give you three names).

Do *not* go by your local hospital. Staff privileges often are given to any applicant who is a licensed physician.

Do *not* go solely by a psychiatrist or psychologist you happen to know. He/she is inclined to favor those practitioners who have the same background or therapeutic approach as his or her own, and may overlook others, equally competent, who do not.

Do *not* go by the yellow pages (classified phone directory). In a large city or metropolitan area it may list both individuals and clinics under such headings as Psychologists, Psychotherapists, and Physicians (with the subgroups Psychiatrists, Psychoanalysts, Child Psychiatrists), but anyone can buy such a listing and the degrees listed after each name can be invented.

HOW TO GET JUST NAMES

For names of reputable practicing psychotherapists in your area—without regard to their orientation or skill—you can call either the nearest branch of the Mental Health Association or the local professional societies for psychiatrists, psychologists, social workers, or psychiatric nurses. If you decide you want only certain ones of these categories, call only them. You can also consult the directories of the various professional organizations, which all have a geographical listing so you can see who lives in your area. Psychiatrists who are board-certified are listed in the *Directory of Medical Specialities;* if not board-certified, they may still be listed in the *American Psychiatric Association Directory.* Psychologists are listed in the *American Psychological Association Directory* and the *National Registry of Health Service Providers in Psychology.* Social workers are listed in the membership directory of the National Association of Social Workers or its *Register of Clinical Social Workers.* All these directories are available in large public libraries and university libraries.

A private or public mental hospital in your area, the psychology department of a nearby medical school, or the counseling service of a college or university also may give you names. However, they are likely to have a vested interest in recommending those practitioners whose background and orientation are similar to their own.

HOW YOU *SHOULD* CHOOSE

Your family doctor or your pastor may be able to recommend someone. With both you can be frank and ask what the outcome of their previous referrals to this practitioner has been. As indicated earlier, they tend to follow up, since they usually continue to see the person as a patient or parishioner and are likely to ask how he or she is doing.

Another good source is a person in the mental health field who has contact with many other mental health professionals but has nothing to gain from recommending one person over another. An ideal choice is a psychiatric social worker in a public mental health center or family service agency. In either case, politics is unlikely to play a role.

Do take into account the recommended practitioner's local reputation. Even if you don't take your neighbors' advice as gospel, when all four of the persons you talk to say that Dr. XYZ or Ms. ABC is wonderful and has helped so many people, chances are that he or she has something going that may help you. Also, if the name of one practitioner is mentioned by numerous sources, you just might try that person yourself.

In all these instances it helps to tell your consultant a little about the nature of the problem. He or she then may be able to suggest a therapist who is very experienced or skilled with that kind of a problem (for example, depression, alcoholism, or phobias).

These are ways to find a competent therapist, but there are three other important considerations: *time, money,* and *compatibility.*

The best therapists often are the ones who are most in demand. Consequently, even if you can locate a highly promising individual, he or she may be fully booked for some time. Nevertheless, it may be useful to see such a person for a preliminary evaluation (one or two sessions), in which you can determine if this is a therapist worth waiting for (if you are able to wait), or, if he or she will have no open time for many months, one who can recommend a less busy colleague with similar characteristics and orientation.

Money is important. There is no point in locating a therapist who costs more than you can pay or than your insurance can cover. Many therapists make some provision for low-income clients—a sliding fee scale, for example—but some will not or cannot (they have to live, too). Depending on your financial circumstances, you may have to abandon the person of your choice and opt for a clinic or other lower-cost solution (see Chapter 10).

Finally, the best-qualified and most highly trained therapist still may not be the person best for you. You don't have to see eye to eye on everything with your therapist, but you should feel comfortable in his or her presence, believe he or she is listening to what you are saying and sensitive to your feelings, and generally find this individual to be someone you can talk to easily and trust. Much of this will be evident in the very first interview, which provides an opportunity for you to size each other up and for you to ask questions about the therapist's education, professional affiliations, diplomas, and experience. Don't hesitate to ask how long he or she has been in practice and if, in broad outline, your problems are similar to those of other clients. Ask if he or she has had personal therapy, and for how long. Psychotherapy is a profound experience, and for insight/analytic/psychodynamic therapy, at least, a therapist who has been through it may be better able to empathize with clients who are undergoing it. (For a fuller description of insight therapy, see Chapter 12.)

YOU MAY NOT HAVE A CHOICE

Depending on where you live, the question of which practitioner to choose may be academic. In 1979, for example, New York State had twenty-six practicing psychiatrists, nineteen psychologists, and ten social workers for every 100,000 of its residents, while Mississippi had only three psychiatrists, 4.5 psychologists, and 0.5 social workers for every 100,000. More than two-thirds of the counties in the United States had *no* psychiatrist. Moreover, only a few hundred physicians each year were entering this specialty. In psychology, about 5,000 students were being awarded their doctorate each year, but not all of them were entering the field of clinical psychology. If you can't find a satisfactory private practitioner, or if you can't find one you can afford, you may want to turn to a clinic. (See Chapter 10.)

CHAPTER 10
Mental Health Care Providers: Clinics

The same kinds of mental health professionals who work in private practice also work in clinics, and sometimes the same individuals divide their time between private and clinic practice.

A clinic is not the same as a *group practice*. A private practitioner works alone in treating clients. Some private practitioners join together in a group practice, which is basically an administrative and financial convenience for them; it does not affect your treatment. In private or in group practice, the therapist you see is the only person responsible for your treatment.

If you use a clinic, however, it is the clinic you pay, and it is the clinic that is responsible for your treatment, not the individual therapist.

In mental health, as in medicine, the name "clinic" is used for a variety of facilities. Though it is basically set up to treat outpatients, a clinic may have provision for inpatients. A clinic may be public or private; profit or nonprofit; charge lower, the same, or higher rates than private practitioners; be part of a hospital complex, university or other educational institution, social service agency, or mental health center, or be independent; represent a group of therapists specializing in a certain approach (behavior therapy, for example) or a special problem (such as alcoholism) or kind of patient (children only), or be eclectic (use many approaches); or be itself a "school" or "institute" for training psychotherapists. Other names for a mental health or psychiatric clinic are *guidance center* and *counseling service.*

The traditional clinic, which originally began as a facility for treating disturbed children, is based on a team approach. The team consists basically of a psychiatrist, psychiatric social worker, and clinical psychologist. In such a setup the psychiatrist directs the clinic and supervises psychologists and social workers who do therapy, and also gives some treatment directly. The psychologist performs testing and conducts individual and group therapy. The social workers also perform therapy and do social casework with patients and their families. Such clinics range in size from the basic team of three to several dozen or more professionals. However, as indicated above, many clinics do not follow this pattern.

In most clinics, a person seeking treatment is assigned to a therapist, which removes the privilege (or burden) of making a choice. Also, in many clinics either the therapist will have some supervision (especially if the clinic is a training institute or the therapist is relatively new to the profession), or there will be peer review—that is, staff meetings where cases are discussed. When this is the case, the client has the advantage of having several professionals consider his or her problems, treatment, and progress.

The most common kinds of mental health clinic are: the outpatient clinic of a mental hospital or a general hospital with a psychiatric service; the VA clinic; the clinic of a prepaid health plan (health maintenance organization, or HMO); a community mental health center; a family service agency; a private clinic; a training institute; and a college or university clinic.

OUTPATIENT CLINIC OF A PSYCHIATRIC (MENTAL) HOSPITAL

Depending on its size, such a clinic generally offers a wide range of services to adults and/or children, including individual, couples, family, group, and behavior therapy, psychopharmacology (administration of psychoactive drugs), vocational services, evaluation and treatment of children's problems (in coordination with schools and other community agencies), and so on. Usually anyone can call to make an appointment at the clinic; one need not be referred by a physician, social agency, or psychiatrist. The initial appointment is with an "intake" person, usually a social worker, who evaluates the client and assigns him or her to a therapist. Medicaid and private health insurance usually cover some or all of the cost for such treatment. For persons not so covered, the clinic may adjust fees on the basis of ability to pay. Although a person is generally assigned to one therapist, a "treatment team" will periodically review the therapy and evaluate progress.

OUTPATIENT CLINIC OF A GENERAL HOSPITAL

Depending on the area served and the size of the hospital, the psychiatric clinic of a general hospital offers a variety of services similar to those of the outpatient clinic of a mental hospital. If the hospital is a teaching hospital (associated with a medical school), the clinic staff may include a larger number of psychiatric residents who work under fairly close supervision. Some hospitals offer outpatient psychiatric care principally for inpatients who have been discharged, but most that offer any outpatient care make it more widely available. Some hospitals have walk-in clinics where anyone can come and make an appointment. In others a physician's referral is required.

VA CLINICS

Veterans Administration (VA) hospitals and outpatient clinics treat veterans who have service-connected mental disorders, and sometimes veterans with problems that are not service-connected (especially if the veteran cannot afford private care or if outpatient care is thought necessary to avoid hospitalization). Occasionally these services are extended to dependents (the veteran's family), primarily when the veteran in question will benefit from their involvement. Family members may be involved in couples or family therapy, and the veteran's spouse may be seen separately by a different therapist, for a limited time. For those eligible these services are free.

In larger population centers, VA clinics may offer a wide range of services. One large outpatient clinic offers the following: a *walk-in clinic,* which screens without prior appointment all new referrals for service for all programs, whether routine or urgent (crisis), schedules in-depth evaluation for candidates for diagnostic evaluation and therapy for all treatment programs, and serves as a crisis intervention unit (see Chapter 17); a *mental hygiene clinic* with numerous psychotherapy programs, which include individual, couples/family, and group therapy, psychopharmacology (providing medication with psychoactive drugs) combined with supportive therapy, and adjunct therapy for medical problems combined with psychiatric problems; a *day treatment center* (see under partial hospitalization in Chapter 17); a *drug dependence center* for treating cases of drug abuse; a *center for problem drinking* for treating alcoholism; and a *compensation and examination section* that performs psychiatric evaluation of applicants for disability compensation and other veterans' benefits programs.

PREPAID HEALTH PLAN (HMO) CLINICS

All prepaid health plans, in which members make fixed regular payments that entitle them to certain services, must, by law, include a number of visits per year for psychotherapy. The law states that they must include "short-term (not to exceed 20 visits) outpatient evaluative and crisis intervention mental health services," although the nature of these services is not spelled out. Like a hospital clinic, an HMO provides a variety of mental health clinicians—psychiatrists, nurses, psychologists, social workers. However, anyone wanting to use their services must be referred by their primary-care physician (family practitioner, internist, or pediatrician) within that health plan. The primary-care physician thus screens out those persons who are thought not to require specialized psychotherapy.

Once a person is referred to the mental health department of the HMO, the individual he or she first sees will usually be the therapist assigned for treatment. Unlike either private or public care, in the prepaid health plan the insurer and provider are one and the same. Therefore there is a strong economic incentive to provide high-quality care quickly and to prevent incurring the cost of either long-term care or hospitalization.

Typically all kinds of problem and illness are handled by the clinic itself, which offers individual, couples, and group therapy. Once the year's quota of visits is used up, the client must pay for additional visits, but the rate tends to be lower—as much as 50 percent lower—than that charged by private practitioners.

As with physical health, prepaid mental health care emphasizes preventive care and cost-effective treatment, and because it is performed in conjunction with primary health care it encourages treatment of the whole person rather than of a specific problem. In the interests of keeping costs down, however, some HMO's may not provide a wide enough range of services, allow too few visits per year, and may not provide care of the highest quality. Critics of HMO's contend that only relatively healthy individuals are permitted to become members in the first place, thereby restricting their use to a small percentage of the population. As of June 1980 there were 236 HMOs in the United States in 37 states (and Guam and the District of Columbia).

COMMUNITY MENTAL HEALTH CENTERS (CMHC'S)

In 1963 Congress passed the Community Mental Health Centers Act, at the time considered a revolutionary action. The law provided $150 million in Federal matching grants to create *local* services for psychiatric care—that is, a group of services, not necessarily all new or under one roof—coordinated to offer continuity of care for all kinds of mental illness within one's own community (or very close to it). The entire country was to be divided into catchment areas, each with a population of 50,000 to 200,000, and each served by its own mental health center. Originally 2,000 centers were planned, and by 1981 about 900 were actually in existence (of 1,500 then planned). Moreover, by 1975 the centers were handling close to one-third of all cases of mental disturbance in which a person sought professional attention.

Many of the centers, whether federally funded or not, receive funds from their respective state, and many are run by the state's mental health department, sometimes as part of a state hospital. They also receive funds from local governments, grants, foundations, and other sources.

In the 1970s, further legislation spelled out the twelve services that a comprehensive community mental health center (CCMHC) must provide: inpatient services, outpatient services, partial hospitalization, emergency (24-hour) services, consultation and education, services for children, services for the elderly, screening, followup, transitional services, alcoholism and alcohol abuse services, and drug addiction and drug abuse services.

Some centers consist of a single building or set of buildings in one location, usually central to their catchment area. Others are decentralized, with several facilities throughout their area.

The principal purposes of the CCMHCs are to keep clients and their treatment within the community, rather than send them off to a remote hospital or other facility, and to provide adequate services for all kinds of mental illness, for clients of all ages and all stages of illness, from diagnosis through treatment and rehabilitation. These goals are very ambitious, and few of the existing clinics meet all of them to the same degree. Nor, in fact, is it really necessary for each service to receive equal weight in every mental health center. Each center serves its own catchment area, and needs vary, depending on whether it is a crowded ghetto in a big city, a thinly populated rural area, a well-to-do suburban area, or some other well-defined population. One mental health center in a large New England city, for example, has a catchment area with an exceptionally large number of elderly persons. Its services therefore include day care for disturbed elderly clients, with door-to-door transportation provided in both directions. Another mental health center about twenty-five miles west of this city serves nine small towns, with a fairly large school-age population. It offers more elaborate children's programs, including a therapeutic preschool program, a children's day treatment service, and considerable consultation to schools and other local agencies serving children.

Not every community mental health center as yet provides the full range of services, but every one operates an outpatient clinic. In most cases a person who calls obtains an appointment with the first available clinician, who may be a nurse, social worker, psychologist, or psychiatrist. This clinician will make an evaluation and, typically, present it at a staff meeting to the "intake" or "case review" committee. At that time an appropriate therapist is assigned, based on availability, particular skills, and experience with similar cases. This process may take anywhere from a few days to a few weeks. If the problem is urgent, however, the intake worker sets up an immediate appointment; in an emergency, a referral is made to the nearest emergency facility (unless the center has one of its own). In some mental health centers all clients simply come to a walk-in clinic, where an appointment is set up either immediately (in an emergency) or for the near future (for evaluation).

All mental health centers have some connection or arrangement with one or more nearby hospitals should hospitalization be needed. Some centers actually started out as hospitals and were converted into centers but retain their own inpatient facility. Payment for services at a mental health center may be through Medicare, Medicaid, and/or private insurance plans. For those who have no insurance of any kind, there is a sliding scale of fees, based on ability to pay. In general the highest fees run much lower than those for private care (often only half as much or even less).

FAMILY SERVICE AGENCIES

The largest network of private, nonprofit social work agencies devoted to family problems in the United States and Canada are the family service agencies. There are approximately 1,000 such agencies, about half of them sectarian (principally Catholic or Jewish), and more than one-fourth accredited members of the Family Service Association of America (most of these are nonsectarian). Originally they were charitable organizations helping the poor, unwed mothers, children needing foster care or adoption, the aged in need of money or medical care, and so on. After World War II this focus changed, as direct relief was taken over by welfare departments and other government agencies. Today the family service agencies focus on assisting individuals and families under stress, and improving their personal and social functioning, as well as acting as agents for social change in areas of society that affect family life. In practice the agencies' main job has become counseling, although they continue to perform such services as providing homemakers, foster care, legal aid, day care, friendly visiting to the ill and lonely, aid to travelers, and so on. Not every agency provides all these services. Those that also offer foster care and adoption programs are usually called *child and family service agencies.*

Since about 1965 a growing number of family service agencies have provided mental health clinic services. Although the agency staff always has consisted primarily of trained social workers, (and still does), such mental health clinics are usually directed by a psychiatrist. The modes of treatment offered are similar to those of community mental health clinics and may be covered by health insurance.

Most clients learn of their local family service agency by word of mouth. Referrals are mostly through private social agencies or the schools, legal agencies (lawyer, court, police), a public welfare agency, or a physician or health-care agency. The problems most often brought by clients are marital (including divorce and single-parent family problems), which tend to represent about one-third of all cases, and parent-child problems, which represent another one-third. Adult personality adjustment is another major area of concern.

Most clients are seen on a short-term basis (fewer than six interviews), and many are dealt with by telephone or correspondence, but a small core of clients tends to be long-term, coming in weekly for six months or longer. Basically, the family service agency provides therapy for neuroses and personality disorders. Its focus is on counseling of various kinds, as well as numerous special programs for particular groups such as the elderly, in its community. It often refers elsewhere those clients who may require hospitalization, medication, or other intensive care, although some of the agencies do take on the aftercare of discharged mental patients.

Anyone who telephones for help talks directly with a social worker. An appointment is either made at once or, if no one is available to see the person, he or she is referred elsewhere. Some agencies have a waiting list; others do not. Usually a client continues to work with the social worker seen at the first interview, where an assessment usually was made. A therapy agreement may be formulated at subsequent sessions.

In addition to individual and family counseling, many family service agencies run workshops in career planning for women, assertiveness training, stress management, parenting, and similar topics of broad interest to the communities they serve.

Family service agencies are funded primarily by United Way and sectarian federations. They also receive donations and bequests, secure grants for special programs, and receive fees from clients for services. Fees charged are always based on income and ability to pay.

PRIVATE CLINICS

As explained above, a private clinic differs from a group practice in that the client pays the clinic rather than an individual therapist, and the clinic (not the therapist) is responsible for the treatment. Other than this basic characteristic, there is enormous variation among private clinics in practically every respect: size, cost, number and kinds of therapists, orientation (one approach, two, three, or many), and so on. Here are profiles of two private clinics operating in a large metropolitan area.

1. "Family Therapy Clinic." The focus at this clinic, which has a professional staff of four psychologists, five social workers, and one psychiatric nurse, is largely on family therapy. It also offers individual, couples, sex, and group therapy, and one of the psychologists works with biofeedback therapy. The clinic conducts a training program for eight students, who are already professional therapists but want additional special training in family therapy

techniques. The clinic's director is well known in this field. There is a special family therapy room with a one-way mirror and television camera whereby students may observe ongoing family therapy sessions. The students' input is brought up at staff meetings, so that a family may benefit from the expertise of a number of therapists at each meeting (although only one conducts the actual session). The average term of treatment is six to twelve months of weekly sessions.

About two-thirds of the clinic's clients are referred by other clients. The rest are referred by doctors, lawyers, school counselors, and pastors in the community. A client who calls for an appointment is assigned to a therapist and is seen within twenty-four hours. Most often the therapist who conducts the initial interview remains the person's therapist. Every client's treatment is periodically reviewed at the weekly staff meeting; both the therapist's written records and TV tapes of family interviews are used for this purpose. There is a 24-hour emergency telephone service and crisis intervention, but this clinic usually does not handle severe disorders that require hospitalization, extensive medication, and the like.

The charges for therapy are comparable to current rates for private care in the community. The therapists at this clinic receive only 45 percent of the fee; the clinic takes the remainder for overhead, administration, and profit. The clinic is licensed by the state and therefore is eligible for Blue Cross and other health insurance coverage. If therapists at the clinic wish to lower their fees to accommodate particular clients, they may do so.

2. "Proprietary Counseling Center." This clinic is a private business corporation that owns and operates three facilities located in different suburban towns. One of the owners, a psychiatrist, serves as overall medical director. The largest of the three facilities has a staff of twelve, including two half-time psychiatrists; the next largest has a staff of ten, including two full-time child psychiatrists and one half-time adult psychiatrist; the smallest has a staff of six. The remainder of the professional staff are clinical psychologists (all with Ph.D.s) and social workers (with master's degrees). The average term of treatment at this clinic is only six and one-half hours, although the overall range is very wide, from one hour for some

clients to several years for others. Clients find out about the clinic through physicians, advertising in the yellow pages, word of mouth, and various community agencies (schools, the police, social agencies). The clinic treats all kinds of mental illness except psychotic individuals requiring hospitalization and long-term mentally retarded persons (although it does evaluate children for mental retardation).

A client calling for an appointment talks to the receptionist, who either sets up an appointment with one of the clinicians or has a clinician return the call. The first interview usually takes place within a week to ten days of the initial call, but emergency treatment can be provided, on a daily basis if a client is in crisis.

Often the person conducting the first interview becomes the ultimate therapist. The clinic holds regular staff meetings at which all current cases are discussed. A case is always brought up after the initial interview, so that the proposed treatment plan can be reviewed, and usually at the end of treatment or after three months (whichever comes first).

All kinds of psychotherapy are used: individual, couples, sex, and group therapy. There are two kinds of group therapy, short-term goal-oriented therapy (parenting, divorce, single-parent, etc.) and long-term therapy. About 10 percent of the clients receive psychoactive drugs as part of their treatment. Individual therapy tends to be of the psychoanalytic, insight-oriented type, whereas family therapy focuses more on interpersonal problems.

The principal emphasis at this clinic is intensive, short-term treatment to avoid hospitalization or long-term care. Consequently its clients pay far less, even though the actual hourly rates are comparable to those for private care within this community.

TRAINING INSTITUTES

A training institute is basically a profit-making corporation that employs a staff of therapists schooled in a particular mode of therapy—most often that developed by a particular therapist whose theories and techniques have become well known. In addition to providing therapy, such an institute serves to train more therapists in its particular method. The training is, in effect, an apprenticeship; it consists mainly of doing therapy under supervision. The quality of such institutes and the therapists they employ varies widely, from highly competent and reputable to downright incompetent and shoddy. Similarly, the rates vary, from relatively low as compared to private care to just as high or higher.

Training institutes vary in the kind of psychotherapy they provide. Those that give advanced training are apt to prefer clients who are willing to commit themselves to long-term therapy. Psychoanalysts, for example, spend four to ten years obtaining postgraduate training at places like the New York Psychoanalytic Institute or the William Alanson White Institute. Consequently, a trainee therapist at such an institute may be quite experienced, but a client may be expected to remain in treatment for a number of years. Other clinics, however, may provide little or no supervision for their trainees and indeed seek out therapists with little experience or inferior qualifications who are willing to work for lower fees (a saving not necessarily passed on to clients). In some respects, therefore, the training institute is as mixed a bag as the private clinic, and it is wise to check carefully the credentials of any therapist assigned to you at such a facility. The "Family Therapy Clinic," described above, is in part an institute, since it trains students in family therapy, but it employs many nontrainee therapists as well; further, it does not confine itself to a single approach, treating individuals as well as families, and combining insight-oriented therapy with behavioral, client-centered, and other methods.

COLLEGE OR UNIVERSITY CLINICS

Most colleges and universities provide some mental health services. Depending on the size of the institution, it may range from a counseling center staffed by a single part-time social worker or psychologist, with a consulting psychiatrist on call, to a full-scale clinic staffed by psychiatrists, psychologists, nurses, and social workers. In the case of the latter, found primarily at large state universities, they may also be attached to the university's medical school and teaching hospital.

Generally, the psychiatric service cooperates closely with other college counseling centers, including the health service (infirmary) and academic counseling, but the usual rules of confidentiality apply, and records are not made available from a counseling service to a psychiatric service, or vice versa, without the student's permission.

In a fully staffed college mental health service the director is usually a psychiatrist but may be a psychologist or social worker. Counseling services ordinarily are run by psychologists, and social workers may belong to either the mental health or the counseling staff. Psychiatrists often serve as consultants to counseling services.

Students usually are seen without any charge beyond the regular health fee, at least for the first few interviews. Most schools, however, must limit the psychiatric services they provide, and if a student needs more extensive help he or she may be referred to either a private therapist or a public clinic. When neither of these alternatives is available (which may be the case in a small town), the college psychiatrist and mental health staff must function as best they can with whatever help they can get from counseling services, academic advisers, and the student's own family physician. In 1977 about 10 percent of the 2,400 colleges in the United States had mental health services that included a psychiatrist, and the majority of the rest could obtain occasional consultation with psychiatrists and psychologists for particular cases.

Here is a profile of the newly established (1980) mental health service of a small private college with 1,200 students, located about half an hour's distance (by train or car) from a large Middle Atlantic city. The staff consists of four part-time mental health professionals and a consulting psychiatrist, collectively the equivalent of 1.5 full-time professionals. They consist of the director, a clinical psychologist (with Ph.D.) who does some therapy; a social worker with a master's degree (who is enrolled in a doctoral program), who sees students ten hours a week; a doctor of psychology (Psy.D.) who provides six hours a week; a fifth-year clinical psychology intern at a nearby medical school who provides fourteen hours; and a consulting psychiatrist who gives two hours of consultation every other week. At least one of these staff members is available to students at all times on weekdays. In addition, the college medical center provides an immediately responsive emergency on-call system with backup hospital care, consultation, and psychotherapy and counseling of the kinds most often sought by students. The health center can reach a mental health staff person by telephone or in person within a few minutes at all times.

The most frequent service sought by students at this college is individual help with personal emotional problems. Some are in crisis but most are not. The number of interviews provided varies. Sometimes one or two sessions to offer guidance and support are sufficient to get a student through a temporary crisis. More often students are seen for a short term of brief psychotherapy once a week, the average term of treatment being six such sessions. Approximately 15 percent of the students make use of the service in this particular college every year, although 8 to 10 percent is the norm in most schools (regardless of size).

College and university mental health services as a rule are available only to the students enrolled at the institution (sometimes also to faculty and other staff members), a highly restricted population. Only in the case of very large clinics at state universities are they sometimes open to the public as well.

CHAPTER 11
Self-Help Groups

The regional calendar of a small-town weekly newspaper serving a dozen neighboring New England communities recently listed the following under the heading "Organizations":

Bereaved Parents Support Group, meets first and third Mondays of every month;

Northeast Singles, Inc., hosts ballroom dancing every Sunday;

Project HIRE, funded by M⎯ Home Care Corporation is registering persons 55 years and over who are seeking employment; many excellent full and part-time openings;

Methodist Church of M⎯ runs drop-in center; topics include alcohol use;

Jewish Family and Children's Service is offering a four-session discussion group for engaged couples called "Surviving the Wedding";

Feingold Association of B⎯ Valley, a support group for parents of hyperactive children, C⎯ chapter meets second Monday of each month;

Widowed Outreach Program is seeking volunteers for one-to-one outreach program, six-month commitment expected, six-hour training program given;

Support group for cancer patients of D⎯ Hospital;

Single Fathers' discussion group;

Women's support groups sponsored by A⎯ women's cooperative;

D⎯ Hospital's Geriatric Team offering support group for family members caring for a person with Alzheimer's disease, meets Tuesdays;

Alcoholics Victorious, meets every Wednesday;

Veterans of the armed services will find help for drug dependency at B___;

Anorexia Nervosa Aid Society offers support services for anorexics, bulimarexics, and their families, ongoing workshops;

Children of Single Parents, Inc., meets Saturday mornings.

These were but one week's listings in an area that, as it happens, has two community mental health centers and two general hospitals, each with a psychiatric service, not to mention a state mental hospital and a large, prestigious private mental hospital. But numerous communities that lack more formal services, or that include individuals who cannot use them owing to lack of funds, or individuals who oppose the established, traditional ways of dealing with mental illness, have set up many self-help groups. Sometimes the groups are founded and run by dedicated persons who want to help others and provide a place to go and someone to talk to. Some of them are professionals, but frequently they are people with relatively little formal training who simply wish to fill a need. Most often they are people who themselves have coped with a particular problem and feel they are uniquely qualified to help fellow sufferers.

Perhaps the best known of the self-help groups is Alcoholics Anonymous, which was begun in 1935 in Akron, Ohio, and became so successful that today there are nearly 30,000 AA groups in ninety-two countries, with an estimated total membership of more than a million. Two other groups formed about the same time were the American Association of Retarded Children and the United Cerebral Palsy Foundation, which both serve not only as support organizations for those afflicted with these disorders, but also as fund-raising and research-supporting bodies.

One of the first self-help programs for mental patients was founded by Dr. Abraham A. Low, a Chicago psychiatrist. He believed that mutual support was essential to his own patients and in 1937 expanded this idea into Recovery, Inc., a lay-directed self-help organization for formerly hospitalized mental patients. Currently

Recovery has more than 1,000 chapters throughout the United States, Canada, Ireland, and Puerto Rico, which welcome anyone with emotional problems, whether or not they were ever hospitalized. Like Alcoholics Anonymous, it uses a directive, inspirational method of group therapy led by members who use Low's book, *Mental Health through Will-Training,* as a source of guidance. Although nonsectarian, the groups have a religious tone.

HOW THEY WORK

Today self-help groups function across America, meeting the needs of people in a variety of situations and problems involving health, mental stress, addiction, social welfare, and rehabilitation. They differ in many respects but tend to have certain basic features in common: they are made up of individuals who share certain symptoms or have undergone a similar experience; they generally offer a face-to-face or phone-to-phone fellowship network that is available without charge; they are likely to be self-governing and self-regulating, emphasizing a community of interests among the members rather than positions of authority within their organization; they advocate self-reliance and require a high sense of commitment to other members; they often have a clear-cut code of beliefs and practices that includes rules for conducting meetings, entrance requirements for members, and ways of dealing with those who "backslide"; they usually are funded by donations from members and friends rather than requiring membership fees or relying on government support or foundation grants.

One of the great strengths of the self-help movement is that those who initially come for assistance stay on to help others. This process of helping others appears to be highly therapeutic. Although some mental health professionals believe there is potential danger in the approach, with untrained individuals taking on problems that confound the experts, many regard them as a valid extension of professional treatment that also helps provide for those who cannot or will not get assistance from more conventional health-care sources. Many physicians refer patients to one or another such group; Alcoholics Anonymous says that about 20 percent of its members are so referred. Certainly self-help groups are less expensive than conventional therapies, and they also are much more personal, informal, and peer-motivated in their approach, with members openly sharing their own experiences and disclosing their private feelings to each other.

There are self-help groups for alcoholics, for their families (Al-Anon), for families with brain-damaged children, child abusers and potential child abusers, children with learning disabilities, parents of Down's syndrome children, the retarded, families with children who have alcohol, drug, or other behavioral problems, compulsive gamblers (Gam-Anon), manic-depressive individuals, drug addicts and their families, people with phobias, ex-psychiatric patients, suicidal persons, compulsive eaters, compulsive self-medicators, homosexuals, runaway children and their families, and just about any other problem one can think of.

HOW TO FIND ONE

Is there a self-help group appropriate for you or for the person you are trying to help? If so, how can you find one? Your family doctor may know of some groups, as may your local county and state medical associations, or your county and state mental health boards. Your local mental health association may sponsor some mutual support groups. In Canada, this information is obtainable from Health and Welfare Canada, Social Service Programs Branch, Ottawa, Ontario K1A, 1B5. You also may be able to get up-to-date information by contacting the Self-Help Institute, Center for Urban Affairs, Northwestern University, Evanston, Illinois, or the National Self-Help Clearinghouse, Graduate Center of City University of New York, 33 West 42nd Street, New York 10036.

CHAPTER 12

Giving Help—
Psychotherapy 1:
Freud and His Descendants

The treatment of mental illness, like that of physical illness, is directed both at relieving symptoms and at eliminating their causes. Even though mental health professionals frequently cannot identify the causes or predict accurately what treatment will work best in a case, mental illnesses often can be treated very effectively.

Three principal kinds of treatment are in current use: *psychotherapy,* essentially a process of talking over one's problems with one or more other persons from whom one receives comfort, support, advice, and/or instruction; *somatic therapies,* also called *organic therapies,* which are administered to a person's body in order to induce changes in his or her feelings and behavior, and which include brain surgery, inducing seizures (convulsions) by means of chemicals or electricity, and changing the body chemistry by means of diet (adding some nutrients, eliminating others), psychoactive drugs, or other chemicals; and *hospitalization,* which involves a drastic change of environment and social relations.

These treatments are used alone or in conjunction with one another. Most often the mildest forms of mental illness are treated with psychotherapy alone. If the symptoms cannot be relieved satisfactorily, psychoactive drugs may be added to the treatment (or, the reverse procedure may be used, drugs being given first to relieve symptoms sufficiently so that a person is able to talk over problems with a therapist). For more severely ill persons, hospitalization may be necessary, and for certain acute or intractable disorders, physical treatment—electroconvulsive therapy or even brain surgery—may be undertaken. The remainder of this chapter and the next two chapters describe the principal kinds of psychotherapy.

Psychotherapy in nearly all its forms is basically an interview process. In one way or another it involves talking over your problem. For the individual with underlying medical problems or with active hallucinations, severe disorientation, or other symptoms indicating that he or she is quite out of touch with reality, no form of psychotherapy *alone* will be of much use. Indeed, it may even be harmful in that it delays more effective treatment.

But the symptoms you or your relative or friend are experiencing, you are told, are often helped by psychotherapy. What kind is for you? There is a bewildering array of therapies to choose from, and each one has its advocates. Psychoanalysis tries to root out problems at their very source. Behaviorists sometimes succeed in curing clients in just a dozen one-hour sessions. Family therapists suggest that help is ineffective unless those closest to the client are also involved. Certainly it would help to know what kinds of therapy there are and how they differ from one another.

FREUDIAN PSYCHOANALYSIS

The ancestor of modern psychotherapy is Freudian psychoanalysis. Although rarely used in its pure form today, some of Freud's ideas underlie many (although not all) of the therapies that are available.

Sigmund Freud (1856–1939) decided that the human mind consists of three areas—id, ego, and superego. The *id* is the area of instincts—inborn, unconscious biological forces and drives that blindly seek to be gratified. The *ego* is the area of rational thought and adaptive behavior. The *superego* is the area of checks and restraints, the voice of conscience and the source of guilt feelings, gradually acquired. Because of their very nature, the id is frequently in conflict with the ego and superego.

The most basic of human drives, said Freud, is the *sex drive.* Suppose, for example, that you, a successful middle manager on your way up to an executive position in your firm, interview a very attractive person, X, for a job opening. X is well qualified for the job and is, on your recommendation, hired. You now find yourself strongly attracted to X and have reason to believe the feeling is reciprocated. *But,* your career would suffer if you became involved with a fellow employee, especially one who is under your supervision. So says your ego, the rational part of you. Further, X is married and has three children, and you, too, are living with someone to whom you are firmly committed. An affair with X would not be fair to X's spouse or to your lover. So says your superego, your conscience. But X is very attractive and has even made some advances. How can I resist, says your id.

This conflict is, of course, on a conscious level, that is, you are fully aware of your feelings. And it will be resolved one way or another. Either you will give in to your strong impulses, with or without subsequent feelings of remorse and guilt, or you will restrain yourself, with or without subsequent regret. Such conflicts can be temporarily troublesome but they rarely cause deep psychic distress.

However, most conflicts between id and ego (and/or superego) as Freud conceived them are *unconscious.* Something is bothering you, perhaps so much that you can't function properly, but you have no idea what it is. Suppose, for example, that X originally had a choice between two jobs. Firm A offered a higher salary, a longer vacation, and better opportunities for advancement. But the person who interviewed X, and who would be his boss at Firm A, bore a striking physical resemblance to X's father. Though X is an ambitious man, he nevertheless took the job offered by Firm B, for less money and vacation but with better benefits and a more conveniently located office. In fact, those are the reasons he gave his wife for his choice, telling her this would give him more time to spend with the family. The reality was that throughout his childhood X felt he could never please his highly critical father, and unconsciously he was afraid that he would not be able to please a boss who looked just like Dad. X thus sacrificed a better opportunity on account of an unconscious, neurotic fear.

Freud believed that the sources of psychic distress inevitably lie in one's past, which includes all experiences from birth on. Indeed, he shocked his colleagues by advancing the idea that the sex drive is present from birth. He went even further, saying that repressed sexual feelings, from as far back as infancy (though more often from early childhood), are the source of most adult neuroses.

Freud had a broad definition of sexuality, to be sure. He saw it as any biologically motivated form of sensual gratification, which takes different forms during the various stages of a person's life. For approximately the first two years of life, he said, an infant's principal source of "erotic" satisfaction is *oral,* the pleasure derived from sucking on breast or bottle. The second stage, during approximately the next two years, is *anal,* directed toward control of elimination (toilet training) and the sense of accomplishment it affords. There follows, during the fifth and sixth years of life, the *phallic* phase, in which pleasure centers about the genitals. This period roughly coincides with a child's sexual interest in the parent of the opposite sex. Freud called this stage the *Oedipal* stage, after the Greek tragic hero who unwittingly killed his father and married his mother. During this period every boy has an unconscious incestuous desire for his mother, ordinarily expressed in the wish for more physical displays of affection, cuddling, and the like. As a result the child begins to regard his father as a rival whom he wishes to displace (also unconsciously). By this age, however, a child has learned enough of society's rules to know that the gratification of these unconscious desires is forbidden. He therefore begins to feel guilty for having them and to fear that his father will punish him, specifically by taking away his sex organs; Freud called this fear *castration anxiety.* It must be emphasized that Freud believed these stages occur in everyone's development, not just in those who later become neurotic. Further, though some children may be quite explicit about their wishes—in one household where the father was leaving on a business trip, his six-year-old son offered to take his place in Mom's bed—they are not consciously aware of them or their meaning.

In a girl the Oedipal stage (which some authorities called the *Electra* stage, after a Greek tragic heroine) takes a somewhat different form. A girl suffers from *penis envy* (rather than castration anxiety) because she lacks what Freud regarded as a highly desirable organ. She blames this condition on her mother and turns to her father for love and gratification.

In both sexes, said Freud, the Oedipal conflict is resolved normally when the child begins to identify with the parent of the same sex. In the example above, when the little boy's offer was turned down, he responded, "Well, don't worry, I'll take care of Mom while you're away." In Freudian terms, he was beginning to identify with what he saw as the father's protective role. The final stage of development, according to Freud, is the genital stage, which characterizes normal adults.

When the Oedipal conflict is not satisfactorily resolved, said Freud, or when development is arrested at any of the pregenital stages, neurosis results. But because these processes are unconscious—the child is not specifically aware of what is going on at the time—they are repressed (buried, forgotten). As a result, neuroses in later life are not easily or directly traceable to their early sources. It is the job of psychoanalysis to discover these sources, to dig out material that has been repressed, which, Freud believed, is chiefly sexual in nature.

There are two principal avenues for this discovery. One is the present-day workings of the unconscious mind, which are more freely expressed at night—that is, through *dreams*. Every dream, said Freud, contains symbols of those parts of the id that the ego and superego will not permit to surface. The second means is a process called *free association*, the seemingly random statements that emerge when a person says whatever comes to mind in whatever order it occurs. The association of ideas one after another is not consciously controlled, and it often enables one to recall events, ideas, and feelings that have long been forgotten (or, in Freudian terms, "repressed").

Dream interpretation and free association are the two principal tools of Freudian psychoanalysis. Moreover, the mechanics of analysis are set up so as to encourage one to bring up as much unconscious material as possible. The person being analyzed, called the *analysand,* is asked to lie down on a couch and say whatever comes to mind. The analyst usually sits behind the couch, more or less out of sight. Both lying down and not facing the analyst are intended to make it easier to relax and talk about anything at all—fantasies, daydreams, distant memories, night dreams, as well as day-to-day happenings and rational ideas.

The analyst says little and plays a largely passive role, in order to encourage *transference*—that is, the analysand begins to direct toward the analyst both positive and negative feelings that originally were directed toward someone else. For example, if a girl regarded her mother as a harsh, punishing person, as a grown woman she might transfer this feeling and react as though her analyst were harsh and punishing. Further, if she knows few actual details about the analyst, it is easier for her to transfer such feelings and so bring them out into the open. For this reason the analyst usually says very little.

Even though analysands understand the ground rule of saying whatever comes to mind, they cannot always do so. Some thoughts may seem too embarrassing, some memories too painful, or sometimes one simply draws a blank. The Freudian term for such blocking is *resistance*. In such instances the analyst usually does intervene and tries to help discover the reason for a particular blocking. Also, periodically the analyst points out connections between seemingly different events, feelings, reactions, or other occurrences in the analysand's life that are not recognized. Except for these interpretations, and dream interpretation, the analyst does little of the talking and takes care to remain noncommittal. Since so much depends on the analysand's talking, it is clear that successful psychoanalysis calls for a relatively intelligent, articulate person.

Classical psychoanalysis as just described is expensive and time-consuming. It ordinarily requires four to five visits to the analyst per week, each such visit lasting about 50 minutes. The total period of time ranges from three to six years or longer. At the rate of $75 per visit being charged by analysts in private practice in 1980, the total cost would come to about $14,000 per year. Since health insurance rarely covers more than a small portion of this cost, few individuals can afford psychoanalysis.

Psychoanalysis is also hard work, for both analysand and analyst.

Its ultimate goal is not just the relief of painful symptoms but a major change in personality so as to lead to better overall adaptation. To be genuine and permanent, such a change can be achieved only after one has surmounted emotional obstacles and acquired *insight* into one's behavior and feelings. It is not enough for the analyst to point out otherwise unrecognized relationships between experiences, memories, behavior, or emotional responses. Nor is the analysand's intellectual understanding of such relationships enough. An insight must be accepted on a detailed emotional level; only then will it begin to change feelings and behavior.

For example, Nancy J., 45, finds that she is always very upset—sometimes to the point of hysterics—when she has to pack a bag for a trip. During analysis she remembers that the feelings evoked by packing resemble her anxiety at the age of five, when her soldier-father left for wartime duty overseas and she helped her mother pack the family's belongings to move to another city. Her mother, preoccupied with her own worries about her husband, was not, at the time, sensitive to her daughter's fears and did little to reassure her. This insight, although perfectly valid, does not change Nancy's anxiety about packing. Only many weeks later, after she has relived the experience a number of times, with a revival and neutralization of the old feelings surrounding the original incident, can she begin to cope better with her distress over departures and separations. This process of incorporating an insight is called *working through,* and it is slow and usually painful. (Freud called it bringing unconscious, id material under conscious, ego control.)

ANALYTIC/INSIGHT/PSYCHODYNAMIC PSYCHOTHERAPY

Partly because of the high cost, partly because the long and arduous training required for analysts greatly limits the number available, and partly because few therapists today agree with Freud in all details of his theory and method, many other kinds of treatment have been developed. In general, those therapies based on the idea that emotional problems have their origin in unresolved psychological conflicts of the past and that symptoms are best relieved through working out these conflicts and acquiring insight are called "analytic psychotherapy," "insight therapy" or "psychodynamic therapy."

These therapies differ from classic Freudian therapy in a number of ways. They do not necessarily regard the prime cause of distress as a sexual problem that was not resolved in early childhood, nor do they consider the sex drive the single most important instinct. They try to facilitate the working-through process with more active participation by the therapist. Rather than delving into the distant past for every detail that can be recalled and relived, they set as their chief goal the relief of those symptoms that strongly interfere with present-day normal life processes; thus, they try to help the client learn how to handle what for him or her are distressing situations, without going into all their underlying causes. Although in general these therapies are more superficial than classical psychoanalysis, they often are very helpful, especially to individuals suffering from neuroses or from disturbances triggered by environmental changes.

The schedule of visits is less intensive and shorter than in classic analysis, and the couch is seldom used. Normally the client sits facing the therapist (often across a desk), although if this posture proves too threatening their chairs may be turned at an angle. Free association is used; dreams also are interpreted, although less than in classic analysis. In general the therapist is more active, both in directing the choice of subject matter and in deciding how long a subject should be pursued. Some therapists even offer advice or make specific suggestions on how to handle ongoing situations that are difficult for the client.

Although the psychotherapist is less careful about remaining noncommittal, transference still takes place. Indeed, some authorities feel that such therapy works mainly when client and therapist like and respect each other, and that the precise details of what goes on during therapy sessions have less importance than a positive relationship.

Whereas drugs such as tranquilizers and antidepressants are little used in classic analysis lest they hamper free association and block dreams, they often are used in conjunction with insight therapy to relieve anxiety and depression. Also, whereas classic analysis is provided only by a highly trained psychoanalyst (see Chapter 8), analytic psychotherapy may be conducted by a psychiatrist, psychologist, social worker, or other professional, and it is widely available in community mental health centers and clinics as well as in the traditional private office.

Because of its focus on specific problems, insight therapy does not take nearly so long and therefore is less expensive than classic analysis. One or two visits per week for a period of one or more years is typical. And finally, although like classic analysis it is rarely used alone for severe mental illness, such as the schizophrenias or manic-depressive illness, insight therapy often is used in combination with other treatments (drugs, electroconvulsive therapy, a hospital setting) for patients recovering from an acute psychotic or depressive episode.

FREUDIAN OFFSHOOTS

Two of Freud's most brilliant associates in Vienna during the early 1900s were Alfred Adler and Carl Jung. Each went on to develop his own theories and methods of psychotherapy, which to some extent are still practiced today.

Alfred Adler (1870–1937) developed the theory that people are directed less by the sex drive than by feelings of inferiority, which drive them to compensate by striving for superiority and power. When such striving is blocked, neurosis results. Later Adler expanded this view, saying that tensions generated in parent-child and sibling relationships can also give rise to neurosis. *Adlerian therapy,* which can be conducted by a psychiatrist, psychologist, or other professional, calls for twice-a-week sessions for a period of several years. The Adlerian therapist takes a more active, directive role than the Freudian analyst, helping the client uncover the original experiences that led to feelings of inferiority and fostering the development of greater self-assurance.

Carl Gustav Jung (1875–1961) also thought that repressed sexual urges alone could not account for neurosis. Rather, he believed that the individual unconscious is a combination of unique personal elements and common racial (cultural) elements. Each individual inherits patterns of conflict common to his or her race. In order to understand a neurosis, therefore, one must go back not only to one's own infancy but to the infancy of one's race. *Jungian analysis* involves much less free association and a great deal of dream interpretation, since Jung believed that dreams reveal much of the "racial" or "collective" unconscious. The Jungian therapist plays a more active role than the Freudian analyst, and the couch is not used much. Jungian therapy also is shorter, usually consisting of one to two sessions per week for a year or so.

Two others in Freud's circle who broke with him and founded their own schools of therapy were Otto Rank and Wilhelm Reich. Rank (1884–1939), whose method is called *will therapy,* said that a patient's quest for treatment expresses his instinctive will to live. He believed that the true source of neurosis is the birth trauma, the shock all human beings experience when they are thrust from the womb. In therapy, the Rankian analyst, who takes a quite active role, leads the client to re-experience the trauma of birth. This time, however, this shocking experience is cushioned by the therapist's love and support for the client. The ultimate goal is to strengthen the client's will and independence. Rank was one of the first to suggest that short-term intensive therapy is effective, and Rankian therapy lasts no more than a few months. However, it has fewer followers than other analytic therapies.

Wilhelm Reich (1877–1957), on the other hand, took Freud's emphasis on the sex drive one step further, saying that this all-important drive, rather than being channeled in other directions, needs to be liberated. In Reich's view an all-powerful *orgone energy* flows through the body, gradually building up a charge akin to an electrical charge. Therefore it must periodically be discharged. But if sexual feeling is suppressed, there is no healthy discharge of energy, and neurosis results. One major symptom of such suppression is chronic muscular tension. It is the job of therapy to relieve such tension, through special breathing exercises and massage, in order to free the body (and hence the mind) of crippling inhibitions. *Reichian therapy,* also called *vegetotherapy* and *orgone therapy,* was one of the first body therapies (See Chapter 13). However, it, like other body therapies, is considered by many professionals to be of dubious validity.

INTERPERSONAL THEORIES

Two other schools of insight therapy differ from both Freudian analysis and the therapies just described in that they place less emphasis on the inner workings of the mind and unconscious drives and more on people's relations with one another. How one gets along with others is, for one thing, far more readily observable than unconscious urges are.

Karen Horney (1885–1952), who was trained as a Freudian analyst in Berlin and came to the United States in 1932, first taught at two Freudian institutes and then, in 1941, set up her own clinic in New York. Freud's views on women in particular led her to formulate her own theories. Horney could not go along with the idea that women's lack of male genital organs accounted for most of their emotional problems. It was not instinctual sex drives repressed in childhood that cause neurosis, concluded Horney, but the insecurity a child feels when the family does not make him or her feel strong and confident. The basic human drive is the search for security. When it is threatened, a person experiences anxiety. Anxiety leads one to move in one of three ways: toward people (socialization, dependence); away from people (detachment, independence); and against people (hostility, aggression). It is the goal of therapy to produce a healthy balance among all three.

Horneyan (or *Hornevian*) *therapy* involves three sessions per week over a period of several years. Both free association and dream interpretation are used, but the Horneyan therapist plays a stronger, more directive role than the Freudian analyst.

Horney's friend and colleague, Harry Stack Sullivan (1892–1949), also considered interpersonal relations more important than inborn instincts. Sullivan maintained that people seek both physical satisfactions and security, which he defined as a sense of feeling accepted. Your concept of yourself, he said, comes from how you think others react to you. When your perception of these reactions is faulty—

for example, when you think everyone in a group hates you—neurosis results. The goal of therapy is to help you see such distortions.

Like Freud, Sullivan traced human development through a series of stages, but rather than defining them in terms of the sex drive (oral, anal, etc.) he defined them in terms of the principal personal relationships at each stage. Thus, in infancy, relations with the mother or mother-substitute are of prime importance. A constantly angry or anxious mother can communicate anger or anxiety to her child, who will then bring this reservoir of unhappiness to later relationships.

Sullivanian therapy, also called *interpersonal psychotherapy*, is centered in the Washington (DC) School of Psychiatry and the William Alanson White Institute in New York City. Its techniques are similar to Freudian analysis except that the search is focused on childhood experiences. Also, it is important that therapist and client form an intense relationship, with the therapist playing a very active role. In effect the therapist listens to the client's problem and asks a great many questions about the client's past. It is during this process that the therapist establishes an intense relationship through which he or she becomes the object of the client's interpersonal relations (and distortions). Then, by explaining how these distortions operate and teaching the client to replace them with healthy reactions, the therapist can relieve the client's neurotic symptoms.

Sullivan himself was one of the few psychotherapists who had some success in treating schizophrenia, but his descriptions of such cases indicate that his success may have been as much a result of his own clinical and interpersonal skills as of his particular methods.

Erich Fromm (1900–1980), schooled in Germany in the analytic technique of Freud, was another founder of the William Alanson White Institute and practiced psychoanalysis. He became very influential through his writings, which dealt with subjects ranging from the alienation of the individual to the sanity of society. In clinical practice he modified Freudian technique considerably, directly confronting the client with his or her problems, dynamically engaging him or her with relevant insights, and working actively toward understanding.

Still one other offshoot of Freudian analysis became fairly widespread. Objecting to the exceedingly long-term therapy called for by classic analysis, although not disagreeing with any of its basic tenets, Franz Alexander and his associates at the Chicago Institute of Psychoanalysis developed a short-term therapy called *intensive short-term analytic therapy* (or *Chicago School therapy*). Unlike classic analysis, the therapist takes a strongly directive role in the client's free association, attempting to lead him or her to those past experiences that appear to be directly connected to the present-day troublesome symptoms. By reviving these painful memories, the client is relieved of the emotional pain associated with them, a process called *catharsis-abreaction*. This process replaces the more tedious, drawn-out working through of insights and focuses on material affecting the specific neurotic symptoms, which are thereby relieved. Therapy involves considerable flexibility. While clients who are intensely anxious may be seen daily, other, less anxious persons may do well on a weekly basis. The couch may be used for some and not for others. In general, the therapy is tailored to meet what the therapist sees as individual needs.

CHAPTER 13

Giving Help—
Psychotherapy 2:
Newer Individual Therapies

Because of Freud's basic premise that the key to neurosis lies in the sufferer's past, the therapies based on his theory tend to be past-oriented. The client tries to understand his or her present behavior and feelings in the light of past experience. However, several kinds of therapy concentrate instead on the present-day symptoms, problems, feelings, and behavior of the client.

Although these therapies differ from one another in many ways, they all are inclined to be more practically oriented. Where insight psychotherapy considers self-understanding the important goal, from which growth, self-control, and self-esteem will come, these newer therapies tend to be more directly supportive, and the therapist plays a more active role in helping the client deal with emotional distress and problematic life situations. Indeed, in some the therapist is quite active, giving advice, speaking openly, and making no attempt to hide or neutralize his or her own personality.

FOCUS ON THE HERE AND NOW

Among those most radically different from Freudian therapy in this respect is William Glasser's *reality therapy*. Glasser saw the individual ego as the mediator between a person and the world around him or her; its general functions to protect the individual and fill his or her needs. The basic cause of emotional disturbances is impaired ego function, so it becomes the therapist's job to restore adequate ego function. The reality therapist deliberately seeks to become involved with the client and to win respect as a reliable authority. Once the client does respect the therapist, the latter proceeds to convince the client that moral and responsible behavior are more desirable than neurotic patterns. In effect, the therapist tells the client to shape up and get well.

Cynics point out that Glasser's approach makes the therapist simply a purveyor of conventional values and conformity. In practice, however, this approach has proved successful with some adolescent delinquents, as well as with persons suffering from a single definable symptom, such as a nervous tic, or a bad habit, such as smoking. The underlying causes of neurotic behavior are not even considered relevant by the reality therapist; only the behavior itself is treated, primarily through a positive therapeutic relationship. (See also behavior therapies below.)

Client-centered Therapy

Another here-and-now approach is Carl Rogers' *nondirective* or *client-centered therapy,* which is based on the idea that every individual has his or her own way of seeing both self and world. The basic drive of all human beings is self-actualization, that is, realizing their potential for growth and development. To promote this, Rogerian therapy concentrates on building the client's sense of self-worth. The therapist is permissive and nondirective, allowing the client to say anything at all, no matter how unimportant or childish it may seem, and expressing empathy for whatever feelings are revealed. In this way the client is free to explore his or her feelings, acquire deeper understanding, and reorganize his or her view of things in general.

The nondirective therapist makes no interpretations and offers no suggestions. For example, suppose Mary complains that her husband was late to dinner twice during the previous week without apology or explanation. The therapist might say, "You feel you deserve more consideration," or "You feel your efforts are not appreciated." Mary presumably then feels free to talk more openly about her marriage and her feelings about related issues.

The non-directive therapist may point out things that the client is not aware of, such as, "You always smile when you are telling me how angry you are," or "You generally face me when you talk, but whenever you mention your father you turn away from me." But the therapist does not give specific advice, praise or blame any action or idea, or suggest areas that should be further explored. All responsibility for the course of the therapy is left to the client. The therapist does not, on the other hand, remain silent or conceal details about his or her own life; in fact, such details may deliberately be revealed if it is thought they will encourage the client to talk more freely.

Rogerian therapy is usually conducted by clinical psychologists rather than psychiatrists, in clinics and mental health centers (as well as in private practice). Some of its techniques have been adopted by therapists specializing in other kinds of therapy, as well as by teachers, the clergy, guidance counselors, and administrators in many lines of endeavor.

Existential Therapy

Existential therapy also aims at a kind of self-realization. Based on existential philosophy and developed mainly by Rollo May in the United States and Ludwig Binswanger and Medard Boss in Switzerland (where it is called *Daseinanalysis,* from the German words *Da sein,* meaning "being there"), it holds that awareness of being is the essence of existence, and that the individual exists principally in relation to other people and things. The goal of existential therapy, which uses a variety of techniques—talk, free association, dream interpretation—is to help the client understand his or her potential. This process requires a great deal of empathy on the therapist's part. Indeed, the therapist is so deeply involved that he or she also expects to be changed by the relationship. Again, the emphasis is on the here-and-now rather than some past source of problems.

Gestalt Therapy

Gestalt therapy, developed by Frederick S. (Fritz) Perls (1894–1970) and others, also is directed toward immediate experience rather than the past. The source of neurosis is thought to be faulty perception, a kind of fragmentation of reality in which a person sees neither himself nor the world accurately. In contrast, the healthy individual is a well-integrated whole (in German, *Gestalt*), fully aware of both self and environment. The goal of therapy, therefore, is to help restore whatever parts are missing until the client is fully aware of his or her own feelings and interactions with others.

Though it cannot be directly inferred from the theory behind it, the process of Gestalt therapy is different from the therapies described so far. The client is encouraged to talk, but only about current feelings and situations. He or she is also encouraged to use nonverbal communication—to act out some of the situations and feelings in dramatic fashion. Gestalt therapy often is conducted in group settings, where perhaps five or six clients get together with a therapist for an entire weekend of activity.

On a one-to-one basis, Gestalt therapy is considerably briefer than other therapies, ranging from three months to a year. The therapist plays a very active role, prodding the client to express feelings, ideas, bodily sensations, perceptions of the immediate environment (treatment room), and the like. The client may be asked to dramatize a particular situation. For example, suppose Martha is very frightened of the therapist, who now asks her to act out her fear. She sits first in one chair and, as Martha, says, "You make me very nervous. I'm afraid that you won't like me when you find out what kind of person I really am." She then moves to another chair and speaks for the therapist, "I am here to help you. You must tell me what you are feeling at this very moment." If Martha is angry at being made to feel afraid, the therapist may ask her to express her anger, by shouting, or by hitting the chair that is made to represent the therapist, or some similar means. Since Gestalt therapy involves vigorous interaction of therapist and client, it often becomes highly emotionally charged, and therefore it is not considered suitable for a severely disturbed person who could not tolerate such intensity.

BEHAVIOR THERAPIES

A number of therapies—both individual and group—have been developed to treat mental illness by, in effect, correcting maladaptive behavior. They differ from analytic (insight) and client-centered therapies in that they generally are less concerned with increasing clients' self-knowledge and self-awareness than with changing their behavior as a means of preventing or treating their illness. Behavior therapists use procedures that bring about learning, their implicit assumption being that one can learn to replace maladaptive behavior with new, adaptive behavior. (They do not, however, attempt to treat severe psychoses such as schizophrenia or manic-depressive disorder in this way alone, although they may use some procedures in conjunction with other treatment.) Behavior therapists sometimes treat the body as well as the mind, as in teaching clients relaxation techniques, but their methods, unlike those of the body therapies (see below), are eminently respectable and are endorsed by the American Psychological Association and other reputable professional groups.

The origins of behavior therapy, also called *behavioral therapy* or *behavior modification,* lie in the learning experiments of Ivan Pavlov, B. F. Skinner, and others, and their extension into the clinical area by Joseph Wolpe and other practitioners. Pavlov, a nineteenth-century Russian physiologist, found he could teach dogs to salivate in response to a bell rather than the actual presence or smell of food, thus establishing what came to be called a "conditioned reflex." Skinner, a twentieth-century American psychologist, found he could change the behavior of rats by reinforcing desired behavior with a reward and negatively reinforcing (deterring) undesired behavior by either withholding food or giving an electric shock, a method that came to be called "operant conditioning." Versions of both methods are used by present-day behavior therapists.

Just as Pavlov taught animals to respond automatically to a different stimulus (a bell instead of food), so can a therapist teach a client to establish a desired reaction to replace an unwanted behavior. Suppose, for example, that Wanda, the young woman who suffers from agoraphobia and experiences anxiety attacks almost anywhere outside her own house, decides to see a behavior therapist. The first step in treatment probably will be teaching Wanda to put herself into a state of deep muscle relaxation whenever she feels the slightest anxiety. Two or three sessions may be devoted to teaching her how to induce relaxation throughout her whole body, muscle group by muscle group, until she can do so at will, both in the therapist's office and at home. Other methods of inducing deep relaxation are transcendental meditation (see page 144) and *autogenic training,* that is, using passive concentration to create an inner sense of warmth, heaviness, and tranquillity, also learned progressively like deep muscle relaxation. Some therapists teach their clients to control the physical manifestations of anxiety— pounding heart, sweaty palms, etc.—by means of *biofeedback,* a method of exercising control over normally involuntary physical functions by means of feedback (information) concerning those functions. With biofeedback, clients can be taught to control their heart rate, blood pressure, peripheral body temperature, and salivation.

Systematic Desensitization

While Wanda is being taught relaxation, she and the therapist also construct a series of anxiety-arousing situations, each of which is more frightening (to her) than the next. The therapist then will ask Wanda to relax completely and to imagine the first situation, which produces the mildest level of anxiety. If she can pretend to experience this situation without panicking, or is able to eliminate her anxiety by relaxing, the therapist proceeds to the next situation, and so on, up to the most anxiety-provoking one (in Wanda's case, perhaps, returning to the supermarket where her first attack of panic took place). If Wanda experiences anxiety at any point, the therapist stops and backtracks to a less threatening situation.

In addition to deep relaxation, a client may be taught to imagine a very pleasurable experience—for Wanda, perhaps a family party staged by her children. Whenever she feels anxiety, then, she not only induces deep relaxation but also pictures herself in this very happy situation, thus replacing her anxious feelings with pleasurable ones. In cases where the client fears specific objects, such as dogs or snakes, *modeling* might be used. Rather than imagining contact with the feared object, the client observes a fearless person (either the therapist or someone else) come closer and closer to the feared object, and gradually is encouraged, under the model's guidance, to do the same.

This entire process is called *systematic desensitization.* It continues until the client can experience in her mind the entire spectrum of frightening situations without experiencing anxiety. Next, Wanda will be asked to do the same outside the therapist's office, gradually exposing herself to each slightly more frightening experience, but retreating at once and practicing deep relaxation at the first sign of anxiety.

A rather different technique is *intense exposure therapy,* also called *flooding* or *implosion.* Here, instead of gradually exposing Wanda to ever more frightening situations, the therapist tells her to imagine the very worst possible experience—for example, being lost in a large crowd in a strange city. Films and tapes depicting such situations are shown to her to make her feel even more anxious. Such "overloading" is intended to collapse her phobic reaction entirely. It is not understood how this technique works to eliminate phobias, but it can be very effective.

Assertiveness Training

Assertiveness training is a form of conditioning that has been effective particularly for individuals suffering from extreme anxiety in social situations. It uses role-playing or behavior rehearsal to teach a person to express his/her views and wishes more effectively in various situations. An assertive person acts as if he/she believes in his/her own self-worth and is not threatened by criticism or disagreement. Assertiveness training does not attempt to go into the causes of low self-esteem but simply teaches a client to respond assertively more often.

Although assertiveness training can be performed on an individual basis, it is frequently used in a group format, with members of the group practicing assertive behavior with one another. This form of conditioning has been extended beyond clinical uses to, for example, individuals who simply wish to improve their negotiating ability in a business setting but are not eager to change their behavior in other respects.

Aversive Conditioning

Aversive conditioning involves the repeated use of an unpleasant or painful stimulus, such as administering an electric shock to a client, or withdrawing positive reinforcers, such as words of praise or candy, whenever undesired behavior occurs. For example, a man with strong sexual feelings for preadolescent girls might be shown pictures and films of such children in various stages of undress. Whenever he exhibited signs of sexual arousal, he would be given a shock. In time, it is hoped, he would come to imagine the pain of the shock whenever he was inappropriately aroused and therefore would curb the feeling and any temptation to act on it. Today aversive conditioning is most often used in conjunction with techniques that establish and reinforce desired behavior, described as operant conditioning.

Operant Conditioning

Operant conditioning is based on the idea that behavior is influenced by its consequences, a notion subscribed to by any parent who has ever rewarded a child's good behavior with a hug or a treat. The behavior therapist calls this *positive reinforcement*. When the desired behavior is complicated or the client seems unable to produce it, *modeling* may be used as a teaching tool.

More elaborate forms of operant conditioning have been devised in mental hospitals and other institutions where, it has been found, even extremely disturbed or profoundly retarded individuals may respond to a system of rewards. Some hospitals use a program called a *token economy,* in which patients are "paid" for good behavior with such privileges as watching television, receiving special food or cigarettes, or extra time outside. In a school—residential or otherwise—good academic work or effort may be rewarded with candy, toys, or extra recess time. *Negative reinforcement* simply consists of withholding the extra privileges.

Such systems may work very well, but they have been criticized on a number of counts. For one thing, in hospitals and prisons they are open to abuse, privileges being withheld unfairly. For another, this is a form of behavior control in which the authorities decide what is desirable behavior and what is not. Prisoners who are rewarded or punished may disagree with the values of the authorities, inevitably causing considerable resentment and undermining the effectiveness of the technique.

The therapy contract described in Chapter 18 is used by some behavioral therapists as an intrinsic part of the treatment—so-called *behavioral contracting.* In such instances the contract specifies the client's obligations to change his/her behavior, in exchange for the therapist's responsibility to provide some desired reward, such as a privilege or special attention. Behavioral contracts can be effective in institutional settings as well, between a hospital patient and a staff member, or child and teacher, with the former agreeing to perform certain tasks without prodding (getting dressed, attending meals/remaining in one's seat, completing assignments) in exchange for desired privileges (extra food, later bedtime/longer recess, a small gift).

Behavior therapy generally begins, as other therapy does, with an assessment based on the client's history and stated problems, as well as direct observation and quantification of the actual behavior. The behavior therapist rarely inquires into the reasons for problems—Why do you become frightened in a crowded place? Why do you punish yourself by overeating? Rather, the therapist is likely to ask specific questions concerning the circumstances under which the client behaves undesirably—What were you doing when you became anxious? Who was with you? How often does this happen? The problems then are defined in a concrete way, and the goals of treatment are established.

What disorders lend themselves best to behavior therapy? The greatest success has been with focal phobias (fear of snakes, dogs, high places, crowds, etc.), obsessive-compulsive behavior (incessant handwashing, for example), and substance abuse of various kinds (food, tobacco, drugs, alcohol), as well as specific problems such as stuttering, and head-banging and other forms of self-injury among severely retarded, autistic, and/or brain-damaged children. Behavior therapy alone has been less effective for depression and other mood disturbances.

Behavior therapy is practiced more by psychologists than psychiatrists, and also by social workers and other mental health professionals. For information about practitioners in your area, you can contact the Association for Advancement of Behavior Therapy, 420 Lexington Avenue, New York, NY 10017. Similar information may be available through the psychology department of a nearby college or university, or through your local community mental health center or mental health association.

COGNITIVE BEHAVIOR THERAPIES

The early behaviorists concentrated on modifying the overt behavior (that is, observable actions) of experimental animals and, later, of human clients. Beginning about 1960, however, a number of therapists began to regard patterns of thought and expressed feelings (called cognitions) as much a part of behavior as overt actions, and similarly subject to modification. Cognitive behavior therapy represents a combination of cognitive psychology, which emphasizes that thoughts influence behavior, and behavioral psychology, which focuses on specific methods to change behavior. Thus it uses the methods of behavior therapy—desensitization, operant conditioning, aversive conditioning, imagery, modeling, behavior rehearsal—

to modify what a client "says to himself" or how he/she "sees himself" before, during, and after overt behavior.

The first important cognitive behavior therapist was Albert Ellis, whose approach is called *rational-emotive therapy.* Ellis maintained that our emotions are caused and controlled by our thinking. A disturbed person is one who has adopted irrational and illogical ideas that lead to and perpetuate emotions that give rise to neurotic actions. In rational-emotive therapy, the therapist helps the client discover what he or she is internally "saying," to question its rationality, and to substitute more rational and realistic "self-talk." In effect, the client is directed to "think positive," to become assertive, and to set sensible goals for getting ahead and enjoying life.

The author of several self-help books, notably *A Guide to Rational Living* (1961), Ellis believed that certain irrational assumptions made by many individuals lead to profound anxiety or depression. Among them are: (1) it is vital that practically everyone I know loves me and approves of me; (2) I must be extremely competent in every undertaking in order to be worthwhile; (3) certain individuals are inherently bad and they should be punished; (4) if things don't go exactly as I wish them to, it is catastrophic; (5) people have little or no control over their sorrows or upsets; (6) it is better to avoid certain difficulties and responsibilities; (7) it is better to depend on others and I need someone strong on whom I can rely; (8) every human problem has a single perfect solution, and it is disastrous if this solution is not found.

For example, David R., 40, is out nearly every night of the week doing community volunteer work. He coaches a Little League team, leads a Scout group, serves on three town boards, and takes charge of several charity fund drives. His job during the day as a bank loan officer is very demanding, and he often must bring work home. Further, at work he becomes very upset whenever he has to turn down a loan application. David begins to develop several distressing symptoms—insomnia, shortness of breath, and finally a bleeding ulcer. After the ulcer has been treated, his family doctor suggests that David see a therapist, and the one he recommends is a rational-emotive therapist. The therapist soon discovers David's specific behavioral problem: he cannot say "No." David has always wanted everyone to like him and approve of him. What people think is terribly important. The therapist points out that it is more important to think well of oneself than to be a friend to everyone, which isn't possible anyway. Through assertiveness training, role-playing, modeling, and other techniques the therapist gradually helps David accept this view.

Similar to rational-emotive therapy is *cognitive therapy,* developed by Aaron T. Beck in the 1960s to treat depression. It, too, is based on the idea that one's moods and emotions are determined primarily by how one construes the world (thinks). These thoughts, or cognitions, are developed from early experience, but tend to be applied whether they are appropriate or not. Thus a person who has little self-esteem may readily develop depression; a person who anticipates personal harm may develop anxiety and phobias; a person who habitually mistrusts others may develop paranoia. Beck's treatment for these misperceptions is behavioral in approach. For example, the cognitive therapist might lead a depressed client like our widow, Jane, through a series of easily accomplished tasks that clearly demonstrate her mastery and competence. He may then help her to identify the specific thoughts she has that make her feel depressed. For example, suppose Jane greeted a friend on the street who did not see her and passed by without response. To Jane, already sad, this appears to be a devastating rejection and makes her feel that no one likes her. The therapist will ask her to examine this interpretation, perhaps by asking how many telephone calls from friends she has received in the past two weeks, to indicate that some people do in fact like her enough to call. One of Beck's classic cases is that of a profoundly depressed college student who believed she was lazy and stupid even though she had a straight A average. Whenever she got an A, she told herself that the class was easy, the grade was an accident, or the teacher was sorry for her. With help she learned to interpret her grades more positively and to recognize that the source of her deep-seated depression was her own misinterpretation of events.

Cognitive therapy usually consists of weekly sessions for a period of six weeks to three months. It appears to work best for clients with depression, anxiety, phobias, and obsessive-compulsive behaviors. It requires the ability to differentiate reality from fantasy and consequently is not suitable for persons undergoing a psychotic episode. It also is not considered very useful for disorders of substance abuse (alcoholism, drug addiction, etc.).

During the 1970s, some cognitive behavior therapists broadened their approach so as to teach clients not only to deal with specific current problems but to prepare them to deal with situations that might come up in the future. In effect they wanted to teach them so-called "coping skills," providing them with a prospective defense for dealing with future stress. Clients were taught broad self-relaxation, to be used whenever they faced problems that might cause physiological arousal (sweaty palms, pounding heart, muscular tension) and also were taught to substitute positive "self-statements" for the habitual anxiety-producing ones that were associated with stress. For example, a client who had experienced one or more phobic reactions in the past would be instructed to follow a series of procedures: assess the reality of this new frightening situation; control any negative thoughts or self-statements; acknowledge the fact that you are aroused (frightened); "psych yourself up" to confront the situation; cope with whatever intense fear you might experience (you're intensely frightened, true, but this object can't really hurt you, nor can the feeling of intense panic, which will soon pass); and reinforce (congratulate) yourself for having coped successfully with this stress. This approach is called *stress-inoculation training.* To the extent that its strategies succeed in avoiding future breakdowns, they represent a form of preventive treatment. (See also Chapter 21.)

SHORT-TERM PROBLEM-ORIENTED THERAPIES

Several other methods of psychotherapy have been developed to treat specific disorders in a relatively brief time (weeks or a few months instead of many months or years). They tend to use a variety of techniques borrowed from other kinds of therapy and they are essentially pragmatic.

One such therapy is *short-term anxiety-provoking therapy,* or

STAPP. Developed by Peter E. Sifneos in the 1960s, it is grounded in Freud's ideas of unconscious conflict but, in marked contrast to the many years required for classic psychoanalysis, it usually entails a total of eight or nine fifty-minute sessions. The basic approach is to make clients confront their troubling feelings, relate them to past events, and work out the current problem. The therapist plays a very active role, asking leading questions, pointing out similarities, and so on.

The client is first asked to select a single emotional problem he or she wants to overcome. The therapist, through skilled interviewing and history-taking, looks for a formulation of the emotional conflicts underlying this problem and concentrates on those conflicts alone, using anxiety-provoking questions to stimulate the client to examine areas of difficulty and help him or her become aware of feelings, experience the conflicts, and learn new ways of dealing with them.

For example, Karen B., 27, is planning to be married in two months to a man she has been living with for three years. She suddenly finds herself terribly anxious about the wedding and goes to an outpatient clinic. The intake clinician she sees suggests STAPP. At her first interview she tells the therapist of her anxiety, which she finds especially troubling because until now her relationship with the young man has been excellent. After getting a full description of her present situation, the therapist asks Karen to describe her general history and any occasions in the past when she felt very upset and anxious. In the next few sessions he raises questions that Karen might find too threatening to bring up herself, such as, "Is your father jealous of your fiancé?" or "Are you afraid that your marriage, like that of your parents, will end in divorce?" After six weekly sessions, Karen determines that it is her parents' bad marriage and bitter divorce that is making her frightened. The therapist helps her separate her own situation from theirs, and to discover that she has tested her relationship with her fiancé sufficiently over the past three years to know that they get on well together.

Another therapy is *short-term interpersonal psychotherapy (IPT)*, a form of brief (twelve to sixteen weeks) treatment that has been used primarily for treating depression. Grounded in the interpersonal theories of Harry Stack Sullivan (see Chapter 12), it is based on the idea that depression occurs in an interpersonal context, so that clarifying and renegotiating the particular context associated with the onset of symptoms can aid recovery. Treatment, which can be used alone or in conjunction with psychoactive drugs (antidepressant medication), focuses on resolving the client's immediate difficulties in his/her important relationships with others (close family, close friends, work associates). The therapist is active (in making suggestions, pointing out contradictions, and so on), supportive, and nonjudgmental. Definite limited treatment goals are set during the first three sessions, which focus on one or two specific problem areas, such as grieving over a loss, marital conflicts, or difficulty in relationships with co-workers. Originally developed by Gerald L. Klerman, IPT has evolved since about 1970 from the experience of the New Haven-Boston Collaborative Depression Project. Dr. Klerman and his associates have developed a program for training experienced therapists (psychiatrists, psychologists, social workers) in the method, and have written a manual outlining the concept, techniques, and strategies of IPT.

Who benefits from such short-term therapies? They tend to work best for a person who is able to identify an overriding problem, is genuinely eager to do something about it, is willing to accept personal responsibility for difficulties, and is able to tolerate some anxiety, anger, and frustration. They are particularly helpful for a client with acute symptoms that occur in reaction to a life crisis—changing schools, marriage, job-hunting, a new baby. They usually are *not* suitable for a person suffering from a chronic psychotic condition, such as severe depression, manic-depressive disease, or schizophrenia.

SEX THERAPY

Sex therapy is a specialized form of problem-oriented therapy that is used to treat sexual dysfunction in men and women. Sexual dysfunction is defined as any disturbance or disorder that frequently or always prevents a person from engaging in satisfying sexual intercourse, and that arises anywhere in the three-stage cycle of sexual response, desire-arousal-orgasm. The most common forms of sexual dysfunction are impotence and premature ejaculation in men and failure to reach orgasm in women.

Sex therapy differs from marital and couples therapy in that its goal is limited to relieving sexual dysfunction. For this purpose it employs a combination of prescribed sexual experiences, which the clients use at home to modify the immediate causes of their problem. Typically a couple is asked to learn first to caress each other to evoke pleasure without thought of completing the act of intercourse, and perform other actions designed to relieve performance anxiety and excessive self-observation, two common sources of difficulty.

Sex therapy can be undertaken by one partner alone but usually requires the participation of both. Most therapists begin with a detailed history of the clients' sex life and give a thorough explanation of the anatomy and physiology of the sex organs and of sexual response. Present-day techniques of sex therapy are based on the work of William Masters and Virginia Johnson, who, about 1960, formed a clinic for treating couples in a series of daily sessions over two weeks. Their work has since been modified by Helen Singer Kaplan and others. The therapy is usually time-limited and fairly short-term (typically twelve to fourteen sessions held weekly or semiweekly) but the exact procedure depends on the individual clinician, who may adapt it to each couple. Therapy is usually terminated when the sex difficulty has been resolved—in effect, when the symptom has been cured, its immediate causes modified, and the clients have enough insight to prevent recurrence. Not all such treatment is successful, of course. Sometimes one or the other partner is found to have an underlying problem that requires individual treatment, or the entire relationship between the partners is pathologic. In other cases the clients may simply give up and either seek relief through some other treatment or decide to live with the problem.

Its very nature makes sex therapy readily open to abuse by unqualified and/or unscrupulous practitioners, and because it is a relatively new field, standards for licensing are not well established. The best way to find a reputable practitioner is through the American Association of Sex Education, Counselors, and Therapists, which will provide names of reputable and experienced therapists in your area.

HYPNOTHERAPY

Hypnotherapy means treatment involving hypnosis, a mental state of heightened concentration and suggestibility, characterized by altered perception and memory. Its first reported use in modern times was by Franz Anton Mesmer (1733–1815), a German physician who practiced what he called "animal magnetism" in Paris, and for some time the method was called "mesmerism." Although the sensational aspects of hypnotism soon led to its dismissal and condemnation by physicians and scientists, it continued to intrigue individuals interested in the human mind, particularly Sigmund Freud. Today hypnotism is still used as a form of entertainment, but it also is useful as a form of anesthesia in dentistry, childbirth, and surgery, for the relief of intractable pain from cancer and other disorders, and in psychotherapy of various kinds. In therapy it is used to recover long-buried memories, which are brought to consciousness while a client is in a hypnotic state (trance); to help induce deep relaxation in clients undergoing systematic desensitization (see above); and to discourage clients from overeating, compulsive gambling, smoking, and other forms of habit abuse. In general, hypnotherapy is thought to be most effective when used as an adjunct to other therapy.

The techniques for inducing hypnosis vary, but they usually involve some procedure to focus the client's attention, inducing him or her to concentrate solely on the therapist.

Exactly what happens in hypnotism is not completely understood. There appear to be several levels of trance—light, moderate, and deep. A hypnotic trance is characterized by extreme relaxation and heightened susceptibility to suggestion, but it does not involve giving up one's will or being controlled by someone else. Rather, while a client is in a trance, the therapist may suggest new ways of behaving and thinking that eliminate an undesirable behavior or habit, or bring recall of a forgotten event that became the source of anxiety or neurosis. Many clients can learn to hypnotize themselves and thus supplement and reinforce the therapist's efforts. In therapy, hypnosis tends to be used in short-term forms of treatment.

Not everyone can be hypnotized. Moreover, hypnotherapy is not completely without risk; on rare occasions a trance brings out latent violence, in the form of a psychotic outburst or a physical attack. Because it is not totally understood, hypnotism is open to abuse by inadequately trained practitioners. Both the American Medical Association and the American Psychiatric Association have published standards for treatment by hypnosis, pointing out the dangers of inappropriate use in clinical situations where it is contraindicated. It requires careful evaluation of clients, their problems, and their total life situations, and is most effectively used by someone well trained in psychological and physiological processes. If hypnotism is suggested as a form of treatment for you, your relative, or your friend, it is wise to check carefully the credentials and experience of the therapist before agreeing to the procedure.

BODY THERAPIES

A number of therapies use what is sometimes called a "holistic" approach, regarding the mind and body as an inseparable whole. None of these therapies has to date been endorsed by a reputable body of professionals, such as the American Psychiatric Association, and all should be viewed with caution, if not skepticism.

Reich, who developed orgone therapy (see page 121), observed that physical tension often was a symptom of mental distress and tried to get clients to release pent-up emotions by deep breathing and laying hands on contracted muscles. His pupil, Alexander Lowen, went further, saying that emotional problems are always expressed in muscular tensions, which "bind up" one's energy so that it cannot be discharged. His system of *bioenergetics* is supposed to get the client back together with his or her body, and help him or her enjoy the life of the body to the fullest. The client must first undress, so as to reveal the body completely. A variety of breathing and other exercises are employed to release tension. Then massage and other physical contact between therapist and client (ranging from touching all the way to sexual intercourse) are used to break down what Lowen considered the conflict between a person's desire for and fear of body contact. This kind of therapy has never been endorsed by any professional organization and is readily open to abuse. If anyone recommends it for you, get a responsible second opinion before undertaking it.

Rolfing, named for its inventor, Ida Rolf (1896–1979), is a method of body reorganization through deep massage. It is based on the idea that the body's muscles literally absorb psychological trauma, which makes them stiff and rigid. By massaging various muscles, allegedly the trauma stored in each is evoked, allowing the client to confront long-repressed feelings. Massage is sometimes combined with guided fantasy, here involving conscious attempts to recall oneself at various early ages, through which one is then supposed to re-experience the painful incidents of the past. Rolfing is usually performed by a kind of physiotherapist who applies pressure to various muscles in a prescribed sequence; occasionally the process is physically painful. The standard term of treatment is a series of ten one-hour sessions, which makes it one of the shortest-term therapies available.

Similar in basis but different in practice is Arthur Janov's *primal therapy.* Janov believes that the source of emotional problems is the denial of a child's basic ("primal") needs—for food, warmth, physical contact—by its parents. The child realizes through such deprivation that its parents do not love him or her, a realization that Janov calls "the primal trauma." Allegedly all neuroses are a response to this trauma. The goal of therapy is to release the "primal pain" by addressing its sources, one's father and mother. Therapy thus consists of reliving the experience of primal pain and responding to it in an uninhibited way, by screaming, kicking, crying, and the like. It usually is begun with a period of twenty-four hours spent in total isolation in order to weaken the client's defenses. This is followed by an intensive three-week course of individual therapy, with daily sessions that last several hours each, during which the therapist tries to get the client to express the deepest possible feelings toward his or her parents. This course may be followed by a period of group therapy in which each individual's primal pain is further explored and expressed.

TRANSCENDENTAL MEDITATION

A very different route to relieving tension—both physical and emotional—is that of various Eastern meditative practices, ranging from yoga to Zen and other kinds of Buddhism, with or without the aid of mind-expanding (psychedelic) drugs. (Such drugs, which include LSD, marijuana, and mescaline, induce hallucinations and, sometimes, psychotic states.)

Meditation has its basis in religion and is much older than any of the other therapies described. Its goal is the attainment of a different state of consciousness, in which the self, the subject and center of ordinary experience, ceases to exist as a separate entity. Instead, the meditator perceives him- or herself as an integral part of the rest of the world. Thus meditation is sometimes described as "losing oneself." Insofar as it employs various breathing and body exercises to induce concentration and a kind of special awareness, it is related to the body therapies.

Meditation is essentially nonverbal. Naming thoughts and feelings is discouraged; rather, the goal is to concentrate so that the ordinary flow of ideas and images lose their ordinary verbal meaning. Strictly speaking, meditation is not a psychotherapy at all, since we defined psychotherapy as an interview process. It does, however, alleviate some of the tensions associated with various neurotic disorders, and it is not incompatible for use in conjunction with other forms of therapy. It also can be and is used by persons not suffering from any particular psychic distress but who are seeking spiritual fulfillment, or looking for a simple means to reduce ordinary, everyday tens'ons.

FEMINIST THERAPY

Feminist therapy is an outgrowth of the women's movement of the 1960s and 1970s and represents a reaction against male-dominated psychiatry (more than 90 percent of American psychiatrists are men) as well as against the theories of Sigmund Freud and others insofar as they pertain to women's "appropriate" roles and sexuality. Feminist therapy incorporates the basic beliefs of feminism, or women's rights, in the approach to treatment. In theory, feminist therapists may be either male or female, but in practice nearly all are women. They do not use any special therapeutic method; rather, each uses whatever mode of psychotherapy she prefers but adapts it to feminist thinking.

Among the ideas most feminist therapists subscribe to is that the traditional role of women as subordinate to men, passive and powerless, should be replaced so that they are—and feel they are—active, equal, and independent. Another central belief is that a therapist should not behave as an authority figure who dominates, intimidates, or patronizes the client. Rather, she should help the client overcome her own feelings of helplessness and dependency, and encourage her assertiveness. To this end feminist therapists often try to avoid technical language, give the client free access to her own records and files, and encourage the client to set her own goals for therapy (rather than rely on the therapist to set them for her).

PSYCHOTHERAPY FOR CHILDREN

Many of the modes of psychotherapy described in this and the previous chapter have been adapted and used for children and adolescents. In addition, some methods have been developed specifically for treating disturbed youngsters.

One such technique is *play therapy,* which originally was used mainly by therapists with a psychoanalytic orientation but today is used by therapists of diverse backgrounds. Most children under the age of ten or twelve are not sophisticated enough to be able to talk about their problems to a therapist. Indeed, most young children are not able to sit still long enough to hold a half-hour conversation with a grownup. Just as conversation is the natural social activity of the adult, play is the natural activity of the child. During a play therapy session the therapist and child play together, usually with any toy or game chosen by the client from a collection made available by the therapist. Play, it is believed, allows children to display anger, fear, anxiety, and other feelings, and to act out fantasies and conflicts. The equipment varies, but there are nearly always dolls and household toys that allow children to act out family relationships and similar matters; soldiers, guns, and other weapons to express aggression; and drawing materials, paints, and clay for less structured means of self-expression.

The analytically oriented therapist uses play therapy to try to understand the symbolic meanings of a child's play in order to clarify the symptoms and underlying pathology. The client-centered Rogerian therapist uses play therapy to allow a child to communicate thoughts and feelings in a comfortable way, and create a permissive, nondemanding environment in which the child feels accepted and comes to accept his or her own feelings. Play therapy is used less often by behavior therapists, who rather focus on reinforcing actual behavior in an ordinary setting, although they may play a game with a child as a form of positive reinforcement.

Psychotherapy for children involves the parents to varying degrees. Some therapists like to see the parents in separate sessions as frequently as they see their child. Others rarely bring the parents into therapy, except to report on progress. Still others may use family therapy—with both parents and the child and siblings present—for some sessions, as well as individual therapy with the child. (Family therapy is discussed in the next chapter.) And some of the behaviorally oriented therapists scarcely work with the child at all but rather instruct parents and teachers in carrying out a reinforcement system of their design.

CHAPTER 14

Giving Help—Psychotherapy 3: Group Therapies

Since about 1950 group therapies have become increasingly popular. There is no one kind of group therapy. Rather, such therapies range from analytical (insight) psychotherapy, which focuses on the problems of individuals but in a group setting, to encounter groups and various kinds of marathon, which offer very concentrated, intense, and brief terms of therapy. Among the individual therapies that have been used in a group setting are Horneyan, Adlerian, Sullivanian, rational-emotive, existential, Gestalt, and bioenergetic.

From the standpoint of cost per session, group therapy is decidedly less expensive than individal therapy. In 1981 it cost about $20 per person per session, approximately one-third (or even less) the cost of individual therapy. However, depending on numerous factors—the problem, the group members, the therapist, the method(s) used, etc.—group therapy may not be as worthwhile as individual therapy.

In conventional group therapy a group of six to ten persons meets, usually once a week for one and one-half hours, with one or two (or more) therapists. (If there is more than one therapist it may be called *conjoint therapy*.) The makeup of the group may be either homogeneous or heterogeneous in terms of age, sex, and kinds of problem. The role of the group leader(s) may vary from very neutral to very active.

FOR WHOM IS GROUP THERAPY?

Group therapy can be undertaken alone or in conjunction with individual therapy. Some therapists invite their clients to join a group after a period of individual therapy, and sometimes a client continues individual therapy, too, with the same or with another therapist. This is sometimes called *combined psychotherapy.*

Since group therapy is used even for extremely disturbed patients in mental hospitals, it would seem to be appropriate for anyone interested in psychotherapy. However, outside a hospital or other setting where there can be very close supervision, group therapy is neither desirable nor suitable for everyone, and for some individuals it may be actively harmful. Who should *not* be in a group therapy?

- A person who is managing, with difficulty, to get along but who is close to a serious breakdown; such a person needs more intensive individual treatment
- A person who is unduly distressed by the ills of others; hearing about the other group members' problems week after week can be overwhelming.
- A person who crumbles under criticism; to such a person even a mildly negative comment by another group member may be devastating.

Further, some individuals may so disrupt or hamper the functioning of a group that it is unwise for them to participate. Among these are:

- A person who wants to monopolize the leader's attention all or most of the time.
- A person unable to share his or her ideas or experiences, and thus is unable to contribute to the group.
- A person extremely insensitive to the feelings of others, who therefore frequently makes wounding remarks and is unable to listen to what others are saying.
- A person who becomes explosively angry.

A skilled and experienced group leader usually screens prospective members very carefully, but even the best leader can make mistakes. If you are considering joining a group, or group therapy has been recommended for you, it is wise to find out as much as you can about the group. In your individual meeting with the group leader—and a group leader nearly always sees each prospective member for at least one session to learn the person's history, evaluate his or her problems, and define goals—you can and should ask the therapist about his or her background (training and experience) and about the makeup and goals of the group, how long it is expected to meet (for a month, several months, a year or more) and whether during that time members will leave and be replaced by new members, how active the therapist will be in group meetings, and any other questions that seem important to you.

Because the interaction of group members sometimes is hard to perceive while it is actually going on, some therapists find it useful to videotape group sessions. Playing back portions of the tape, either to individual members or to the entire group, makes it possible to review exactly what happened and enables individuals to see how they behave in a group setting. If the therapist does videotape your group, you may want to know what happens to the tapes, in order to preserve confidentiality. Often such tapes are not stored at all, but are used, erased, and re-used, which avoids the need for legal release forms and preserves privacy.

Note, however, that group members, unlike the therapist, are not legally bound to respect confidentiality. Therefore what is said in a group does not have the same confidentiality value as a comment made to an individual therapist.

Who *should* consider group therapy? As indicated above and further described below, there are many different kinds of group therapy, and groups have been used to treat a huge variety of problems, ranging from chronic severe mental disorders such as schizophrenia in long-term institutionalized patients to individuals coping with alcoholism and drug abuse. Some mental problems seem to lend themselves more readily to group therapy than individual therapy. Among them are:

- The shy, lonely person who is very dependent and in fact very isolated. The group process makes him or her realize there are others in the same boat. This approach is very useful for some adolescents.
- The person in individual therapy who has become overdependent on the therapist. Group therapy forces him or her to share the therapist's attention with the other members and fosters a greater degree of independence.
- A person who has trouble getting along with others. The group may focus on the precise sources of the difficulty and teach ways to overcome them.
- Persons with a problem seen as unusual or shameful—an embarrassing phobia, addiction to alcohol or drugs, obesity. A group made up of individuals with this same problem can offer mutual emotional support.
- Couples with marital difficulties. Groups made up of married couples experiencing problems can benefit from observing each other's interactions in a group setting. Also, with more than one couple present, the therapist is in less danger of being drawn into the role of judge between two warring individuals.

If you are interested specifically in some form of group therapy, you may be able to obtain the names of practitioners in your area from the American Group Psychotherapy Association, 1865 Broadway, New York, NY 10023.

Insight group therapy can take several forms. It may focus primarily on the individual members and how they react to the group setting, or it may address itself to the group as a whole and let individual problems arise as they may. For example, consider a therapy group in which one person, Tony, tends to dominate meetings. Whenever anyone brings up an issue, he offers his opinion or brings up a similar event in his experience. Today Laura is trying to tell the group about her difficulties with her teen-age daughter, and Tony, who has no children himself, constantly interrupts her. John tries to stop Tony so that Laura may talk, but he is ignored. If this is a group concentrating on individuals, the group leader, Phyllis, might stop Tony and suggest that he is interrupting Laura for several reasons. She might point out that he feels uncomfortable unless he is the center of attention; he cannot just sit back and listen. Also, Laura seems to find John attractive, and this might remind Tony of his childhood, when his mother seemed to favor his younger brother. On the other hand, if this group is one in which the collective process is in focus, Phyllis might point out that here Tony was bossing the meeting and giving Laura a hard time, but the other members of the group, except for John, were doing nothing to stop him. They were sitting back and allowing these events to take place, even when they had nothing to gain (and something to lose, in terms of time, attention, etc.) from their inaction.

PSYCHODRAMA

A commonly used technique in group therapy is borrowed from psychodrama, invented by Jacob L. Moreno (1889–1974). Some members of the group act out a particular situation or issue, while the rest of the group act as an audience. After the "performance," everyone is asked to make comments and offer interpretations of what they have observed. Thus Laura might be asked to play the mother, John her teen-aged daughter, and Tony would play Laura's husband. First Laura might express anger at her daughter for always staying out much later than her curfew and refusing to help with household chores. John might respond that he thought "Mother" was always picking on him. And so on. John, although playing the role of Laura's daughter, inevitably will reveal some of his own background (perhaps his own experience as a teenager), which makes the drama helpful for analyzing his feelings and behavior as well as Laura's problem. Other psychodrama techniques include *role reversal* (next John might play the mother and Laura the daughter) and the *mirror method* (Laura sits back and observes while some other group member acts out her role).

FAMILY THERAPY

Family therapy is a specialized form of group therapy, usually involving a single family. It was developed in the 1950s, growing out of the treatment of mentally ill children and their mothers, a focus that expanded to family processes, that is, all the relationships within a family. Today most people go to see a family therapist when they have problems involving their marriage or one or more of their children. When no children are involved or the basic problem is a marital one, it is usually called *marital* or *couples therapy.*

Family therapy may be analytically oriented, concentrating on the conflicts each individual has with other family members, or it may use any or several of the other individual or group psychotherapy approaches described above. It may be the only method of treatment or it may be combined with other treatment, one or more members of the family also receiving individual therapy and/or being engaged in other group therapy.

The underlying theory of family therapy—no matter which of the various techniques of group therapy is used—is that a family is a system or group that has definite functions, among them survival, security (safety of its members), economic viability (having enough money to live on), identity (who belongs and who doesn't), power and control, affection and intimacy, and so on. A family's behavior becomes maladaptive (emotionally ill) when it emphasizes some functions at the expense of other, equally important ones, or if the parents' leadership function is impaired. For example, in one family certain members (the parents) may consider identity so important that they do not allow the children to have friends but insist they come straight home from school and limit their social life to the members of the family. In another family, making money and acquiring property may become so important to the parents that they spend little or no time with or energy on their children other than buying them expensive clothing and toys. In still another family the father might withdraw from all disciplinary, decision-making, and other functions that would normally involve agreement with the mother, leaving her to perform all these duties yet covertly undermining her decisions. In all these cases the relations among family members may readily become distorted, so that there is a trend toward recurring crises, and eventually one or more of the family members may break down.

There are three main approaches to family therapy. The *insight-awareness* approach is basically insight therapy adapted to the family; that is, observation, clarification and interpretation are used to foster understanding. The therapist listens to the family, keeps a "therapeutic distance," and tries to form a therapeutic relationship with family members. This is essentially individual insight therapy practiced in the presence of other family members. The second approach is *strategic-behavioral* (also called *systems, communications, or structural*). It focuses on patterns of behavior and attempts to change them for the better. The therapist plays a far more active role, sometimes assigning specific tasks both in and out of the treatment sessions, manipulating mood, focusing on specific symptoms, interrupting repetitive behavior patterns to point them out, explain them, and prescribe certain behaviors. The third approach is the *experiential-existential,* in which the emphasis is on what the therapist sees and what family members perceive and feel. The therapist may act either as a role model or as an advocate for the family members, and the overall goal is to change the ways family members experience and react to each other. It is to some extent the counterpart of Gestalt therapy applied to a family. (A fourth approach combining elements of these is described in Chapter 23.)

A number of specific techniques have been developed and/or used by family therapists. Among them are:

- Family tasks. The therapist assigns tasks to be performed during or between sessions, for example, undertaking an outing that includes all the family members, or instructing a husband and wife to discuss a family secret.
- Paradoxical prescription/intention (also called symptom scheduling, negative practice, or reverse psychology), in which symptoms are made more intense and/or more frequent so as to de-mystify them; for example, a couple who constantly argue may be told to argue about which restaurant they will go to *before* dinner, so they can enjoy their meal without arguing (see also page 327).
- Coaching, in which the therapist directly coaches family members in their various interactions during a therapy session.

- Home visiting, where the therapist goes to the clients' home, school, church, etc. and meets the individuals and agencies that influence their lives.
- Guided fantasy, in which the therapist helps a family member share his or her personal fantasies with other family members.
- Family sculpture, in which the therapist asks one or all of the family members present to create, at a given moment during the therapy session, a physical representation of their relationships by arranging their bodies in space.
- Psychodrama and role playing (see above).
- Video- and audiotaping of a therapy session, with an immediate playback to help family members see how they interact and communicate, both verbally and nonverbally (through gestures, facial expression, etc.).
- One-way mirror, used in a number of ways: by the therapist, who leaves the family in the treatment room and observes them through the mirror, or by one of the family members leaving the group and observing the others, or by one of a pair of therapists (cotherapists), with one remaining in the room and the other observing.
- Weekend family marathon, where one or several families get together for eight to twelve hours of intensive encounter (see also encounter groups and marathons below).
- Multiple family group therapy, bringing together several families to meet together.
- Network therapy, in which the family, friends, and all other individuals who have any bearing on a person's problems meet together in three to six biweekly, four-hour sessions at the client's home (there may be as many as forty-five persons at such a meeting).

How Family Therapy Works

Even if not all the family members agree to enter treatment together, a family therapist may want to see all of them for a single session, for purposes of evaluation. This first meeting can reveal a great deal about the family, just in the way they enter the room and sit down—

who sits with whom, who speaks and who listens, who smiles and who frowns, and so on. The therapist can take note of how the members talk to each other, what they choose to talk about, what they choose to avoid, and what they reveal through "body language" (gestures, posture).

Suppose, for example, that Harry and Mary H., the couple in their thirties described in Chapter 1, decide they must do something about seven-year-old Mark's tantrums, and their pediatrician suggests they see a family therapist. At the first session, Harry, Mary, Mark, and five-year-old Judy attend; Harry's two children from his former marriage, who visit him every other weekend, have refused to come. Mary leads the way into the room, followed by the children and then Harry. She walks briskly, he drags his feet. She sits in the chair nearest the therapist, the children stand very close to her, and Harry takes the chair nearest the door. Already some of the interactions of this family are evident. It is Mary who has come for help and seeks an ally in the therapist. The children align themselves with their mother, and the father remains in an alien position, near the door, as though he were ready to walk out any time (and, you may recall, he has actually walked out on the family several times earlier).

In the course of therapy, the H. family and their therapist will focus on defining the causes of problems, improving communication among family members, learning to cope with stress, and involving the children in this and other processes. If most or all of the family members remain in the group, therapy is sometimes called *conjoint family therapy;* if it is decided this family will benefit from meetings with one or more other families, it becomes *multiple family therapy;* and if a team of professionals—not just one or two family therapists but perhaps a psychologist to test and evaluate Mark, an individual therapist to treat Harry separately, and a social worker who sees Mary alone—is brought in, it is called *multiple impact family therapy.*

Family therapy tends to be relatively short-term, typically consisting of weekly hour-long sessions over a period of six months to a year. It is appropriate for a wide range of disorders, but especially when interpersonal conflicts in the family strongly affect one or more of the members. It is also considered very useful in treating children, on the theory that a shift in parental relations and parent-child relations can free a child from anxiety and reduce his or her need to act out parental and family problems in maladaptive behavior.

When is family therapy *not* appropriate? According to Nathan W. Ackerman, one of the experts of family therapy:

- When the family is about to break up anyhow, and it is too late to stop the process. (Then, however, divorce mediation (see Chapters 8 and 21) might ease the breakup for parents and children.)
- When one parent has a major mental disorder, particularly severe paranoid delusions, or is determined to behave destructively.
- When one or both parents cannot be honest. Deeply rooted deceit makes family therapy useless.
- When a deeply held religious, cultural, or economic belief of the family is opposed to this form of intervention. The family members must *want* to change things for the better, or change cannot take place.
- When one or more of the family members has extremely rigid defenses that, if broken down, may trigger a crisis—a psychotic episode or physical assault.
- When one or more members has a disease or other disability of a progressive nature that rules out their participation.

TRANSACTIONAL ANALYSIS (T.A.)

Transactional analysis is a technique developed in California in the early 1950s by a Canadian-born psychiatrist, Eric Berne (1920-1970). Berne maintained that our social needs are as important as our biological drives (hunger, sex, etc.), and that we all have a basic need for love and recognition. The human personality has three basic aspects, or *ego states*: Parent, Child, and Adult. Unlike Freud's supergo, id, and ego (see Chapter 12), to which they are roughly comparable, Berne's states are directly observable in behavior. The Parent is essentially critical and judgmental; the Child is a leftover of childhood, dominated by intense feelings; the Adult is the rational decision-maker, responding to real-life situations and mediating between Parent and Child. When either Child or Parent dominates the way we behave towards others—what Berne called our *social transactions*—our behavior is maladaptive.

The Child or Parent state express themselves by means of "games," repetitive behavior with hidden meanings. For example, "Kick me" is a "game" played by the Child that asks for the very rejection that is feared.

Although T.A. can be an individual therapy, more often it is carried on in groups. In T.A. groups, the members interact and confront one another, and the leader explains and interprets the "games" they are playing. Often T.A. is combined with other techniques, especially role playing and psychodrama. The therapist, whose background may range from advanced training in psychiatry or psychology to a few months' training in T.A. alone, is very active, as are all the group members. Everyone is encouraged to clarify points, intervene to discuss a member's behavior, confront a passive member, point out contradictions, etc. If you are specifically interested in T.A., you may obtain the names of practitioners in your area from the International Transactional Analysis Association, 3155 College Avenue, Berkeley, CA 94705.

ENCOUNTER GROUPS AND MARATHONS

The basic purpose of encounter group therapy is to overcome emotional alienation and isolation by means of intimate encounters with others. Also called *T-groups* (for training groups, referring to training mental health professionals in methods of group therapy) and *sensitivity groups,* they tend to be intensive in nature and short in duration. The first important encounter group was formed in the 1960s at Esalen Institute at Big Sur, California. It consisted of ten to fifteen persons who met in several sessions over a short period, ranging from several days to several weeks. One form is the marathon, consisting of a single long session that extends over a day or a weekend, in which both verbal and nonverbal contact (confrontation, hugging, massage), as well as various structured exercises are used. Honest and open communication are stressed. Participants are encouraged to pay close attention to their feelings and to their bodies, and to obey such rules as "Fight when it feels right," "Take off your clothes if it feels useful," and "If possible express yourself physically rather than verbally."

Another form of encounter group is called *est,* for *Erhard Seminars Training.* Its inventor, Werner Erhard, is a former management consultant with no formal training in mental health. Est consists of two long sessions, held on consecutive weekends, and three evenings, at a cost, in 1982, of $400 per person. Each group involves approximately 250 persons in a single large room, such as a hotel ballroom, with a leader, called a "trainer." During the sixty or so hours of est, the emphasis is on various forms of physical discomfort—no eating or drinking is allowed, and only limited absences for toilet use—and constant repetition of the est message: "If you are willing to acknowledge that you are the cause of your own experience, then you can run your own lives instead of being run by them."

Many mental health professionals schooled in more traditional methods regard encounter groups and est as expensive hoaxes, useless for permanent accomplishment of any kind and potentially harmful to individuals in need of treatment for mental disorders. One element common to nearly all such groups is direct confrontation. For example, a group member who makes a statement such as "I'm really nervous when I'm with someone who's bigger than I am" may be asked to repeat that statement individually to every person in the group. This tactic can be very threatening to some individuals.

Another frequent criticism is that such groups tend to be run by persons with little or virtually no training in mental health. The same criticism applies to another kind of group therapy—that of the peer, *self-help groups* described in Chapter 11—but in this case the members all have had experience with the same problem (alcoholism, drug addiction, recovery from mental illness, or whatever) and consequently are less likely to cause serious harm.

"ECLECTIC" THERAPY

We have described the most important modes of psychotherapy currently being practiced, and even these represent just a fraction of the total (there may be as many as 300 different methods and schools; a book describing more than 250 was recently published*). Some, as has been indicated, are more suitable for certain disorders than others, and some should never be undertaken by certain individuals. Nevertheless, it would be difficult to choose a therapist by orientation or method alone. However, we are *not* suggesting you should do so (see the section on how to choose a therapist, Chapter 9); rather, this should be just one factor in your choice. Further, you may not have to, because many therapists today— some suggest as many as half—consider themselves "eclectic," which means they draw on the theories and techniques of a variety of schools and try to adapt them to the unique needs of each client.

Here is a profile of one therapist who describes herself as "eclectic." Dr. P. holds a master's degree in counseling and a doctor of education degree (Ed.D.) in psychology. She began her career as a high school teacher, found herself spending an increasing amount of time counseling students, and returned to school to obtain advanced training. She has been in private practice for six years, and performs individual, couples, family, and group therapy. As a clinical psychologist, she cannot prescribe medication, so she uses a psychiatrist she knows well as a backup. However, she prefers to avoid the use of medication on a long-term basis. The clients she sees, on the average of once a week each, have disorders ranging from alcoholism to depression, personality disorders, and various neuroses. She usually refers persons with active schizophrenia and other psychotic conditions to other clinicians.

Dr. P's formal training was principally in client-centered therapy (see Chapter 13), but in her practice she takes a much more active role than the traditional nondirective therapist. She draws on analytic, insight therapy, using dream interpretation and guided fan-

*Richie Herink, ed., *The Psychotherapy Handbook* (1980).

tasy*, and in group therapy she frequently uses psychodrama (see above). A strong believer in "the whole person," she advises her clients on diet, exercise, and recreation, maintaining that a healthy body makes for a healthy mind. The average term of treatment with Dr. P. is one year. Clients do not enter into a formal treatment contract with her but she emphasizes frequent re-evaluation of the direction of treatment.

Eclectic therapy would seem to have advantages in that it can draw on any or all schools of thought. In practice, however, many therapists today who say they belong to one school or another would freely admit their debts to other theories and methods. Moreover, the experienced therapist of any persuasion tends to recognize his or her limitations and, if honest, will admit that not every client will be helped.

The very multiplicity of theories and therapies indicates at least two important realities. First, the state of understanding of mental illness—indeed, of mental activities in general—is still too primitive to enable anyone to say that any one of the theories of personality now in existence is correct. Human personality is so complex that no simple theory can be formulated for any but its grossest aspects, and some don't even do that well. Second, for a psychotherapy to become popular, it must help some people. The element that seems common to psychotherapies (and also to treatment by faith healers and witch doctors) is that of a reliable, authoritative person who is presumed to understand the mysteries of the illness and whom the troubled person trusts for help.

Which mode of psychotherapy is right for you? As the Russian playwright Anton Chekhov said, "Where there are many remedies, the disease is incurable." That is partly true of psychotherapy, in that a person is seldom "cured" of his or her illness. But many people *are* helped. In Chapter 18 we discuss how you can tell if psychotherapy and other forms of treatment are helping you, or your relative or friend.

---

*Guided fantasy is a technique in which the therapist describes some imaginary situation to the client—"You are entering a large room full of strangers," for example—and asks the client to enlarge on this theme, in as much detail as possible. Originally used by Freud, this method to foster insight is now employed by therapists from various schools, including some behavior therapists.

CHAPTER 15

Giving Help—Treatment With Psychoactive Drugs

The somatic or organic therapies treat a person's body in order to bring about changes in emotions and behavior. They include brain surgery, inducing seizures by means of chemicals or electricity, and changing the body chemistry through diet, drugs, or other chemicals. The most widespread somatic therapy used today is the administration of psychoactive drugs.

WHAT ARE PSYCHOACTIVE DRUGS?

The use of drugs to alter mental states was common among ancient and primitive peoples, who discovered various natural substances that would induce hallucinations. The modern clinical use of drugs to alter mood and behavior, which began about 1950, revolutionized the treatment of mental illness. For the first time, violent patients could be reliably controlled instead of having to be locked up or put in physical restraints like straitjackets. First tested on a large scale in 1954, the antipsychotic drugs have reduced the hospital population in some areas by as much as 75 percent. It is impossible to estimate how many suicides have been prevented by antidepressant drugs, or how many manic-depressive individuals have been able to lead useful lives since their mania has been controlled by lithium carbonate.

161

COMMONLY USED PSYCHOACTIVE DRUGS

	Generic Name	*Brand Name*
Antianxiety drugs (minor tranquilizers or anxiolytics)		
benzodiazepines	chlorazepate	Azene, Tranxene
	chlordiazepoxide	Librium, Menrium
	diazepam	Valium
	flurazepam	Dalmane
	lorazepam	Ativan
	oxazepam	Serax
	prazepam	Verstran
	temazepam	Restoril
propanediol carbamate	meprobamate	Equanil, Miltown
barbiturates	amobarbital	Amytal
	pentobarbital	Nembutal
	phenobarbital	Luminal
	secobarbital	Seconal
antihistamine	hydroxyzine	Atarax, Vistaril
beta-adrenergic antagonist	propranool	Inderal
Antidepressant drugs (mood elevators)		
tricyclic	amitriptyline	Elavil, Endep
	desipramine	Norpramin, Pertofrane
	doxepin	Sinequan, Adapin
	imipramine	Tofranil, Imavate
	nortriptyline	Pamelor, Aventyl
	protriptyline	Vivactil
monoamine oxidase inhibitors	isocarboxazid	Marplan
	pargyline	Eutonyl
	phenelzine	Nardil
	tranylcypromine	Parnate
psychostimulants	dextro-amphetamine	Dexedrine
	methylphenidate	Ritalin
	pemoline	Cylert
Antimanic drugs (mood stabilizers)	lithium carbonate	Eskalith, Lithane, Litholate

	Generic Name	Brand Name
Antipsychotic drugs (major tranquilizers or neuroleptics) phenothiazines	acetophenazine	Tindal
	butaperazine	Repoise
	carphenazine	Proketazine
	chlorpromazine	Thorazine
	fluphenazine	Prolixin
	mesoridazine	Serentil
	perphenazine	Trilafon
	piperacetazine	Quide
	prochlorperazine	Compazine
	thioridazine	Mellaril
	trifluoperazine	Stelazine
thioxanthenes	chlorprothixene	Taractan
	thiothixene	Navane
butyrophene	haloperidol	Haldol
dihydroindoline	molindone	Moban
dibenzoxazepine	loxapine	Loxitane

Like most powerful chemical agents, psychoactive (also called *psychotropic*) drugs are a mixed blessing. Some are addictive, causing a person to become physically and/or psychologically dependent on them. Some have side effects serious enough to make them either a treatment of last resort or quite unusable in certain individuals. Some are widely prescribed by numerous kinds of practitioner—family physicians, internists, gynecologists—to patients for whom they are of little or no benefit. Their use then can represent a form of drug *abuse*. In an emergency the wrong drug can cause considerable harm; for example, an antipsychotic drug given to a person delirious because of drug withdrawal can dangerously lower the blood pressure. Different individuals react differently to psychoactive drugs, so the proper dosage can be difficult to determine. And finally, practically every reputable clinician encounters some individuals who are "hooked" on one or more drugs that are not helping them at all, and may be hindering other, more appropriate treatment.

Despite these drawbacks, the psychoactive drugs are undeniably valuable in treating not just the most severe mental illnesses, but also some less serious but distressing disorders. As with any treatment, the risks must be weighed against the benefits. More often than not, the benefits of these drugs do outweigh the risks if they are administered under competent medical supervision.

What should you do if a physician suggests a psychoactive drug for you, your husband, or your friend? As indicated earlier, it is vital to have a medical checkup before undergoing any physical or chemical treatment. Further, be sure the mental health practitioner knows your medical history, particularly with regard to allergies and adverse drug reactions. If you regularly take other medications of any kind—whether they are over-the-counter remedies or prescription drugs—be sure the prescribing physician knows about them, lest they are compounds that can interfere with the new drug's action or the new drug will interact with them. Finally, be sure to ask about possible side effects, restrictions on your activities or diet while taking the drug, and, if you are a woman of childbearing age, the effect of the drug on pregnancy and breast-feeding. Also ask how long a drug's influence persists; in some cases it may not be flushed out of the body for a week after it has been discontinued.

There are four main classifications of psychoactive drugs, based on their major uses: antianxiety drugs (minor tranquilizers, anxiolytics); antidepressant drugs (mood elevators); antimanic (mood-stabilizing) drugs; and antipsychotic drugs (major tranquilizers, neuroleptics).

ANTIANXIETY DRUGS (TRANQUILIZERS)

The principal antianxiety drugs, also called *minor tranquilizers* or *anxiolytics,* are the benzodiazepines, which include flurazepam (Dalmane), chlordiazepoxide (Librium), and diazepam (Valium), among others. Although these compounds were discovered in 1933, it was only in 1960 that one of them, chlordiazepoxide, was found to have a calming effect on wild animals, and thereafter began to be used in human patients.

The antianxiety drugs have four principal effects: they sedate, they combat anxiety, they relax muscles, and they act against convulsions. Although all of them act in this way to some extent, flurazepam often is used as a sleep inducer, and diazepam as an anticonvulsant and muscle relaxant.

The benzodiazepines are long-acting drugs, remaining in the system long after they are taken. The individual drugs vary in how fast they are eliminated from the body, some taking as little as five to ten hours and others thirty-six to 200 hours (for half to be eliminated). Since these drugs can make one drowsy and lethargic, anyone taking them should be cautious about driving, operating machinery, or undertaking other activities requiring alertness and good coordination. Also, these drugs enhance the effects of alcohol, so that even a small amount of liquor can be intoxicating.

The benzodiazepines frequently are prescribed by doctors other than psychiatrists. In fact, diazepam (Valium) was, in 1981, the fourth most frequently prescribed of all drugs in the United States (in the mid-1970s it ranked *first*). To some extent these drugs are addictive. Abrupt withdrawal from Valium, for example, has been known to cause seizures, an effect that is avoided if the dosage of the drug is reduced gradually. They also can cause depression or deepen an already existing depression.

Another widely used antianxiety drug is meprobamate (Equanil, Miltown), which was developed in 1954. It, too, has some muscle-relaxing and anticonvulsant properties, but its principal effect is sedative (calming) and hypnotic (combating sleeplessness due to anxiety and tension). Its side effects are similar to those of the benzodiazepines, and if it is used over a long period it can be addictive.

The *barbiturates* have been used as sedatives and sleep inducers since 1912. Today the mildest of them, phenobarbital, is used mostly to provide daytime sedation or to control epileptic seizures. Some of the stronger ones—amobarbital, secobarbital, pentobarbital—are sometimes used as antianxiety drugs. For this use, however, they are less effective and have more side effects than the benzodiazepines. Also, they are addictive.

Other antianxiety drugs include one of the antihistamine (anti-allergy) drugs, hydroxyzine (Atarax, Vistaril), and propranolol (Inderal), a drug useful against hypertension (high blood pressure) and certain heart conditions, which is associated with numerous side effects (fatigue, dizziness, insomnia, hallucinations, depression).

ANTIDEPRESSANTS

There are two main kinds of antidepressant, the tricyclic antidepressants and the monoamine oxidase inhibitors. In addition, certain central nervous system stimulants have been used against depression.

The tricyclic antidepressants were discovered in 1958 by a Swiss psychiatrist, Ronald Kuhn, who was looking for a compound effective against schizophrenia. Instead he found one that relieves depression; from it imprimamine (Tofranil) and related drugs were developed. Antidepressants appear to work by enhancing the action of a group of neurotransmitters called the trigger amines (epinephrine, norepinephrine, serotonin), which are believed to be central to regulating and maintaining moods. The tricyclics, so called because of their three-ring chemical structure, are thought to block the breakdown of norepinephrine, and consequently result in higher levels of this neurotransmitter (see Chapter 23 for a discussion of neurotransmitters).

The benefits of the tricyclic antidepressants often are not perceived for two to five weeks after beginning treatment. They frequently are beneficial against depression, helping at least 70 percent of patients. However, they do not work in every case, and even when they are effective their side effects sometimes are severe or hazardous enough to make it necessary to discontinue them. They can cause such unpleasant symptoms as a dry mouth, drowsiness, blurred vision, urinary hesitation, and constipation—all of which often disappear after a few weeks' use or when the dosage is lowered—as well as more serious symptoms, such as low blood pressure, cardiac arrhythmias (irregular heartbeat), and seizures in epileptic patients. They must be used with extreme caution by persons with glaucoma, epilepsy, prostate gland enlargement, asthma, kidney disease, liver disease, or heart disease. Long-term use may cause a craving for sweets and a consequent weight gain. A large overdose (ten to thirty times the normal daily dose) is lethal, so depressed patients usually are given only small amounts at a time.

Tricyclics are not addictive but they should not be discontinued abruptly. Once the symptoms of depression subside, a daily main-

IF YOU TAKE AN MAO INHIBITOR FOR DEPRESSION
you <u>must</u> avoid:

all fermented cheeses or cheese products
pickled herring
sardines
anchovies
chicken livers
canned or processed meat
pods of broad beans (fava beans, etc.)
canned figs
yeast extract
red wine*
beer
more than two ounces a day of:
    sour cream
    yogurt
    cottage cheese
    American cheese
    mild Swiss cheese
    chocolate
more than two cups per day of regular coffee (decaffeinated coffee may be drunk)
nasal decongestants in the form of nose drops, cough drops or cold remedies†
diet pills of any kind
stimulant drugs of any kind
any other medications unless your physician approves them specifically

*Occasional single cocktail or 2 to 3 ounces white wine are permitted
†Permitted cold remedies: aspirin, acetaminophen (Tylenol), guaifensin (Robitussin cough syrup), cepylpyridinium (Cepacol gargle).

tenance dose—the minimum needed for a response—may be continued for three months, after which the dose can be gradually reduced. If symptoms do not recur, the drug can then be stopped. Tricyclics may be used in combination with an antianxiety drug.

The second main category of antidepressant are the monoamine oxidase (MAO) inhibitors, which work by increasing the concentration of available neurotransmitters (by preventing their metabolism by the enzyme monoamine oxidase). Soon after these drugs were introduced, it was discovered that they cause some individuals to develop severe hypertensive reactions and cerebral vascular accident (strokes). Further, since the newly developed tricyclics seemed to work very well for many depressed persons, the MAO inhibitors were for a time abandoned. Then it was discovered that patients taking MAO inhibitors who avoid foods high in tyramine, a chemical compound present in many foods but particularly concentrated in red wine, beer, aged cheeses, pickled herring, and other fermented foods, are less likely to have an adverse reaction. Tyramine, it appeared, causes too great a release of the neurotransmitter norepinephrine, which in turn can cause not only hypertension but severe headache and cardiac arrhythmias. A similar response can be triggered by substances present in many over-the-counter cold and hay fever remedies (nose drops, sprays, antihistamine preparations), as well as some local anesthetics, which therefore also must be avoided. MAO inhibitors should not be taken by persons with a history of liver disease, congestive heart failure, or a previous blood clot or hemorrhage in the brain, or persons with adrenal disorders or epilepsy.

Despite the potential hazards, MAO inhibitors work very well in cases of severe depression that, unlike the typical severe endogenous depression (see Chapter 4), are accompanied by anxiety attacks and phobias, especially agoraphobia. Usually, however, practitioners prefer to give tricyclic antidepressants an extensive trial before they prescribe MAO inhibitors.

A third class of antidepressants are *psychostimulants* (central nervous system stimulants) such as dextroamphetamine (Dexedrine) and related drugs. They work by stimulating the release of neurotransmitters that in turn are activated by the release of norepinephrine. After a time, however, they can deplete the supply of norepinephrine and cause either depression or a psychotic episode similar to schizophrenia. Because of this danger, and because they are addictive and subject to abuse, the amphetamines are considered less desirable antidepressants than either the tricyclics or the MAO inhibitors.

ANTIMANIC DRUGS

The principal antimanic drug in use is lithium carbonate, a compound that was first used against mania in 1949 in Australia by Dr.

John J. Cade and began to be commercially produced in the United States in 1970. Until then the same antipsychotic drugs (see below) were used for both schizophrenia and manic-depressive disease. Lithium, however, proved more useful as a maintenance drug, that is, one given over a long period of time after the manic episode had ended, because it appeared to prevent subsequent manic, and also depressive, episodes. Since lithium takes five to ten days to take effect, initially the antipsychotic drugs may be used along with it to control mania. Long-term use of lithium can cause enlargement of the thyroid gland (goiter), which, however, returns to normal size again when the drug is stopped.

The administration of lithium requires periodic monitoring of its concentration in the blood to keep it at safe and effective levels in the body. Minor side effects of the drug are stomach upsets (mild nausea, diarrhea), increased thirst, a dazed feeling, muscular weak-

DRUGS THAT INTERACT WITH ALCOHOL

- Antialcoholism preparations (Antabuse)
  Use of alcohol with this medication results in nausea, vomiting, headache, high blood pressure, and possible erratic heartbeat; it can result in death.

- Antidepressants (Elavil, Tofranil, etc.)
  Alcohol may cause an additional reduction in central nervous system functioning and lessen a person's ability to operate normally. The combination of alcohol and the MAO inhibitors can cause a high blood pressure crisis, potentially life-threatening.

- Antipsychotics (Mellaril, Thorazine, etc.)
  Alcohol may cause additional depression of central nervous system function, which can result in severe impairment of voluntary movements (walking, using one's hands, etc.). The combination can also cause a loss of effective breathing function and can therefore be fatal.

- Sedative hypnotics (Nembutal, etc.)
  Alcohol further reduces central nervous system function, sometimes to the point of the loss of effective breathing (respiratory arrest) or consciousness (coma). This combination can be fatal.

- Antianxiety drugs (minor tranquilizers; Valium, Librium, etc.)
  Alcohol will cause reduced central nervous system function, especially during the first few weeks of drug use. This results in decreased alertness and judgment, and can lead to household, automotive, and industrial accidents.

ness, and fine tremors of the hands or mouth; all these usually subside as the dosage is adjusted. Toxic levels of the drug are marked by sluggishness, drowsiness, slurred speech, a coarse tremor, muscular twitching, vomiting, and severe diarrhea.

Despite its possible dangers, lithium succeeds in controlling an estimated 75 percent of cases of manic-depressive disorder. Before beginning treatment, a physical examination should be made that includes laboratory studies of electrolytes and blood urea nitrogen, a urinalysis, and an electrocardiogram.

ANTIPSYCHOTIC DRUGS

The antipsychotic drugs, or *major tranquilizers,* are used to treat serious psychiatric disorders, principally schizophrenia, acute mania, and acute confusional states. They produce a state of emotional quiet and indifference, technically called *neurolepsy,* and are therefore also called *neuroleptics.*

There are five main classes of antipsychotic drug, and although they differ in potency, effectiveness, and side effects, they all act by blocking the effects of the neurotransmitter dopamine, which, it is believed, is how they inhibit psychotic symptoms. The more they block dopamine, the more effective they are. The principal serious side effects of antipsychotic drugs are sedation (drowsiness and lethargy) and hypotension (low blood pressure). Other common but less serious side effects are dry mouth, blurred vision, constipation, appetite increase and weight gain, tachycardia (rapid heartbeat), and, in some persons, a syndrome of muscular stiffness or tremor. These side effects tend to disappear when the dosage is reduced or the drug is stopped.

Another serious side effect seen in persons who take these drugs in high doses over a period of several years (as chronic schizophrenia patients sometimes do) is tardive dyskinesia, a syndrome of uncontrolled repetitive movements of the tongue, mouth, jaws (grimacing or chewing movements, for example), and sometimes of the limbs. This effect may be permanent (it does not go away when the drug is stopped), and as yet no cure has been found.

The five classes of antipsychotic drug in current use are the phenothiazines (which include chlorpromazine, or Thorazine, thioridazine, or Mellaril, and trifluoperazine, or Stelazine), thioxanthenes, butyrophenones (including haloperidol, or Haldol), dihydroindolones, and dibenzoxazepines. They usually relieve such distressing symptoms as thought disturbances, delusions, hallucinations, and agitation. Some individuals require a daily maintenance dose for many months and even years; without it they relapse and need to be rehospitalized. Others seem able to stop the drug after a year or two without relapse. In most cases of schizophrenia, those who receive antipsychotics immediately do better in the long run than those for whom drug therapy is delayed.

Antipsychotics are given in tablet or liquid form, or are injected into a muscle. They usually may be taken once a day, but one of the phenothiazines, fluphenazine (Prolixin), is available in a long-acting form that can be injected weekly or biweekly. The initial effects usually are felt within 48 hours.

There are two basic methods for determining the proper dosage for effectiveness, which varies considerably among individuals. One approach begins with a low dose and increases it very gradually, until the symptoms are under control. The other approach, called "loading," begins with a high dose in order to control psychotic symptoms quickly and then decreases gradually until the minimum needed to control the symptoms is found. This method is somewhat chancier and is used only when the risk of the illness is greater than the risk of serious side effects.

DRUGS FOR HYPERACTIVITY

Three kinds of central nervous system stimulant—the amphetamines (Dexedrine, Benzedrine, etc.), methylphenidate (Ritalin), and pemoline (Cylert)—have been used to control hyperactivity in children. Although in adults they act as stimulants, in children they tend to have a calming effect, enabling them to sit still longer and concentrate better. It is not known why the drugs work in this way, and they do not work for all children. Their effectiveness should be carefully monitored by parents and teachers, and examination by a physician at frequent intervals also is important in order to assess the effects of the treatment and make sure there are no serious side effects. The most common side effects are sleep difficulty (insomnia), loss of appetite, weight loss, and rapid heartbeat—similar to the side effects of these stimulants in adults. They usually can be eliminated by reducing the dosage or discontinuing the drug.

ANTIALCOHOLISM DRUGS

The drug disulfiram (Antabuse) is a very potent agent that, when taken alone, is innocuous, but when taken in combination with alcohol, produces a painful and frightening reaction, which includes nausea, irregular heartbeat, and a severe headache. Drinking any alcoholic beverage within twelve hours of taking the drug will cause this reaction. The intensity and duration of the reaction vary, depending on the amounts of the drug and alcohol in the system, but one to three hours is typical. It is extremely unpleasant and can be life-threatening if the doses involved are very large.

Disulfiram must be taken on a daily basis in order to ensure a reaction. At first it may cause drowsiness, fatigue, headaches, skin rash, and other reactions, but these usually disappear within a week or two. A person considering the use of disulfiram should be carefully checked by a physician; it should not be used (or only with extreme caution) by persons suffering from disorders that predispose them to cardiovascular complications (particularly diabetes and liver, kidney, or thyroid disorders), and it should be avoided entirely during pregnancy.

Disulfiram is useful for alcoholism in two ways. First, its effects last ten days, so that a person cannot change his or her mind rapidly and take a drink, but must wait until the drug is out of the system. Further, stopping the drug means he or she intends to resume drinking. Thus the drug is a useful test of a person's seriousness about giving up alcohol. An alcoholic who really wants to stop is likely to recognize the "crutch" value of the drug in helping to stop drinking and usually is willing to take it. A person who is unsure about stopping usually is unwilling to take it and tends to resume drinking soon.

Some authorities believe disulfiram may cause some brain damage if it is used over a period of years. Consequently it may be necessary to weigh the risk of such brain damage against the risks of other damage caused by continued alcohol consumption.

Alcoholics Anonymous, the largest network of alcoholic self-help groups (see Chapter 11), opposes the use of disulfiram and other drugs on philosophic grounds, maintaining that inner strength alone is effective in keeping a person from drinking.

In summary, it should be noted that many mentally ill persons do not like to take drugs. They do not like to depend on them, and they may be distressed by their side effects. In cases of serious and more or less chronic disorders that can only be controlled by regular use of drugs, such as chronic schizophrenia or manic-depressive disease, discontinuing medication nearly always leads to a revival of symptoms, often to the point where a person must (again) be hospitalized. In the case of less serious disorders, which in time often respond to one or another kind of psychotherapy or counseling, medication may be very useful to control distressing symptoms sufficiently so that, in effect, psychotherapy has a chance to work. In such cases there often is no need to continue medication for more than a matter of weeks. Here, however, the decision as to whether or not to use drugs is more open to disagreement. Psychiatrists, who are physicians and may write prescriptions, often are more likely to favor medications than psychologists and social workers, who are not physicians. This certainly is not true of all individuals, yet to some extent the answer you get may depend on whom you ask. (See also the section evaluating somatic therapies, including drugs, in Chapter 18.)

CHAPTER 16

Giving Help—Other Somatic Therapies

Like drug treatment, most other somatic therapies for mental illness are carried out by physicians, principally psychiatrists and neurosurgeons. The chief exception is treatment with vitamins and other nutritional therapy, which, if it does not involve a prescription drug, can be administered by anyone.

At the risk of being repetitive, we emphasize again that anyone considering medical treatment for mental illness should first have a physical checkup. Further, whoever prescribes treatment for a mental disorder should know the results of this checkup and be acquainted with the person's medical history, especially with respect to allergies, drug reactions, and chronic conditions such as high blood pressure, heart disease, or diabetes. Before you decide to accept any medical treatment for mental illness, ask about the possible side effects of the treatment. Should you avoid certain substances (alcohol, foods, other medications) while undergoing treatment? (For example, see the chart on page 169.) Will there be any expected side effects or lasting aftereffects?

If, after discussing the treatment with your doctor, you have any doubts about a therapy that is being recommended, by all means get a second opinion, preferably from a physician who has no professional connection with the doctor who prescribed the treatment.

174

"SHOCK" THERAPY

"Shock" therapy is a method of changing brain activity by chemical or electric means. In the late 1920s a Viennese psychiatrist, Manfred Sakel, observed that an overdose of insulin given to a drug addict appeared to lessen his withdrawal symptoms. Sakel then began to treat schizophrenic patients with insulin, which in large doses produces profound hypoglycemia (low blood sugar) and coma.

Insulin coma therapy (ICT), also called "insulin shock," was introduced at a number of American mental hospitals in the 1930s. Patients first were given large doses of insulin to reduce their blood-sugar level and induce coma; after an hour or so they were revived with large doses of glucose (sugar). Although insulin therapy does appear to benefit schizophrenic patients in particular, it is a fairly elaborate procedure that requires a specially trained staff, and the method has been largely abandoned in the United States, mostly because other chemical therapies work as well or better and are much simpler to administer. However, it is still widely used in some other countries.

In the mid-1930s a Hungarian psychiatrist, Ladislav V. von Meduna, discovered that injections of camphor brought on convulsions, and that many schizophrenic symptoms seemed to disappear after such a convulsion, or seizure.* The results with camphor injections were very uncertain, and often a patient underwent not one but a series of seizures. Another drug, pentylenetetrazol (Metrazol), proved to be more reliable. However, this drug caused the patient to have a terrible sensation of impending death just before onset of the seizure, so its use was strongly resisted by patients.

Convulsions also can be induced by means of inhaling flurothyl vapor, a procedure in which three to four respirations are forced into the lungs by means of an oxygen bag. The effects are similar to those of bilateral electroconvulsive therapy (see below), although

---

*A *seizure* is a sudden pattern of electrical discharge of a network containing about 100,000 brain cells. Exactly where in the brain this discharge occurs and how widely it spreads determines the seizure's clinical manifestation. Uninhibited spread throughout the brain is a *grand mal seizure;* the occurrence of such seizures spontaneously is a disorder called *grand mal epilepsy.*

with somewhat less memory loss and somewhat more post-treatment confusion. Many patients also develop nausea, vomiting, and dizziness immediately after treatment, and since the method is slightly more cumbersome than electroconvulsive therapy it is not used as often.

ELECTROCONVULSIVE THERAPY (ECT)

In 1938 two Italian psychiatrists, Ugo Cerletti and Lucio Bini, who were searching for a cure for schizophrenia, used electricity to induce a grand mal seizure in a disturbed patient. His condition improved, and in subsequent years the procedure became a common treatment for a variety of mental disorders, both in Europe and America, particularly since it did not evoke nearly as much resistance from patients as chemically induced seizures. Interestingly, electrical therapy had been practiced as long ago as the first century, when ancient Roman physicians used the shock of electric eels on patients with severe, intractable headache.

With the development of psychoactive drugs, the use of electroshock therapy (EST) or electroconvulsive therapy (ECT), as it often is called, declined considerably, and at the same time doubts arose as to its safety and effectiveness. A 1978 survey conducted by the American Psychiatric Association revealed that about one-third of its members had reservations concerning ECT. The treatment continued to be used and is presently regarded as very helpful for patients with a major depression who either are not helped by or cannot tolerate (because of heart disease or some other physical condition) antidepressant medications. An estimated 100,000 persons a year undergo ECT in the United States.

Persons undergoing ECT first are injected with a short-acting anesthetic, and then a muscle relaxant to prevent the sudden muscular contractions that, in the early days of ECT, occasionally caused broken bones or chipped teeth. An electrocardiograph may be used to monitor heart rhythm, and oxygen generally is administered from the time the patient falls asleep until spontaneous breathing resumes. Electrodes are attached to the head, and an electric current is applied for a fraction of a second. The voltage is 80 to 100 volts, a small amount of current but enough to cause a brain seizure that can be traced on an electroencephalograph.

The patient regains consciousness within a few minutes but may continue to be groggy and confused for a time. Normally ECT is given in a series of treatments, usually three a week for two to three weeks. The principal side effect is memory loss. Patients often do not recall either the treatment itself or any events immediately before it; some lose recollection of events during the entire two- or three-week period of treatment. Some also find it difficult to retain newly learned information for a time after treatment.

It has been found that it is the seizures that cause clinical improvement and the amount of current used that influences memory loss. Therefore, research has been directed at finding a way to induce a grand mal seizure—one that affects both hemispheres of the brain—with the smallest possible amount of electric current. One way of doing this is to apply the stimulating electrodes so as to deliver current to only one side of the brain—the nondominant hemisphere. (It has been known since the time of the ancient Babylonians that the right hemisphere of the brain controls the left side of the body, and the left hemisphere the right side.) For a right-handed person, therefore, the electrodes are placed so as to elicit a seizure on the right side of the brain, which controls the left (nondominant) side of the body. This so-called *unilateral* (one-sided) technique reduces loss of memory (of both past events and newly acquired information) and also reduces the confusion immediately following treatment. It is not definitely known whether it is as effective as bilateral (both sides of the brain) treatment or whether a larger number of treatments is required for the same effect.

How and why ECT works are unknown. Some authorities believe it stimulates the brain cells in certain critical areas to produce neurotransmitters (see Chapter 23) they had for some reason been failing to produce. Whatever the mechanism, there is no doubt that ECT will often relieve a major depression in the 20 to 30 percent of cases that do not respond to drug treatment or for which drugs are considered unsafe. An estimated 90 percent of such patients experience improvement provided that enough ECT treatments (six to eight) are given.

At first glance, ECT may seem to be an extreme and frightening procedure, and in the past there were some settings in which it was overused. However, the American Psychiatric Association maintains it is both safe and effective, and the tendency toward using it too much has been reversed.

What should you do if ECT is recommended for you, your severely depressed relative, or your friend? Unless immediate intervention is essential, as it may be if the person is actively suicidal, more conservative treatment should first be considered. (It should be noted that a determined person may commit suicide despite strong precautions and virtually constant supervision, but once ECT has been begun suicide is extremely rare.) If there is no state of emergency, however, and there is time to use other treatments, antidepressant medication should certainly be tried. If it is decided to use ECT, a medical history should be taken and a complete physical examination performed, including routine blood tests, urinalysis, chest X-ray, and for patients over 40 or those with a history of heart disease, an electrocardiogram. No individual suspected of having a brain tumor or intracranial bleeding should undergo ECT unless that condition has first been ruled out. Under such conditions ECT can cause serious injury or even death. This, however, is the only physical contraindication to ECT. Also, one should not take anything by mouth for six hours before treatment (the usual precaution when general anesthesia is administered).

It is advisable to find a practitioner who has wide experience with the treatment, and a setting where it is often performed (usually a hospital). ECT frequently is done on an outpatient basis, but if it is, a relative or friend should be available to take the patient home (about one hour after awakening). If this cannot be arranged, patients should remain in a recovery area until they have been examined and cleared for release in their own care by the physician. Relatives should be warned to keep a patient who is confused or has lost his/her memory immediately after a treatment away from normal social contacts until adequate functioning resumes. Further, patients should not try to conduct business or legal affairs until their confusion and amnesia have disappeared.

After a course of ECT, those patients who continue to receive antidepressant medication tend to have fewer relapses. Without such medication, about one-fourth may experience a relapse into profound depression within six months (some studies indicate a smaller percentage, and others a larger one).

Are there any indications for ECT other than a major depression? In manic-depressive disease, about 10 to 20 percent of patients in the manic phase do not respond to either lithium or antipsychotics. For such patients, who are in an acute manic phase characterized by overactivity to the point of exhaustion, ECT given twice a day for two to three days may control the overactivity. At that point they may either be given lithium, or ECT may be continued at the normal rate of three times a week until the course of treatment (six to ten treatments) is complete.

In schizophrenia, ECT is occasionally effective with patients who are not responding to antipsychotic drugs, although the rate of success is less than that with either depression or manic-depressive disease. The course of treatment usually is longer—ten to fifteen treatments in all—and is most effective in those cases of acute schizophrenia where the onset has been rapid and recent (during the first six months of the illness) and where the symptoms are either paranoia (persecution delusions) or catatonic excitement.

ECT does *not* work for persons with organic psychoses, neuroses, personality disorders, or senile dementia. It should not be used in conjunction with antipsychotic drugs (described in Chapter 15).

ECT is covered by medical/surgical insurance. Those who have no insurance can expect to pay between $50 and $350 for a course of six treatments.

NUTRITIONAL THERAPY

Treatment of mental illness with large doses of food supplements, such as vitamins *(megavitamin therapy)* and trace minerals, has been used since the early 1960s. Large amounts of such vitamins as B_1, B_6, B_{12}, C, and E have been used for patients with schizophrenia, on the theory that most (some say 60 percent or more) schizophrenics have hypoglycemia (low blood sugar). To date this finding has not been verified by reliable independent investigators. Hypoglycemia is said also to appear in hyperactive children, autistic children, and the mentally retarded. (Genuine hypoglycemia is relatively rare. It is caused by the body's inability to metabolize sugar properly and is diagnosed by means of a glucose tolerance test, which should be a six-hour test to ensure accuracy; it is treated with a diet high in protein and low in sugar.)

The name *orthomolecular psychiatry* was coined in 1968 by Nobel Prize-winning chemist Linus Pauling, who defined it as "the provision of the optimum molecular environment for the mind, especially the optimum concentration of substances normally present in the body." By the optimum (best) molecules Pauling means megavitamins (huge doses of the above-named vitamins) as well as protein concentrates and supplements of certain trace minerals, such as zinc. Another idea is that schizophrenics have too much blood histamine, which responds to zinc and manganese supplements.

A related theory is that food allergy plays a role in many mental disorders. Supporters of this notion insist that certain foods must be avoided, particularly cereals (wheat, rye, oats, barley, etc.), sugar, dyes and other food additives, and any particular foods that cause an allergic reaction in the individual being treated. In addition, vitamin and mineral supplements are given. This therapy may be used in conjunction with psychoactive drugs, but in exceedingly low doses. Treatment is said to be required for varying periods, from a few months to a lifetime; the end is determined by withdrawing nutritional supplements after the patient has been free of symptoms for a long period.

Nutritional therapy has had its most fervent support among parents of children with learning disabilities and hyperactive behavior. Their symptoms are said to be reduced or disappear entirely when their diet is free of all foods containing chemical additives (colorants, flavorings, preservatives) and includes essential nutrients they may have been lacking. The principal proponent of this regimen was

Benjamin F. Feingold (1900–1982), a pediatric allergist who wrote two books* and many articles in scientific journals.

Vitamin therapy as such is not dangerous, provided it does not involve those vitamins—A and D— where large doses actually can cause serious damage. However, the claims of vitamin therapists have not been substantiated to the satisfaction of the American Psychiatric Association, and their studies have never been duplicated by independent, unbiased researchers. Many mental health professionals regard both theory and practice in this field as so much hogwash. They point out that giving and withholding food are potent weapons with respect to young children, that the very careful attention required by a special diet may itself be what a hyperactive child benefits from, and that many hyperactive youngsters outgrow their hyperactivity in time. Therefore it is impossible to tell if improvement is caused by a change in diet.

Supporters, on the other hand, claim that American health practitioners traditionally know little and care less about nutrition, that the American diet is loaded with "junk food" containing few nutrients and numerous chemicals, and that our understanding of the connections between diet and brain activity is very limited.

What, then, should you do if nutritional therapy is recommended for you or your child? If a thorough medical checkup reveals no medical condition that contraindicates a change of diet, it may do no harm to try it, at least for a time. The principal drawback of nutritional therapy is that it may not help. Moreover, it may delay seeking treatment of a condition that will respond to other therapies. Given these factors, and the lack of reliable evidence concerning its effectiveness, it seems unreasonable to rely on nutritional therapy alone.

OTHER PHYSICAL THERAPIES

Hydrotherapy consists of using warm water baths, usually in a hospital, to calm disturbed individuals. The patient is placed in a tub

---

Why Your Child is Hyperactive (1975) and *The Feingold Cookbook for Hyperactive Children* (1979).

of warm water at a carefully maintained temperature and is covered with a sheet so that only his or her head remains out of the water. In order to maintain the temperature, an attendant must remain nearby. Hydrotherapy is rarely used in America today, since tranquilizers and other drugs calm most individuals more reliably, but it is still used in Europe.

Modern *sleep therapy* was invented in 1922 by a Swiss psychiatrist, Jakob Klaesi, who used drugs to induce long periods of sleep, as much as a week at a time. Patients were awakened only for feeding and toilet use. It, too, is believed to be a very old treatment, used intermittently since ancient Egyptian times. Today it is rarely used in America but occasionally is used in Europe.

Kidney dialysis, regular treatments on an artificial kidney machine, began to be used in the late 1970s to improve symptoms of schizophrenia in persons who had no kidney disease. The treatment is based on the idea that some forms of schizophrenia are caused by either an excess or a defective form of endorphins or enkephalins, opiate-like molecules in the brain, and that the artificial kidney filters out these substances. An expensive procedure, dialysis had at this writing not been used on many mental patients and was considered a highly experimental therapy at best.

SURGERY

Human skulls found in ruins testify to the fact that long before men and women learned how to record events in writing, they attempted to cure diseases of the brain and/or mind by means of surgery. These efforts were confined to *trephination,* the simple act of boring a hole in the skull in order to let out the evil spirits or blood or pus or whatever was thought to be causing a problem. The actual content of the skull—the brain—was inaccessible to surgeons until the nineteenth century.

The first brain operation in which a surgeon knew where to look for disease inside the skull was performed in London in 1884, and this occasion marked the beginning of modern brain surgery. However, the mortality rate for such operations remained astronomically high until the mid-twentieth century, when the need to treat traumatic head wounds inflicted on the battlefields of World War II, the Korean conflict, and the Vietnam War spurred the development of increasingly successful techniques and procedures. While these have been of enormous benefit to persons whose mental illness is caused by brain tumors, blood clots, or other lesions that can, sometimes, be successfully repaired, they have had little effect on the many others whose mental illness has no definite organic cause. Nevertheless, surgery attempting to cure functional (non-organic) disorders has been used, and sometimes it has even succeeded.

The term *psychosurgery* was invented to define surgical procedures that are undertaken not to correct visible brain lesions, such as repairing a wound or removing a tumor, but rather to produce behavioral change. One such kind of surgery was introduced in 1935 by Nobel Prize winner and neurosurgeon, Egas Moniz. The procedure he developed, *leukotomy* or *frontal lobotomy,* involves cutting nerve fibers that run from the frontal lobes of the brain to the deeper limbic system, portions that are associated with the ability to experience emotion. It was widely used in the 1940s and early 1950s to treat uncontrollably violent mental patients, and it did indeed make them less troublesome. However, it also induced in them a state of total mental apathy, so that they stopped caring about or reacting to anything at all. In effect they became emotional vegetables.

Because of its drastic results and the simultaneous development of psychoactive drugs that, in most cases, control violent patients more safely, psychosurgery was used much less in the United States from the late 1950s on. About 1970, however, there was renewed interest in it as more sophisticated surgical techniques were developed and as some patients were found to experience undesirable side effects from long-term use of certain drugs. Indeed, surgical techniques have been greatly refined, so that less brain tissue is damaged and the risk of personality changes is decreased. However, in about 25 percent of cases it results in no improvement.

These issues, and also the experimental use of psychosurgery in some patients, occasionally even in hyperactive children, caused growing concern about its misuse. Consequently the Mental Health

Association in 1973 issued a statement maintaining that psychosurgery was still to be classified as experimental and should not be used except in those instances where: (1) a patient is in such great distress from a mental disorder that he or she, by choice, elects to have such surgery; (2) all other alternatives have been considered or adequately tried according to the patient, the patient's family, and at least two reputable physicians, one of them a psychiatrist; (3) the procedure has been reviewed and approved in writing by at least two independent neurosurgeons; and (4) the patient's own lawyer is present when any final decision to operate is made.

Those who favor or engage in psychosurgery today are a distinctly small percentage of mental health professionals. Most are conservative neurosurgeons who only operate in response to desperate appeals from patients and their families. The majority of mental health professionals take a very cautious position regarding psychosurgery and would not consider its use except in very rare instances.

If someone suggests that surgery is appropriate for you, your relative, or your friend, by all means seek at least a second opinion from another physician, preferably a psychiatrist but perhaps also from another neurologist. In any case be sure it is a physician whose practice is in no way connected to the physician who proposed surgery.

CHAPTER 17

Giving Help—Hospitalization

Every year more than 1.5 million Americans become patients in psychiatric facilities. In 1981 it was estimated that at any one time, nearly 395,000 hospital beds in the United States are occupied by mental patients.

Being hospitalized for mental illness may still seem, to most people, a very frightening alternative. But today's forms of inpatient care are a far cry from the "snakepit" conditions that were the norm as recently as 1940. To be sure, there is a small core of psychiatric patients who are hospitalized for life, for whom no treatment of any kind has been effective and who therefore have become permanent residents of the so-called "back wards." Such wards exist mainly in state and county mental hospitals because, given the costs of hospitalization of any kind, even a very wealthy person's financial resources cannot keep up with the cost of private care for more than a limited time. In 1955 there were an estimated 559,000 chronic patients in public mental hospitals; by 1981 this number had declined to fewer than 150,000.

THE HISTORY OF ASYLUMS

Hospitalization for mental illness has been with us for a long time. Mental patients were hospitalized by the Arabs in the 8th century at Damascus, and again in the 10th century at Basra, in both instances in general hospitals. There is mention of a hospital devoted exclusively to mental patients at Mandu, in India, about the year 1000. The Turks had hospitals that admitted mental patients in various centers throughout the thirteenth century, and in Europe, St. John's Home in Ghent admitted mental patients, along with vagrants and paupers, in 1191. In Europe the insane at first were admitted along with the physically ill into shelters or hospitals. The first European hospital exclusively for mental patients was opened in 1409 in Valencia, Spain.

In America during colonial times, public provision for the mentally ill took the form of poorhouses, workhouses, and jails. In these settings they were treated no better than criminals and often worse, since their keepers regarded them as no different from animals and subjected them to humiliation and torture. In 1793 Philippe Pinel removed the chains from inmates of Bicêtre, a mental hospital in Paris, and began a new era in treatment of the mentally ill in Europe and America. The 19th century saw a spate of "moral reformers" who aroused public indignation over inhuman conditions in institutions. The reformers attributed mental illness to an underlying social disorder and regarded the mentally ill as victims of forces beyond their control who deserved philanthropic treatment. From these humanitarian convictions arose the cult of asylum, a haven of safety and good treatment. Dorothea Dix, one of the principal leaders of the reform movement, traveled across the nation to encourage state governments to establish or enlarge mental hospitals, and her personal efforts led to increases in institutional services to the mentally ill in twenty different states. In 1847 Congress passed a bill that provided aid for the development of public mental institutions run by state and local governments, but President Franklin Pierce vetoed it. Despite the lack of Federal support, a system of institutions soon spread across the nation. In 1810 only a few eastern states had private asylums. By 1850 there were state care facilities throughout the northeast and midwestern states, and by 1860 public institutions operated in twenty-eight (of the then thirty-three) states.

Because mental illness was believed to result from social and economic ills, it made sense to isolate the mentally ill from those forces in the community that had caused their illness. The asylums therefore were located in remote rural areas. Visits from family and friends, and other forms of outside contact, were discouraged.

Rather, life in a well-ordered environment was supposed to restore the ill to normality. Therapy consisted of a highly structured life, with meals and all other activities following a rigid schedule. Repetitive and simple chores, usually farming and workshop crafts, occupied the day, the performance of work being considered therapeutic. It was assumed that with this regimen patients would recover from their illness and rejoin the labor force.

In fact, however, most patients were not cured. Some recovered (spontaneously, no doubt) but most remained there, becoming chronic patients. The asylums continued to grow, and by the end of the nineteenth century they had become huge, overcrowded institutions. Staffing was inadequate, and patients who could not work simply did nothing at all. Treatment was negligible or nonexistent. The abuses of institutional care began to come to light, and horror stories of cruelties reached the public, but no practical alternative to institutionalization presented itself for many years. The superintendents and other asylum employees had a vested interest in the existing system and argued that the public needed protection from dangerous mental patients, who not only might become violent but might somehow infect others with their disease. Their custodial treatment, they argued, represented a necessary service to the community.

This legacy still taints the popular view of mental hospitals and in fact lies behind the movement for deinstitutionalization that began in the 1950s. Its supporters argued that institutions made people worse, not better. Moreover, this more recent "reform" movement could address itself to long-term and chronic mental patients who, thanks to the development of psychoactive drugs in the late 1950s, now constitute a relatively small percentage of cases. Hospitalization for mental illness today can be as brief as twenty-four hours, and the average hospital stay for most mental patients is well under one month.

WHO SHOULD BE HOSPITALIZED?

Although not everyone in crisis needs hospitalization, most who are hospitalized are indeed undergoing a crisis. As we saw in Chapter

2, a person likely to commit suicide or presenting a threat to others needs constant supervision, at least for a short time, and that can best be provided in a hospital.

Second, a person who needs to be kept away from alcohol or drugs similarly needs constant supervision for a time.

Third, a person unaware of his or her own illness, either unable or unwilling to cooperate in treatment, or whose illness has become worse despite treatment, may require the intensive care available only in a hospital.

Fourth, a person in need of treatment or tests that are better or more safely performed in the hospital, or a person who has physical needs (special diet, physical rehabilitation) or other illness requiring medical treatment is best off in a hospital.

Fifth, a person whose home setting is contributing to the illness or is undermining, in one way or another, the effectiveness of treatment may be at least temporarily removed from that setting by means of hospitalization.

Sixth, a person whose illness has made it impossible to function independently may have to be hospitalized. In fact, it is this category of patient that accounts for the majority of very long-term or chronic inmates of mental institutions.

Finally, a person whose illness is thought to respond to milieu therapy—that is, a healing environment provided by means of interaction with other patients and a multidisciplinary professional staff—is hospitalized so that an intensive course of such treatment can take place.

KINDS OF INPATIENT FACILITY

Up to about 1950 the only facilities that admitted seriously ill mental patients were state or county mental hospitals and Veterans Administration mental hospitals, supplemented somewhat by private mental hospitals (some of which were prohibitively expensive). Today about half of those hospitalized for mental illness still use these facilities, and the other half go to a general hospital with a psychiatric service. The principal reason for this change appears to be the use of psychoactive drugs. Until they came into use, a person ill enough to require hospitalization usually had symptoms that made him or her very difficult to manage; today the worst symptoms often can be controlled with medication.

As a rule, in order to devote some of its space to psychiatric patients, a general hospital must have 100 or more beds. However, some smaller hospitals (with fifty or so beds) may have a psychiatric unit if there is sufficient demand. In 1981 about 1,000 general hospitals in the United States had psychiatric units of one kind or another, ranging from a fully staffed service comparable to that of a full-scale psychiatric hospital to just a few beds set aside for mental patients. Of the large hospitals (with 500 or more beds), 75 percent had an inpatient psychiatric unit, usually a fairly well staffed one. Still, in less densely populated areas—in Idaho or Montana, for instance—it may be hard to find a general hospital that admits mental patients.

Another major change generated by the use of psychoactive drugs is the much shorter duration of hospitalization. About 85 to 90 percent of all mental inpatients leave the hospital within a few months, and many leave much sooner. In 1956 the median length of stay in county and state mental hospitals was eight years; today it is twenty-six days.

Most authorities today agree that a long-term stay in the hospital—one of years—may do more harm than good. Over time the hospitalized patient becomes more and more passive, lethargic, and dependent. The long-stay patient is likely to show less and less interest in his or her surroundings, withdraw from social contact, begin to neglect personal grooming, and rely wholly on others to make decisions and provide for needs. Even if patients must eventually be readmitted—and a great many are—current thinking holds that it is better for them to be released as soon as possible, even only temporarily, rather than to remain in the hospital for a long period.

Most general hospitals admit only patients who are in crisis or who will stay for a foreseeable short time, ranging from a few days to a few weeks. Those who do not recover in that time often are referred elsewhere for extended care, frequently to a state mental hospital or VA mental hospital, although some patients are referred to private mental hospitals.

Further, general hospitals accept only voluntary patients, that is, patients who are not forced to be hospitalized by means of certification or commitment (see Chapter 22 for a discussion of these legal terms). Private mental hospitals, of which there were an estimated 200 free-standing ones in the United States in 1981, generally accept both voluntary and involuntary patients, and, depending on the individual hospital, may or may not accept patients for long-term care. County and state mental hospitals are more likely to accept involuntary patients, and they take both short- and long-term patients.

The most common disorders for which a patient goes to a county or state hospital are schizophrenia and alcohol dependence; the main diagnoses in general hospitals with a psychiatric service are depressive episodes and schizophrenia.

CRISIS INTERVENTION/BRIEF TREATMENT

One of the more dramatic innovations of the past thirty years is the brief treatment unit or crisis intervention center, to which patients are admitted for twenty-four hours to one week in order to obtain help during a difficult period. The underlying theory of such treatment is that rapid and appropriate intervention at a critical time can prevent the development of maladaptive behavior leading to more serious illness and so avoids the need for more extensive treatment. In addition, it is hoped that the prompt resolution of a crisis can help promote healthier adaptive patterns for the future.

Crisis intervention often may be handled on an outpatient basis, provided a qualified professional is able and willing to commit a large block of time to the individual in need. Unfortunately this is not always the case. Many hospital and community health center emergency services consist of a 24-hour telephone service that arranges for immediate referral, but rarely is there a trained person available at all times to stay with a suicidal person or help someone deal with acute alcohol withdrawal symptoms. Most individuals needing such supervision are referred to an inpatient unit, which may be part of a community mental health center but more often is part of a general hospital. (Mental hospitals, either private or public, tend to define short-term or brief treatment in terms of a month rather than a week.)

Although the precise regimen varies from hospital to hospital, the general approach to crisis treatment is essentially the same. The length of hospitalization is limited to as brief a time as possible, as little as twenty-four hours and rarely more than seven days. From the start, the patient is encouraged to plan for discharge, often actually being informed that he or she will not be permitted to stay in the hospital beyond a certain time. Treatment is intensive, and usually involves individual therapy at least once a day. Psychoactive drugs are prescribed as soon as possible to relieve symptoms, and the family, friends, and, if necessary, social agencies are involved at once in order to set up the supports that will be needed after discharge. The treatment plan is formulated quickly, the immediate—and sometimes the only—goal being to find a solution to the immediate problem that precipitated the crisis. For example, a woman who became suicidally depressed on learning that her only child was incurably retarded might be treated with electroconvulsive therapy (ECT), which tends to work faster than antidepressant drugs; her husband would be called in for counseling, to help her cope after discharge; and a temporary hospital stay for complete evaluation might be set up for the child, to begin when the mother was discharged so that she would not have to care for the child at home immediately.

Hospital units for brief treatment tend to be highly flexible in their procedures. There may be a daily patient and staff meeting to plan the day's activities and to review each patient's progress, but other scheduled activities are held to a minimum. The transition to home life might begin with giving patients a pass to go to work during the day for several days but returning to spend the night in the hospital, or making short visits before actually spending a whole day at home. Patients are encouraged to take as much responsibility for themselves as they can.

The patient is discharged when the acute symptoms of distress are under control and there appears to be enough support to allow him or her to survive at home. If symptoms do not subside enough or if the home situation remains problematical, a patient may be referred for further hospital care, either in a longer-term unit at the same hospital or in another facility. Often the staff of the crisis unit will follow a patient for some time after discharge, remaining available to provide support and perform therapy if needed.

The team format is standard in most hospital psychiatric units— that is, a team of professionals, including a psychiatrist, psychologist, social worker, nurse, and aide, is assigned to each patient for evaluation and treatment. In crisis intervention this approach is considered virtually essential, because so much work must be done in such a short time. Often several teams are enlisted, one to work with a patient, another with the patient's family, and perhaps still another with the appropriate social agencies. Because of time pressure, many of the activities—meetings with family members, therapy sessions, and so on—must take place during evenings and weekends rather than being confined to the ordinary hours of the work week.

The goal of brief treatment is to provide temporary relief of symptoms and enable an individual to return to normal activities as quickly as possible. It appears to work well for persons with a temporarily serious or suicidal depression, or for those experiencing a mild manic episode. It is less (sometimes not at all) effective for very severe illnesses, such as a severe schizophrenic reaction, psychotic depression, or full-blown mania, or for the confusion and other symptoms of organic brain disease. For these disorders it usually takes more than a week to control symptoms. However, brief treatment may be very useful for a patient with chronic schizophrenia whose symptoms are normally controlled by medication but who has experienced a mild to moderate increase in symptoms owing to some unusual life stress.

INTERMEDIATE TREATMENT/TWO TO NINE WEEKS

Critics of short-term intervention units maintain that they tend to concentrate entirely on the life events that sent a person to seek emergency help and pay no attention to an underlying illness. Such short-term units, it is held, take too great a risk by discharging very disturbed and/or suicidal individuals before they are ready, or they may force a person to make important life decisions without taking time to consider the alternatives and long-term implications.

A somewhat longer term of inpatient treatment may be provided. In a general hospital such "intermediate" terms usually mean more than one week and up to two months; in psychiatric hospitals it may refer to a term of four to eight months.

Again the treatment plan is made as quickly as possible, and a treatment team is assigned to the patient, but there is less pressure on returning a person to the community quite so fast. It is no coincidence that many private insurance plans cover two months of hospitalization for mental illness in a general hospital's psychiatric unit. This appears to be an adequate time of treatment for the majority of those who require hospitalization.

Here is a profile of a 211-bed general hospital, nonprofit and private, that offers both brief and intermediate care. Although the average stay for patients is sixteen days, some stay only one day and others have stayed for as long as a year. (The latter tend to be elderly patients who are too disturbed to be admitted to a nursing home and for whom no other appropriate facility can be found.)

This hospital serves as the main inpatient facility for a nine-town catchment area of a community mental health center in eastern Massachusetts. It has thirty-one beds devoted to psychiatric (including alcoholic) patients. It accepts any patient aged fifteen or older, unless he or she is uncontrollably violent or considered a danger to self or others; such patients are immediately referred to the acute-care unit of a nearby state mental hospital or a private mental hospital.

The psychiatric unit's staff consists of twenty-five full-time counselors and nurses, as well as three staff psychiatrists, a psychologist, full-time social worker, occupational therapist, alcohol specialists, and unit teacher (to instruct nurses). Patients are admitted to the unit straight from the hospital's emergency room or are referred by the police, the community mental health clinic, a physician, family member, themselves, or some other source. There is no waiting list, and no one must wait more than twenty-four hours to be admitted. Each patient has an attending physician and also is immediately

HOSPITALIZED PATIENTS' RIGHTS
These are the basic rights of every patient at Emerson Hospital:*

Equality of Care
You can expect to be treated with consideration and with respect regardless of your race, sex, religion, national origin, or the source of payment for your care.

Emergency Treatment
You have a right to prompt, life-saving treatment in an emergency, regardless of your ability to pay.

Complete Information
You have a right to be fully informed about your treatment and a right to consent to or decline such treatment. For example, a patient suffering from any form of breast cancer has the right to complete information on all alternative treatments which are medically viable.

Privacy
You are entitled to privacy during the rendering of medical or any other kind of care, to the best of our capacity. At all times you can expect that your privacy and dignity will be respected.

Confidentiality
You can be sure all your records and communications about you will be kept confidential to the extent provided by the law.

Identification of Staff
You have a right to know the name and specialty of the physician (or any other person) responsible for your care or the coordination of your care. You also have the right to know the affiliations of the physician and any affiliations of Emerson Hospital with educational institutions or other health-care facilities as these may be related to your care.

The Right to Say "No"
You may refuse to be examined, observed, or treated by students or anyone from the hospital staff who is not involved with your treatment. Even so, you will receive our very best care—whether it be psychiatric, psychological, or medical/surgical care and attention.

You may also refuse to serve as a research subject, or you may refuse any care or examination when the primary purpose is educational or informational rather than therapeutic or diagnostic.

Access to Your Medical Records
You may ask to inspect your medical records and may even request a copy for yourself. We will ask you to pay for copying expenses.

Explanation of Your Bill
You may ask for an itemized bill and an explanation of each item. In addition, you may receive a copy of any bill or statement of charges to any insurance company or third-party payor. If you wish, you may also receive information we have about financial assistance and any free care that may be available.

A Copy of Regulations
You have a right to obtain a copy of any rules and regulations of the hospital which apply to your conduct as a patient.

Response to Your Concerns
Finally, you have a right to expect that all reasonable requests will receive prompt, courteous, and adequate attention.

Your Responsibilities
Along with the rights and privileges of being a patient, there are also some responsibilities. We ask that you respect these responsibilities so that we can do our job of giving you the best possible care.

- Please keep your appointments. When unable to do so, notify us promptly.
- When we ask, do provide us with accurate information about your medical history, present condition, medication, and other pertinent facts about your health.
- Please follow all instructions given for your care. Ask questions whenever you do not understand the instructions or cannot comply with them.
- Please follow hospital regulations and be considerate of the rights of other patients as well as those who serve and care for you.

Questions?

If you have any questions or problems concerning your care or your rights as a patient, let us know. Your nurse or physician are always ready to discuss your concerns.

In addition, a *Patient Representative*—whose *only* job is to listen to you—is available to talk with you about your rights or any questions or problems you may have. This person is *your* representative, a well-trained volunteer who is interested in your rights and well being and who will try to make your hospital stay as pleasant as possible.

Please feel free to consult with the Patient Representative. Dialing extension 345 (from 8:30 a.m. to 5 p.m.) will put you in touch.

*A general hospital in Concord, MA. In addition, Massachusetts Law, Chapter 214 of the Acts of 1979, known as the Patient's Bill of Rights, is available upon request.

assigned to a "key person"—that is, a particular nurse or counselor who is in contact with the patient's family, physician, outside agencies, and the patient, on a daily basis if necessary.

Treatment is begun almost at once and is quite intensive. It includes individual therapy, where the major thrust is to restore the patient to functioning well enough to leave the hospital. There also are "milieu groups," which include all the patients in the unit as well as the staff, and which meet three times a week. (Milieu therapy is further described below.) Further, where it is appropriate there may be couples and/or family therapy. The patient, staff, and physician together devise an individual treatment plan.

Although there are no locked doors, each patient requires his/her physician's approval for leaving the unit floor and, even with such approval, is expected to inform his/her key person when leaving and to sign out and in at the nursing station. Medications must be specifically prescribed by the physician and are distributed in the medication room. Visiting hours are liberal, from 8 A.M. to 8 P.M., but no visitors are allowed during the three scheduled milieu group meetings or during two smaller group therapy meetings.

This hospital always refers patients who are being discharged to some form of "aftercare," usually to the community mental health center. In fact, a member of the treatment team, most often a nurse, actively follows the patient into the aftercare program. Part of the patient's treatment team—typically the social worker, nurse, and counselor—are designated to serve as an aftercare team and, after discharge, function as "case managers" to help with the patient's life problems. This service, performed to prevent rehospitalization, is an unusual one—few hospitals provide it—and, it is believed, is the main reason why this hospital has such a low rate of "return" patients; its readmission rate is 30 percent, a figure that includes alcoholic patients, who typically have a 75 percent or higher return rate.

MILIEU THERAPY

Psychotherapy (individual, couples, family, group) and somatic therapies (medication, ECT) all are forms of treatment that can readily be performed on an outpatient basis. Hospitalization offers several forms of treatment that require use of the hospital setting. One is *milieu therapy; milieu,* a French word meaning "environment," refers to a patient's surroundings, which consist of the physical surroundings, all the individuals with whom he/she comes in contact (other patients as well as hospital staff), and the planned activities (therapy, meals, recreation, etc.). All these elements are part of the treatment. Thus the hospital setting in effect becomes a therapeutic community, and the social organization, with the intensive interaction it promotes, is considered curative. In contrast to the older model of the "sick" patient, milieu therapy consists of active efforts directed toward getting a patient involved with others, including the assumption of some responsibility for others, in the hope of making him/her ultimately responsible for him/herself.

Although very short-term hospitalization in a crisis unit can include milieu therapy, there may not be time enough to establish relationships with all the other patients and staff. The focus there is on getting better fast so as to get out of the hospital. Intermediate-term hospitalization usually involves milieu therapy, often in a quite intensive form.

In the general hospital described above, the psychiatric unit has no private rooms; each patient has at least one roommate, so complete isolation is discouraged. Meals are served in a community dining area; there also is a small kitchen adjacent to it, where patients can prepare their own snacks.

A schedule of each day's activities is posted in the dining area, and patients are encouraged to participate in unit activities unless their individual treatment plan conflicts. Community group meetings are held for an hour each Monday, Wednesday, and Friday morning, attended by all the patients and much of the staff. Individual problems and concerns may be discussed during these gatherings, and patients are encouraged to share their ideas and feelings. Small group meetings are held on Tuesday and Thursday afternoons, and attendance there is required as well. In addition, alcohol group meetings, run by the special alcohol counselors, are held every weekday, and although they are specifically recommended for patients with alcohol-related problems, other interested patients may attend as well.

The occupational therapy program offers a variety of activities. An arts and crafts session held each weekday is designed to help develop concentration and attention span, increase self-esteem through the successful completion of projects, and possibly develop a hobby skill that can be used after discharge. One day a week a work discussion group focuses on handling job problems and the importance of balancing time between work and recreation. One morning a week a meal-planning meeting is held, and the dinner that is planned is actually prepared by patients, with some help from staff, the following evening. Patients may invite relatives and friends to this meal, which is followed by a relatives' group meeting for patients and their families, where common problems can be discussed.

Other activities are a three-times-a-week exercise group, a weekly relaxation group, and art therapy. In addition, outings to sports and cultural events in the community are organized periodically by patients and staff.

An essential idea underlying milieu therapy is that all the staff participate in the treatment, not just the physician or the individual therapist or group therapy leader, but nurses, aides, social workers, art therapists, and so on. This function is facilitated in the meetings where anyone may express an opinion, describe any problem, and propose solutions. Patient groups and patient government organizations give the patient a strong voice in decisions, and open, easy communication with the staff is stressed. This is in marked contrast to the older approaches to hospital care, where the patient's activities were chosen and directed by the staff much as a small child's are by the parents, encouraging a dependency that serves as little preparation for life after discharge.

Another form of treatment requiring an institutional setting is *social learning therapy*. It is based on the principles of operant conditioning (see under behavior therapies in Chapter 13), and a comparative study of its use over a decade among chronic mental patients indicates it can be very successful.* In contrast to milieu

---

*Gordon L. Paul and Robert J. Lentz, *Psychosocial Treatment of Chronic Mental Patients* (1978).

therapy, in which patients are held responsible for their own behavior, social learning therapy tries to teach new and desirable behavior by demonstration, prompting, direct instruction, and the use of a token economy. Patients receive tokens, which they can later redeem for rewards, whenever they behave appropriately (get up in the morning, dress themselves, attend meals and assigned activities, etc.). Undesirable behavior, on the other hand, is ignored entirely if possible and is never rewarded.

PRIVATE MENTAL HOSPITAL VS. GENERAL HOSPITAL

A private mental hospital offers the same kinds of short-term and intermediate care as a general hospital, although, as noted above, the interpretation of "short" and "intermediate" tends to be longer. In addition, it may offer long-term care, for a period of a year or more. Since few patients can afford long-term private care, for most it is not an option. Admission to a private hospital may be either voluntary or involuntary (commitment), whereas general hospitals usually accept only voluntary patients. Many private hospitals do not accept children. In general hospitals they may be admitted, but sometimes to the pediatric service rather than to a psychiatric unit (as is the case in the above-described general hospital).

In the private mental hospital every staff member is to some extent trained and experienced in caring for mental patients; in a general hospital the nursing staff may rotate among the different departments. In the mental hospital a therapy team such as that described above is the rule, whereas general hospitals cannot always assign one. A private mental hospital may have either an *open staff,* in which case a patient's own psychiatrist may continue to treat him/her during hospitalization, or a *closed staff,* where certain physicians work for the hospital on a salary basis or in partnership and only they can treat patients hospitalized there. With the latter, a private psychiatrist who is not a member of the staff must refer the patient to another psychiatrist on the staff who will take over the treatment. Most general hospitals have open-staff arrangements.

About two-thirds of the 200 American private mental hospitals are proprietary, that is, they are operated for a profit. Compared to nonprofit private mental hospitals, the proprietary ones tended to have fewer beds, higher rates of patient turnover, shorter lengths of stay, and lower expenditures per patient day. The typical general hospital psychiatric unit has about thirty beds; the typical private mental hospital has about eighty beds, although some hospitals are smaller and others much larger. Although some people disapprove of profit-making facilities in the health care field, contending they are more interested in making money than in providing high quality care, others believe that they are filling a large gap, providing psychiatric services where previously there were none, and that their profits come from increased efficiency rather than poor-quality or decreased treatment.

Private mental hospitals tend to concentrate on inpatient care, whereas general hospitals with a psychiatric service often have outpatient clinics, and some also have 24-hour walk-in emergency service, partial hospitalization (see below), and other services.

A stay in a mental hospital—public or private— is likely to involve more restrictions on a patient's activities than a stay in a general hospital. There may be regulations regarding the use of the telephone, for example, or no telephone privileges, and rules concerning relationships with staff and other patients. There also may be a system of privileges that are extended or denied, such as, for example, the privilege of walking freely about the hospital grounds.

Here are profiles of three mental hospitals. Hospitals A and C are private, and Hospital B is public. None is typical—and indeed there may be no typical facility.

Hospital A is a large, prestigious, private nonprofit hospital. It is affiliated with one of the nation's finest medical schools and has an excellent reputation, both as a teaching hospital and as a research institution. Unlike many other private mental hospitals, therefore, it offers multiple outpatient services. It also has 328 beds for inpatients. The total number of patients treated in an average year is about 3,700, of whom about 40 percent are hospitalized.

Of its 328 beds, 44 are in a separate building known as the children's center and are reserved for children. The rest are divided among fifteen treatment buildings, about half of which house specialty programs (for particular kinds of problems) and half are general units, serving patients with a variety of disorders. All are coeducational, have multidisciplinary staffs, and draw on a wide range of treatment methods. All of them use milieu therapy, that is, they use daily hospital life as part of the therapy. Some of the wards are open and others are locked.

About half of its inpatients are referred to Hospital A by physicians (emergency ward doctors, psychiatrists, family doctors), 25 to 35 percent come of their own accord, and the rest come through the police and court system. Emergency cases generally are sent first to a general hospital for evaluation of their physical status. The decision as to whether or not to admit a person is based on a number of factors—past history, ability to pay for care, and the like. Approximately 95 percent of the patients admitted are covered for varying degrees of the costs by some form of insurance (Blue Cross, major medical, Medicare, CHAMPUS, etc.). Medicaid patients are not accepted as inpatients.

The average length of stay is fifty days or a little more, a reduction of 50 percent from 1970. However, this figure is somewhat misleading, since 70 to 100 beds are occupied by long-term patients, hospitalized for six months or more. The decision as to which ward a patient will be assigned to is made at the time of admission. A patient usually remains on the same ward for the entire stay (there is no "progress" from locked to unlocked ward) because it is felt that the relationships established with the staff and other patients are important and should not be disrupted.

A core group of professionals is assigned to each unit in a building. This group, called the "hall team," is usually made up of a psychiatrist in charge, psychiatric residents (since this is a teaching hospital), nurses, and social workers. The psychiatrist in charge has overall responsibility for planning and managing the treatment plans of every patient there. Each such unit has ten to twenty-one patients. As soon as a patient arrives, one of the nurses is assigned as the patient's "coordinator." This person has frequent contact with the patient and is familiar with his/her treatment plan.

Soon after admission, a planning conference is held, involving professionals both from the unit and outside. This group carefully reviews the patient's history, and each member brings his/her special training to bear on the planning process. The coordinator, for example, usually knows what the patient has been doing and how he/she has been feeling from day to day; the social worker usually presents information obtained from contact with family members; the psychologist may report results of psychological tests; the vocational counselor may be familiar with career strengths; and so on. At the end of the conference the staff selects from available therapeutic methods those it believes will best meet this patient's needs. Among them are individual therapy, group therapy, family therapy, medication, electroconvulsive therapy (ECT), and milieu therapy.

Hospital A uses a privilege system. As a patient's ability and willingness to handle daily living situations increase, more and more privileges and responsibilities are assigned. (See the accompanying chart.) When the time for discharge approaches, a gradual transition is planned, which may include part-time participation in a community work project or workshop, a job-training program, or a therapy group that focuses on leaving the hospital. The plan may involve enrolling in a partial hospitalization program, a halfway house, or a mental health clinic in the patient's own community. Those who live nearby may even return to their unit several times a week for a time to take part in a therapy group or clinic.

Hospital B is the inpatient facility of a community mental health center in an urban area, which makes it a public mental hospital. It has eighty beds for adults and ten for children, and admits approximately 450 patients a year, of whom 80 percent are readmissions. (This unusually high rate is accounted for by the nature of the area it serves, which has a high proportion of elderly persons and a high incidence of drug and alcohol abusers.) The average length of stay is 56.5 days, but some patients stay only a few days and others several months. Most are admitted through the center's walk-in clinic.

The hospital has no locked wards but there is a seclusion room for violent patients. The most common diagnoses are chronic schizophrenia, depressive illness, and drug abuse. All kinds of treatment are used — about half of the hospitalized patients receive medication of some kind—and most patients who leave the hospital go

PRIVILEGE SYSTEM IN A MENTAL HOSPITAL

DEFINITION OF PRIVILEGES

STAFF TWO TO ONE—A patient may leave the hall accompanied by two staff members.

STAFF ONE TO ONE—A patient may leave the hall accompanied by one staff member.

PATIENT ESCORT—A patient may leave the hall accompanied by another patient who is responsible for him.

GROUP ESCORT—A group of patients may leave the hall for a specified activity accompanied by a staff member.

MUTUAL ESCORT SYSTEM (M.E.S.)—Two patients may go to a designated place each being responsible for the other.

FAMILY ESCORT—A patient may go to specified areas accompanied by a designated member of his family.

DESTINATION PRIVILEGE(D.P.)—A patient may go unaccompanied to a specified "locked supervised area." Staff on the patient's hall and staff in the "locked supervised area" keep each other informed of when the patient is expected to leave and arrive at either location.

CALL BACKS (C.B.)—A patient may go unaccompanied to any specified place, but must call his hall on arrival and again when he is ready to leave to report his next destination.

LIMITED GROUNDS (L.G.)—The patient may go unaccompanied to limited areas on hospital grounds, as specifically prescribed.

FULL GROUNDS (F.G.)—A patient may go anywhere within the designated patient areas of the hospital by himself.

FULL TOWNS (F.T.)—A patient may take trips to town freely by notifying the charge nurse of his intended departure and return.

OVERNIGHTS—The patient may leave the hospital for one or more nights, as prescribed.

through various transitional aftercare programs before returning to the community. This hospital, too, is affiliated with a fine medical school, so the staff includes medical interns and residents.

Hospital C is a sixty-eight-bed private, proprietary, closed-staff psychiatric hospital. Most patients are admitted voluntarily but some are committed. The hospital accepts patients with all degrees of illness, from the age of twelve upward. Many of the patients are teenagers, and the hospital has developed special services for this age group, including a school, educational testing, and vocational testing. All kinds of therapy are used, from individual to family and group psychotherapy, drug treatment, and electroconvulsive therapy (ECT). Patients receive a complete physical examination on admission. The average time of stay is twenty-eight days, but many patients remain for longer or shorter periods. There is an affiliated halfway house where patients may go for day care after discharge. The hospital also offers some outpatient services, including psychological testing of various kinds, psychotherapy, and daily psychopharmacology (drug) clinics.

THE STATE OR COUNTY MENTAL HOSPITAL

It is rare to gain admission to a public mental hospital by simply walking in and asking to be admitted. Though each of the fifty states has its own laws, most require some form of commitment or certification. Further, as a result of the deinstitutionalization policies that have become the predominant public mental health outlook since the 1970s, it has become much harder to get into a public mental hospital. Deinstitutionalization has resulted in cutting the public-mental-hospital census from 559,000 patients in 1955 to fewer than 150,000 in 1981. Those who remain in state and county hospitals tend to be the most violent, incompetent, or suicidal—a danger to themselves and/or the community—and also those most resistant to treatment. Of necessity this patient population reduces the feasibility of group therapy, for one thing. Yet public hospitals are by law required to provide treatment, not just custodial care. Sometimes the only therapy that is carried on, other than medication, is a minimal form of milieu therapy (described more fully above).

Among the greatest problems of public mental hospitals are the shortage of staff and the difficulty of recruiting competent staff. The reasons are logical: their patients are hard to treat, there are too many of them, and mental health professionals tend to find better pay and more satisfying work in the private sector. Many public hospitals therefore resort to hiring foreign physicians, who may be well trained and willing to work but whose knowledge of the English language and of American customs may be quite limited, and who therefore cannot communicate well with patients. In the end, staff shortages may drive even the best-intentioned staff members to overmedicate patients and/or put them in seclusion too frequently, simply because the high ratio of patients to staff leaves them no alternative.

A state or county hospital admits patients requiring either short- or long-term care. Usually a program of intensive treatment is begun soon after admission in order to discharge the patient as soon as possible. Those who do not respond within a reasonable time become chronic or long-term-care patients and receive much less treatment of any kind.

Intensive treatment includes the use of drugs and electroconvulsive therapy (ECT), and group psychotherapy. Individual psychotherapy is rarely performed because there are not enough therapists to go around. There usually are recreational and occupational therapy programs as well, which often depend heavily on the services of volunteers recruited from the surrounding communities. About 90 percent of the patients are discharged within a few months. However, the rate of readmission—the return of previous patients through the so-called "revolving door"—can be discouragingly high, as much as 80 percent in some institutions.

The outlook for improvement in a state or county hospital depends a great deal on the hospital's ability to provide intensive treatment for a sufficient period of time. Since most such facilities are understaffed, they generally cannot do much for very long.

Most state hospitals are situated away from community population centers. They consist of a group of buildings that can house 1,500 to 5,000 patients. Owing to deinstitutionalization, many are now half-empty. Patients live either on wards or in "cottages" that house 25 to 100 patients each. Only about one-third of the nation's state mental hospitals have facilities for children. They either house children with adults or in a separate unit or wing. Although a few state hospitals bring in teachers to provide schooling for child patients, most do not.

VETERANS ADMINISTRATION (VA) HOSPITALS

Both VA mental hospitals and VA general hospitals with a psychiatric service are among the best facilities of their kind. Unfortunately they often limit admissions to veterans with service-connected disorders. If the hospital has a free bed and a veteran cannot afford other care, he/she may be admitted with a mental disorder that is not service-connected. Dependents (the families of veterans) are not admitted, but they may be involved in the treatment on an outpatient basis when it is judged to be beneficial to the veteran. There are about sixty VA mental hospitals in the nation, and about an equal number of VA general hospitals with psychiatric units. Both give the same kinds of care as other mental hospitals and psychiatric units, but generally are very well staffed and well equipped, and able to provide thoroughgoing intensive treatment for as long as necessary. Their services to veterans are free, paid for by tax dollars.

RESIDENTIAL FACILITIES FOR CHILDREN

Children and adolescents who need hospitalization for severe mental illness can be placed either in the psychiatric or the pediatric unit of a general hospital, or in a psychiatric hospital. The former, however, may accept children only for short-term care, and they may exclude some categories of illness entirely. Private psychiatric hospitals often do not accept any children, and, as indicated above, two-thirds of the state hospitals have no facilities for them. Sometimes children are admitted but then are placed together with adults, which rarely is beneficial. Some psychiatric hospitals do deal primarily or exclusively with children, but they are few and far between (four in 1975).

Another kind of facility for mentally ill children is the *residential treatment center* (RTC), which provides long-term care in a protected environment for children too disturbed to function at home or in school. These centers usually provide schooling (either in the center or in the community) and various forms of psychotherapy. They tend to be small, rarely accommodating more than fifty patients, and they, too, are few in number (331 in 1976) compared to the need for them. Residential treatment centers are run by various agencies, usually private but often with the assistance of some public funds. Most children remain in a center for no more than one or two years; some stay a considerably shorter time. Some RTCs accept psychotic or autistic children, but others do not.

Another residential facility, principally for adolescents, is the *group home* or *group shelter,* which provides a supervised living arrangement for disturbed youngsters. Frequently funded entirely or partly by the state, such homes generally are affiliated with a community mental health center or a mental hospital.

Because of the shortage of 24-hour residential facilities for severely mentally ill children, it may be easier to find a special day care center or day school that caters to such youngsters. These facilities provide psychiatric treatment and schooling similar to those of residential centers but the patients return to their own homes for the night. Some day care centers are part of a community mental health center. Day schools are more likely to be private schools specializing in the care of emotionally disturbed children, often along with mentally retarded and learning-disabled youngsters.

Day schools, day care centers, RTCs, and hospitals that accept mentally ill children all are listed in *U.S. Facilities and Programs for Children with Severe Mental Illnesses,* a directory published by the National Institute of Mental Health. It can be obtained either through your library or by writing to NIMH, Public Inquiries, 5600 Fisher's Lane, Rockville, MD 20857.

NURSING HOMES

Nursing homes, also called *extended care facilities,* are used as mental health care facilities primarily for elderly persons with mental illness (either alone, or, more often, in association with physical illness), for middle-aged and elderly persons suffering from Alzheimer's disease or some other form of senile dementia (see Chapter 4), and for elderly patients who must leave a public mental hospital but still require considerable round-the-clock supervision and care. In 1981 an estimated 5 percent of all Americans over the age of sixty-five had enough mental impairment so that they could no longer care for themselves, and 80 percent had at least one chronic physical disorder.

The elderly vary tremendously in their response to drug treatment, far more so than younger people, and they often suffer frequent and severe side effects. The simultaneous presence of several physical and mental disorders may necessitate using several medications, which can complicate the picture. Consequently it is much more difficult to control psychiatric symptoms in the elderly by means of drugs.

In 1981 more than one million Americans resided in nursing homes. About 90 percent of them were over sixty-five and fully half had been diagnosed as "senile." The majority relied on Medicare and Medicaid to cover most or all of the cost of their stay. More than three-fourths of all American nursing homes are proprietary, that is, in business to earn a profit. In 1981 they represented a $15 billion industry. Some of them give excellent care; many others do not.

Basically three kinds of nursing home accept patients with mental illness: intermediate care, skilled nursing, and extended care. *Intermediate care nursing homes,* which represent the majority of all nursing homes, are supposed to give nursing supervision and such personal care services as help with eating, bathing, dressing, and walking. Therapy and other services may be provided, but in reality many such facilities offer little more than custodial care. Medicaid may reimburse the cost of intermediate care completely; Medicare does not cover it at all.

A *skilled nursing facility* must provide round-the-clock nursing and preventive care, rehabilitation, therapy, and other services as needed. Skilled-care facilities are covered by Medicare and Medicaid (although some are covered only by Medicaid) and are eligible for accreditation by the Joint Commission on Accreditation of Hospitals. An *extended care facility* is supposed to supply round-the-clock skilled nursing and medical supervision; in effect it is intended to serve as an extension of hospital care on a long-term but not necessarily permanent basis. It is covered by Medicare and by some private health insurance plans, and is eligible for accreditation by the Joint Commission on Accreditation of Hospitals.

A person's eligibility for Medicare coverage depends on the illness. Physicians must periodically certify that a patient needs a given level of care, or Medicare won't pay for it.

To locate a nursing home for an elderly mentally ill relative, ask your relative's physician, rabbi or pastor, a local family service agency, the local board of health (which checks to see if local homes comply with the health code), a local Social Security Office, your community or state council on aging (or elderly affairs), or senior citizens organization (they may have first-hand knowledge of local homes). Two national organizations to contact (for information and also for making specific complaints about a home) are the American Health Care Association, 1200 15th Street, NW, Washington, DC 20005, for proprietary (profitmaking) homes,* and the American Association of Homes for the Aging, 1050 17th Street, NW, Suite 770, Washington, DC 20036, for nonprofit homes. Ask for the names of *licensed* facilities that are eligible for the kind of reimbursement you or your relative will be relying on.

Each state has its own licensing requirements. In most states this requires regular inspection of a home by the Department of Public Health, as well as by local bodies that make sure it meets sanitary codes, fire ordinances, electrical codes, and other safety requirements. It is wise to see these licenses, which indicate that the home meets some minimum safety standards.

There are some excellent guides on how to select a nursing home. Every one of them urges you to visit the home for at least an hour or two and look it over from top to bottom, including not only bedrooms and toilets but halls, lobby, dining room, kitchen, activity rooms, and grounds. Note particularly how staff members treat patients (kindly, politely), how patients look (clean, dressed, not in obvious distress), and the appearance of the food (try to time your visit during a meal). See the administrator personally and ask him or her detailed questions concerning medical and nursing services (is there a physician?), activities (is there physical therapy? occupational therapy?), rules, licensing, eligibility for Medicaid and Medicare, extra charges if any, and so on.

*Write them for a free copy of *Thinking About a Nursing Home?* which includes a list of state nursing home associations.

Your state office of elderly affairs or human services or welfare may issue a brochure or guidelines to investigating local nursing homes. *Nursing Home Care,* published by the U.S. Department of Health, Education and Welfare, is available for a modest price (less than $1) from the Superintendent of Documents, U.S. Government Printing Office, Washington, DC 20402.

HOW TO PICK A HOSPITAL

Let's assume that you or your relative need to be hospitalized. Frequently hospitalization is arranged by your doctor, but sometimes one doesn't have a doctor or the doctor offers several hospitals from which to choose. In that case it certainly is desirable for the patient and his/her family to take part in the decision.

Length of stay, costs and insurance coverage, and the age and legal status of the patient all are factors that limit one's choices. As indicated above, some hospitals do not offer long-term treatment, some will not admit patients unless they have hospitalization insurance or can demonstrate their ability to pay, and many do not accept children at all. Unless a person is legally committed it is unlikely that he or she can be admitted into a state hospital, where charges are based on ability to pay. Most often, the only facilities among which one can choose for a voluntary admission will be either a general hospital or a private mental hospital.

Ideally a hospital is a therapeutic community where the patient is protected from outside influences that have contributed to his/her illness, where therapy of many kinds is available, including appropriate recreational and occupational therapy, and where he/she may receive attention from a variety of competent and concerned specialists. In practice this protective environment may be prisonlike, with locked rooms, the use of physical restraints, and rigid rules to which all patients must conform. Moreover, you cannot judge from appearances alone. Repression can take place in an attractive setting, too.

Staffing can also be deceptive. A high ratio of staff to patients can look wonderful on paper, but what is the reality? For example, in one state hospital thirty-four employees were assigned to a unit of fifty-eight acutely ill patients: twenty on the day shift, seven on the evening shift, and another seven on the night shift. The day employees were eleven "therapy aides," only four of whom were actually there; two psychiatrists, one of whom left daily at noon; one treatment team leader; one nurse; one social worker; and three other professionals, a practical nurse, psychologist, and rehabilitation specialist, who also were not there (they had resigned six months earlier and still not been replaced). The evening shift consisted of six aides and one practical nurse, and the night shift of seven aides. Since no registered nurse was on either of these shifts, any emergency arising between 4 P.M. and 8 A.M. had to be handled on a catch-as-catch-can basis by a "nurse management team" that was responsible for several hundred other patients as well. As pointed out before, state hospitals have severe staffing problems, so this situation is not altogether surprising. However, the staff on paper was a far cry from the staff present in the hospital.

What, then, should you look for in selecting a hospital? At the minimum, the hospital should have a *license,* which means it reports to the state department of health. You can ask to see a copy of the Department of Mental Health inspector's last report, which should be on file in the administrator's office.

The hospital should be *accredited* by the Joint Commission on Hospitals, which means it has been inspected by the commission, filled out an extensive questionnaire, and undergoes a survey every two years.

Another question concerns the patient's legal status. In most general hospitals a patient can leave the hospital any time he/she wishes to, whether or not the staff agree, provided a paper is signed releasing the hospital from any responsibility. In some psychiatric units of general hospitals and in most mental hospitals (public or private) a patient must give notice before leaving, and if the staff disagree his/her departure may be delayed for several days.

Ultimately, your most important questions concern the hospital's quality of care, which is harder to judge. For a general hospital, which might be your first choice for a case requiring either short- or intermediate-term care, consider the hospital's *reputation* in the community. Is it well regarded? Here you can rely on the opinion of local doctors not directly concerned in mental health care, as well as psychiatrists and other mental health professionals.

What *kinds of treatment* are available? If individual therapy is given, how often and for how long, and by whom? If there is group therapy—and there generally is— how often do groups meet and how large are they? Is milieu therapy part of the regimen? It is in most hospitals today, so if not, you should find out why not. Is there occupational (activity) therapy? If so, what kinds of activities are available? Do they seem appropriate for the patient for whom you are inquiring?

You can ask all these questions over the telephone, when you also should inquire about the *number of beds,* the *kinds of accommodation* (ward, semiprivate room, how many beds per room), and any limitations on *length of stay.*

Who will be treating the patient? Is there a treatment team? Is there an individual *treatment plan* for each patient? Does the patient know what it contains, and can he/she request changes in it once it is made? Do the professional staff meet to discuss each patient's progress or lack of it? How often? A treatment plan is not just a schedule of activities. Rather, it states specific goals for a patient, which are to be reached (it is hoped) in a specified time. Since these goals involve the patient's behavior and/or symptoms, he/she should know precisely what they are.

What is the overall goal of treatment for you or your relative? Is it to bring the patient through a current crisis, or to prepare him/her for discharge and care as an outpatient? When does the hospital expect to discharge the patient? Are there plans for both discharge and aftercare? In a good hospital the goals for treatment are set during or almost immediately after the patient's admission, and a treatment plan is devised almost at once. Treatment actually begins on the day of admission, and so should a plan for discharge.

This may seem like an enormous amount of information to obtain, and indeed there may not be time to find out all these facts in the critical period when a decision must be made. However, many of them can be raised with the referral source, and if admission can be put off for a day or so, as it often can, a great deal can be learned on the telephone if one is persistent and patient.

Most hospitals publish a brochure for patients and their families that lists the names of the chief administrators and gives basic information about clothing, mail, telephone, laundry, visiting hours, and the like. Be sure to ask for such a brochure and read it carefully. It may answer some of your questions in advance, so that you can reserve the others for telephone or personal inquiry.

On admission, ask *who will be in charge* of the patient's treatment—who is the person to ask the many questions that may arise in the course of hospitalization. Is this the same person who will be in touch with the patient's family? If not, whom should family members call to inquire about progress? Are there restrictions on *visiting?* Is visiting ever prohibited?

How does the hospital deal with a violent or disruptive patient? Is *seclusion* used, and if so, for how long, and how often? Seclusion means confining a patient in a special room, usually containing only a mattress, in order to calm him/her down. It is rarely used in general hospitals, since they tend to refer unruly individuals elsewhere, but it is frequently used in both private and public mental hospitals. Generally there are strict rules on how seclusion is to be used; find out what they are.

During admission you should ask exactly what hospital care is included in the published rates and what is extra. Even if the hospital will be paid through Blue Cross or some other insurance plan, ultimately you are paying and you should know exactly what you will get.

Treatment in a general hospital tends to be more expensive than in a private mental hospital, since the latter usually does not need to maintain special medical equipment, laboratories, operating rooms, or the like. Some psychiatric hospitals are very expensive indeed, but as a rule they are less expensive than a general hospital. Treatment in a general hospital usually is almost fully covered by standard insurance plans like Blue Cross for a certain period of time, most often sixty days; it also is covered by Medicaid and Medicare. Treatment in a private mental hospital may be covered in part by such private plans, but usually for a shorter time, and Medicaid will not cover treatment for any patient between the ages of twenty-one and sixty-five in private mental hospitals (as of 1981).

A good private mental hospital is likely to have more staff available for treatment. Individual therapy may be given as often as three times a week; group therapy may be conducted by more highly trained therapists. Or it may not. The variation among private hospitals is enormous in every respect: cost, quality of care, staff-to-patient ratio. Some private hospitals refuse certain kinds of patient—the psychotic, the drug abuser, the alcoholic. Others specialize in certain disorders. There is an Association of Private Psychiatric Hospitals which requires its members to meet certain standards, but some very good hospitals simply do not choose to belong to it. Accreditation by the Joint Commission on Accreditation of Hospitals, however, is a must.

LEAVING THE HOSPITAL: AFTERCARE

Lack of support and followup treatment after being hospitalized for mental illness can, and often does, lead to a relapse, which in turn can lead a patient right back to the hospital. For many individuals an appointment once or twice a week with a therapist is not enough, at least not at the beginning, during the initial period of recovery and adjustment that follows discharge. Where the hospital stay has been very brief, and the focus of treatment has been on controlling the worst symptoms, with no time taken to deal with or even investigate possible underlying problems, *aftercare* of some kind is even more important.

Ideally, planning for discharge should be part of the overall treatment from the start. Merely instructing a patient who is being discharged to visit the hospital outpatient clinic (or community mental health clinic) once a week is not enough. The patient may never get there. Preferably the same therapist should be available for treatment after discharge. When that is not possible, and often it is not, some other arrangement for followup therapy should be made. If at all possible, the patient should have some say in the choice of the new therapist and arrange to meet him/her *before* discharge.

Sometimes more elaborate aftercare may be needed, such as visiting a day care program or returning to the hospital every night for a while. From daily visits, treatment can gradually taper down to a few hours a week, until it is no longer needed. If these arrangements are being considered, it is a good idea for the patient to visit the facility *before* hospital discharge.

PARTIAL HOSPITALIZATION

In addition to normal 24-hour hospitalization, some mental health centers and hospitals provide *day care,* where patients come to the facility to spend a certain number of hours every day but return home at night, or *night care,* where patients work or attend school during the day and return to the facility for the evening and night. These facilities provide individual and/or group therapy, as well as activities judged to be therapeutically useful, in a safe, controlled atmosphere. They are intended to serve either as a transition between the hospital and the community (that is, a form of aftercare for patients leaving the hospital) or as alternatives to full-time hospitalization.

Here is a description of a day care program run by a community mental health center. This program serves clients from three suburban towns. Transportation is not provided; the clients must get to the program on their own.

Approximately twenty-two clients per day use the center. Each is assigned to a staff person to plan the individual's daily schedule and periodically (every three months) re-evaluate it. The schedule consists of therapeutic groups—in effect a setup similar to the milieu therapy practiced inside the hospital. Most clients come either for certain groups or for the full day (9:30 A.M. to 3 P.M.). All of them receive additional therapy, either at the mental health center clinic or privately.

The average stay in the program ranges from six months to a year. Clients usually begin the program on a part-time basis, and then leave it in stages when departing for a job or school. The staff is multidisciplinary, including a half-time psychiatrist, a psychologist, occupational therapists, social workers, nurses, and students of nursing, occupational therapy, and social work.

Clients range in age from eighteen to eighty or older. Most have problems that have been diagnosed as severe: schizophrenia, manic-depressive disease, severe depression. The majority are young adults who are learning to lead independent lives. There also is a group of women, which fluctuates in size, who are dealing with problems of middle age: departing children, re-entry into the job market, separation and divorce.

The cost of attending this day care program is usually covered by medical insurance (up to $500 for Blue Cross), Medicaid, and other plans. A person paying for the service entirely out-of-pocket in 1981 would be charged $29 per day.

The schedule (see the accompanying illustration) consists of therapeutic groups, which are either task-oriented (that is, they work on specific group projects, such as meal preparation) or verbally oriented (engage in verbal group therapy); some groups do both. There is a daily community meeting attended by everyone present that day. The medications group (nearly all the clients receive psychoactive drugs) discusses kinds of medication, why one takes certain drugs and not others, increases and decreases in dosage, side effects, and so on. The skill-building group undertakes individual projects designed to examine what skills a client has, what tasks can be performed, the level of concentration, the need for supervision, etc. The healthy eating group prepares lunch one day a week. On other days clients either bring a bag lunch or go out to local restaurants. Every client is expected to attend the activities and groups listed on his/her schedule, and is asked to plan appointments and personal errands outside program hours. Clients are not supposed to take naps while attending the program, unless there is special staff approval.

Who needs a part-time hospital?

- A person who needs more treatment than visits to a psychiatrist or other mental health professional can provide but who does not

WEEK'S SCHEDULE IN A DAY HOSPITAL

Appointment Schedule   January 26, 1981-Rotation

A.M.	Monday	Tuesday	Wednesday	Thursday	Friday
8:30					
9:00					
9:30	Coffee	Coffee	Coffee	Coffee	Coffee
10:00	Comm. Mtg.	Comm. Mtg.	Comm. Events Mtg.	Comm. Mtg.	Comm. Mtg.
11:00	Med. group / Newspaper	Healthy Eating / Other's point of view	Current Events / Ind. Living	Skill Bldg. / Taking care of yourself	Arts & Craft / Open Verbal
12:00	Lunch	Lunch	Lunch	Lunch	Lunch
P.M. 12:30	Recreation	Recreation	Recreation	Recreation	Recreation
1:00	Outing	Art Therapy	Medication Group	Social Club	Women's group / Movement
2:00		Work Exploration	Prevocational		Communications
2:30					
3:00					

require full inpatient care. Suppose Mary H., who has been quarreling constantly with her husband and whose children are showing signs of disturbance, becomes acutely depressed by her situation and finds it increasingly difficult to meet the normal day-to-day demands of her family. She is spending more and more time sleeping. A day hospital program, where she can receive therapy and support while her children are in school, may be a valuable alternative for her; full-time hospitalization might not be necessary for her treatment needs and would also have the disadvantage of disrupting the family to a much greater extent.

A person whose illness is under control but who is not ready to resume work or school. For example, suppose Donald's schizophrenia has been brought under control with medication, but he is not ready to return to college. He continues to live at home and is enrolled in a day care program for adolescents, some of whom attend a special school. This school offers a computer course that he finds interesting, and in the structured environment provided along with daily group therapy and numerous therapeutic activities, he might improve enough to re-enroll in college by the next semester.

RESIDENTIAL AFTERCARE

There also are community residences, called *halfway houses* and *quarterway houses,* which serve either as transitional steps between the hospital and the community or as alternatives to full-time hospitalization, as well as *long-term residences.*

Quarterway houses often are sections or wards in a mental hospital that serve as a transition to discharge, encouraging skills in everyday living. Halfway houses often are located in the community but have an on-site staff and programs. They tend to serve younger, more vocationally able patients who have retained ties within their community. Long-term residences also are based in the community but tend to have more staff than halfway houses and are intended for persons who may stay more than a year (as opposed to those who use the halfway house as a transitional living arrangement).

Those nursing homes that are extended-care facilities (see above) may be used as a form of aftercare, but more often they serve as a substitute for long-term hospitalization, particularly for elderly patients.

Hospital A, the large private mental hospital described earlier, runs five community residences: a twenty-four bed facility for anyone in psychiatric treatment who is at least seventeen years old and has a bona fide program to occupy him or her during the day (a job, school, day hospital care); a seventeen-bed residence for persons twenty-one or over with chronic psychiatric problems who do not require hospitalization but cannot live in the community without special supervision; two five-bed units for recovering alcoholics who have been discharged from the hospital's own inpatient alcoholism program; and an eight-bed residence for younger adolescents (fourteen to nineteen) who are enrolled in a hospital treatment program and its special high school but who do not need inpatient care.

Hospital A's residential programs are among the very best obtainable. They are small, comprehensive, and rarely available elsewhere. More common are the group homes or shelters for adolescents (see above), but they, too, are limited in size and number, and there may be a considerable waiting period before one can get in.

With the deinstitutionalization program of the 1970s and its large-scale attempts to move long-term chronic patients out of huge, overcrowded state hospitals, a growing need has arisen for placing these patients. Many if not most have no families to which to return, and they cannot manage life on their own in the community. Some have been institutionalized too long to remember how to shop, cook, do laundry, and otherwise perform the simple tasks of everyday life. Some are still too disturbed to behave reliably.

Consequently a variety of residential aftercare programs have sprung up, ranging in quality from very good to abysmally bad. One kind is the *cooperative apartment* or *house* where the occupants help one another, both emotionally and in running the household. During the week they may attend a day care program, or perhaps hold jobs or attend school; evenings and weekends they are on their own, without supervision. The cooperative apartment usually is either leased by a mental health agency or by a related nonprofit corporation, and/or their leases are shared with the tenants. The tenants live in groups of two to five. They pay their own rent, share in household chores, and have professional supervision, with crisis intervention available.

Another alternative is the *supervised apartment,* where staff members of the sponsoring organization live in a building containing several such apartments and provide supervision, therapy, and other forms of support. In rural areas, *work camps* may serve those persons who cannot yet survive in independent housing but do not need a full-scale institution. Such camps generally function as working farms, with daily chores and work, and supervision available as needed.

These arrangements require a level of independence that some discharged patients cannot undertake. For them a *foster home* may be found with a family in the community, or they may go to live in a *licensed community boarding house* (in some places called a *board-and-care home*). Foster care, based on a centuries-old program in Gheel, Belgium, involves placements that are run by a non-clinical caretaker, who provides housing for one to four persons. Often such persons are elderly or mentally retarded. Other necessary services are provided in the community, foster care being essentially custodial in nature.

Private (proprietary) facilities consist of hotels (welfare or single-room occupancy) or homes for adults. Usually they provide neither relief from social isolation, since there are no common activities in which the occupants can join, nor appropriate rehabilitation or treatment. The latter two arrangements, unfortunately, are open to abuse by untrained and unscrupulous providers. Although some private homes and boarding houses provide a genuinely homelike atmosphere and family-style activities, many others are dreary, dismal places where the family or boarding-house operator has no interest in the occupants other than the rent and board they pay and may in fact treat them abusively.

The entire question of how to provide for deinstitutionalized mental patients is still relatively new, and at this writing no large-scale satisfactory solutions have yet been developed. Community resistance often forces residences to be established in rundown or undesirable neighborhoods, creating, in effect, an "ex-mental patient ghetto." Funding is limited, and local regulations for obtaining funds and establishing housing alternatives can be very cumbersome; at one point forty-seven separate steps to obtain approval from various bodies were required in one state.

Those ex-patients who are lucky enough to find good housing still need psychosocial rehabilitation to manage the tasks of day-to-day living—transportation, grooming, shopping, personal hygiene, banking, and so on. In recent years some centers have emerged that combine housing, socialization, and rehabilitation—centers such as Fountain House (New York City), Horizon House (Philadelphia), Threshholds (Chicago), Rose Garden (Rockford, Illinois), Council House (Pittsburgh), Hill House (Cleveland) and Portal House (Los Angeles)—but far more facilities of this kind are needed. The state and county hospitals, woefully inadequate as they may be, still can provide custodial care for those who cannot function in any other setting. As yet no community shelters have been built to replace them.

CHAPTER 18

Is It Working? How to Evaluate Treatment

How can you tell if the treatment you have gone to so much trouble and expense to obtain is any good? Is it helping? Is it making you worse? Or is it neutral, a virtual stalemate (and therefore a waste of time and money)?

Again, there is no easy answer. Even in cases where the goal of treatment is limited and obvious—to remove a particular symptom, such as impotence—and the method of treatment is very specific, as it usually is in sex therapy, you may end up being able to enjoy sexual relations more but discover that you have a whole set of new problems.

Suppose you don't like your therapist. Should you change to another? What if you start having trouble sleeping and have bad dreams about issues brought up in therapy? Does this mean you are getting worse? Or suppose the medication you have been given to make you feel less tense and anxious is leaving you too groggy to do your work at the office? Or your therapist keeps asking you about past events when you really want to talk about your present problems? What if your therapist makes sexual advances? Or suppose your therapist never says much of anything and your sessions are increasingly taken up by long silences? Does this mean you are finished, that you have gone as far as you can go?

GOALS OF TREATMENT

To a large extent your judgment of whether or not your treatment is effective depends on what you expect it to accomplish. Do you want to be rid of troublesome symptoms? If so, exactly what symptoms are you talking about?

In your very first interview with a therapist, whether it is a private practitioner who has been recommended or the intake person at your mental health clinic, you will probably be asked just what brought you (or your relative or friend) here. If no one does ask, you should certainly bring it up yourself, and without delay. Says one psychiatrist:

When I see a person, I am most concerned with how they function, usually in a major area of life. People usually come to me with a problem for which they—or someone else—wish to have help. I suppose if a person came to me and said, "How am I doing? Do I need help?" I would try to assess what they were doing with their lives in terms of how they were functioning at work, what they were achieving in relation to their potential, how they were getting along with others (harmoniously or in conflict), how much they were suffering subjectively, how confident they felt, how much they were able to do what they wanted, how they were facing their problems, and so on.

During your first session the therapist—any therapist—is looking you over, trying to assess just what is the matter and what can or should be done about it. You may know that help of some kind is needed, or you may simply be responding to someone's recommendation (that of your doctor, perhaps, who can find no organic cause for your frequent stomach upsets). In that case, you may be seeing the therapist in order to find out if he or she thinks therapy is indeed the right course of action for you. That in itself is an appropriate goal—to find out if therapy is indicated—and some authorities suggest it should be the very first goal for everyone. In other words, the decision to be evaluated in order to find out if therapy is needed and the decision to enter therapy with a particular practitioner are two separate matters.

The process of assessing symptoms was discussed in Chapter 3. The therapist (or intake person) will (or should) obtain from you a history of the present problem, a detailed past history, including some family history, and take account of your present mental status in order to come to some conclusions about your condition. At a clinic this initial interview becomes the basis for choosing a mode of therapy and a therapist for you (the client rarely has much choice, at least not initially), or, if no appropriate therapist is available or no appropriate treatment is given there, for referring you elsewhere. With a private individual therapist (or one who is screening you for membership in a therapy group) it becomes the basis for an initial diagnosis.

It is at this point that you should ask some questions. We are assuming that you have already inquired, before even coming to the first interview, about this therapist's fees and whether or not he/she has time to take you on. (See Chapter 9 on how to choose a therapist.) If for some reason you have not obtained this information, now is the time to ask. Let us assume, however, that you already know you can afford this therapist (or your insurance covers it adequately) and he/she has time to take another client. Essentially you are now determining how compatible you find him/her.

First, you may want to know the therapist's training and background, and general philosophy of treatment. Does he or she use one or another method exclusively or primarily? Is this the method proposed for your problem? Has he or she had experience with this kind of problem, and if so, what were the results? Does he/she agree that your problem is . . . , or does he/she believe it is really something else (and if so, what)? What does he/she consider the primary goal of treatment? Approximately how long might it take to achieve this goal (six months, a year, three years)? The response to this last

---

ASK YOUR POTENTIAL THERAPIST:

1. What do you think my problem is?
2. How do you propose to help me?
3. How do you feel about working with me?

question may well be that it is too early to tell, but ask it anyhow; you certainly will want to bring it up again some time.

A variety of other issues may be of special concern to you, so feel free to ask about them. Among them are:

- May you telephone the therapist? Is there any special time for doing so? Does he/she ever discuss therapy issues on the phone, or schedule an emergency interview if you need it?
- What provisions does the therapist make for vacations and/or out-of-town trips? Is there someone who covers?
- Do you have to pay for a cancelled (by you) appointment? How much notice is required to avoid payment?
- Does the therapist prescribe medication or have it prescribed by a consulting physician? If so, what if any precautions are taken (concerning side effects, allergic reaction, etc.)?
- How does the therapist feel about using ECT?
- How does the therapist feel about getting a second opinion? Is he/she agreeable to consultation should the need arise?
- Is the therapist willing to draw up a treatment contract (see below)?
- If after a time the fee becomes too high and more therapy is indicated, is the therapist willing to adjust the fee?
- Is the therapist willing to see one or more members of your family (once, occasionally, or as the need arises)?
- Has the therapist ever been in personal therapy?

In the end, however, what is most important is your overall impression of this person, in whom you may be confiding some intimate details of your life. Does he/she seem to understand what you are saying? Does what he/she says make sense to you?

An elaborate research study of the interpersonal skills of an effective therapist came up with three particular characteristics: accurate empathy, nonpossessive warmth, and genuineness. In terms of how well clients respond to treatment, the ideal therapist, according to this study, is a person who can really understand what people are saying, who can readily get on someone else's wave length (accurate empathy). Moreover, this person has a genuine liking and concern for others, accepting them with all their faults and foibles just as they are (nonpossessive warmth), and is able to convey that feeling to them. Finally, the ideal therapist is not a phoney. He/she does not pretend to know everything, or to be superior to his/her clients. He/she is not defensive about his/her own shortcomings, and does not feel threatened when you ask questions about his/her background and orientation.

In another, less formal study, twenty-three psychotherapists were asked what *they* consider important in choosing their own therapists. The qualities mentioned again and again were "warmth," "liking," "caring," and "support." They looked for someone who would give them a feeling of being "approved," "appreciated," "respected." They rejected therapists whom they described as "cold fish," "too distant," and "ungiving."

Against these criteria, how does your therapist measure up?

It may take more than one interview for you to make these judgments, or it may take some time and thought after the first interview. There is no need to decide immediately, or to schedule another appointment at once. If you are not sure, say so—feel free to tell the therapist about your hesitations and reservations—and say you will think it over and make another appointment if you decide to proceed.

If you do think this is the right person for you to see, you may want to propose drawing up a treatment contract or plan that will spell out the goals of treatment and some kind of timetable for achieving them.

THE THERAPY CONTRACT

Strictly speaking, a contract is a promise or set of promises whose performance the law recognizes as a duty and for breach of which the law gives remedy. The therapy contract is a more flexible agreement. Rather than intended to be legally binding, it establishes an explicit mutual understanding and accountability between client and therapist. Basically it defines the agreed-on goals of therapy and the basic ground rules—when and where therapy will take place, and for what fee. It does not guarantee results. The stated goals may or may not be fulfilled. They may even be changed in the course of the therapy. But at the very least a written contract makes the client decide on his or her priorities—why therapy is being undertaken and what it is intended to accomplish—and it makes those priorities clear to the therapist.

A contract may take several sessions to draw up, a time during which your goals can be clarified. The therapist will provide input, too. Some of your goals may be unrealistic, or, on the other hand, they may not be ambitious enough. A problem that was years in the making, a habit you have had for a long time, may take more than a dozen sessions of therapy to understand and change.

The therapist will learn a great deal about you in the formulation of the contract, and, conversely, the therapist's reactions will tell you a good deal. Not all therapists will react favorably to a contract. Some may feel it limits therapy too much to certain issues at the expense of other, equally important ones. Others may find it puts too much responsibility in the hands of the client, whom they may judge to be too disturbed to make rational decisions. Still others may feel it presupposes a certain approach to treatment on their part, with which they may not agree. Even a therapist not opposed to the basic idea of such a contract might feel that for a client to think through problems and feelings enough to formulate a contract is too much to ask. In some cases no doubt it is, but even if it can't be done at once, it could be done after a few sessions when, with or without medication, the client presumably would be feeling well enough to begin sorting out goals.

A good therapy contract is flexible. It allows for changing goals at all times, even within the period of the contract. After all, one of the basic purposes of therapy is to get a new, informed perspective on your feelings and behavior. This often results in a redefinition of goals and even of the problems that brought you to a therapist in the first place.

The basic elements of the therapy contract are:

1. Names of each party to the contract.
2. Dates of the beginning and end of the agreement.

3. The length of each therapy session.
4. The goals of the sessions (stated as specifically as possible).
5. The cost per session and when payable.
6. The definition of the therapist's services.
7. Provisions for cancellation of the contract and of any sessions.
8. Renegotiation at the end of the stipulated period.
9. Allowance for changing goals.
10. Definition of the nature of the services; no guarantee of results; guarantee of good faith.
11. Establishment of access to medical record; guarantee of record's confidentiality and its content and use of any information therein.

WHAT ABOUT GROUP THERAPY?

Although the above-described therapy contract and the accompanying sample contract are designed for individual therapy, there is no reason why it could not be adapted for group therapy as well. Here, however, unless the group can agree on a set of general goals and expectations that apply to all members, each group member would have to state his or her specific goals and make them known to the other members of the group.

As indicated in Chapter 14 in the general description of group therapy, most group leaders hold at least one individual meeting with a prospective member in order to see whether or not that person will fit into the group. This is the time, as we noted, for you to ask about the therapist's background, the makeup and goals of the group, how long it will meet, and how members enter and leave the group. In addition, you may consider your first session or sessions with a therapy group as a period of evaluation similar to the first interview or two with an individual therapist. Some groups actually have a trial period of a set number of sessions during which a new member may decide whether or not the group is appropriate for him or her, and the group decides whether the new member will fit in.

What should you be considering in evaluating a therapy group?

SAMPLE THERAPY CONTRACT

I, Jane Doe, hereafter referred to as CLIENT, agree to join with Mary Jones, hereafter referred to as THERAPIST, every Tuesday evening at 7:00 P.M. until 7:50 P.M. beginning October 5, 1982 until November 23, 1982. During these eight fifty-minute sessions we will direct our mutual efforts toward the following goals:

1. Relieving my chronic headaches.
2. Explaining to my satisfaction my frequent temper outbursts at my husband.
3. Exploring the possibility of my returning to work.

I agree to pay $55 per session for the use of Therapist's resources, training, and experience as a psychotherapist. This amount is payable within thirty (30) days of each session.

If I am not satisfied with the progress made in attaining the above-named goals, I may cancel any and all subsequent appointments for these sessions provided that I give Therapist three days' notice of my intention to cancel. In that event I am not required to pay for sessions not met. However, if I miss a session without such forewarning I am financially responsible for that missed session. The only exception to this arrangement is unforeseen and unavoidable accident or illness.

At the end of eight sessions Therapist and Client will agree to renegotiate the terms of this contract. We include the possibility that stated goals will have changed during this period. I understand that this agreement does not guarantee that I will have attained all my goals in full in the stipulated time. However, it does constitute an offer on my part to pay Therapist for access to her resources as a psychotherapist and her acceptance to apply all those resources in good faith.

I further stipulate that this agreement become part of the medical record, which is accessible to both parties at will but to no other person without my written consent. Therapist will respect my right to maintain the confidentiality of any information communicated by me to Therapist during the course of therapy. In particular, Therapist will not publish, communicate, or otherwise disclose, without my written consent, any such information which, if disclosed, would injure me in any way.

Date	Signature of Client	Signature of Therapist

Adapted by permission from *Through The Mental Health Maze* by Sallie Adams and Michael Orgel, Courtesy of Health Research Group, Washington, DC.

Here you must take into account two factors, the group members and the group leader. Are the other members very different from you? If so, are they *too* different—in background, education, goals, life style—for you to understand and help each other? What kind of help are the others seeking? Is it very similar or very different from what you need? For example, some groups function principally in a low-key, supportive fashion, allowing each member to talk about his or her special concerns and problems with little attempt on anyone's part to work on solutions. In contrast, another kind of group may use psychodrama, role playing, and a variety of techniques to hasten the process of individual change. Is the group leader active or does he/she sit back and let the group run itself? In an insight-focused therapy group the leader may in effect be conducting individual therapy with the members in turn, rather than using the presence of other members in a constructive way. Or, if the approach is client-centered, nondirective counseling, the leader may say little or nothing during meetings, even allowing the group to bog down in trivial or irrelevant conversation. Does the leader attempt to draw out a shy person and curb an overtalkative one? Although beginning sessions with a group can be an alarming experience, making the newcomer feel as shy and anxious as a child on the first day of school in a new town, you should make an effort to learn as much as you can about the group and its leader in order to decide whether or not this is indeed the right place for you to seek help.

IS YOUR THERAPY WORKING?

The immediate effect of any psychotherapy is a sense of relief. You have taken a giant step ahead. You have looked around and found someone who, you think, will be able to help you. You feel less anxious and unhappy just because you are seeing someone, and are comforted by the very process. Even more than most physical illnesses, mental illnesses are sensitive and responsive to care, at least initially. This is the psychic counterpart of the placebo effect, when the very fact of a relationship with a therapist brings some relief from pain and discomfort.

After this initial period, however, things may change. If you have decided on a very brief period of therapy, such as six or eight sessions of STAPP (see Chapter 13) or a couple of months of cognitive therapy, you will soon be expecting positive results of a more permanent nature. Some of the goals you set forth originally should begin to look attainable, or begin to give way, perhaps, to somewhat different goals. From the example shown in the sample therapy contract, Jane Doe's headaches may be less intense or less frequent, and she may begin to make some connections between her outbursts at her husband and his habit of bringing home work every night and every weekend. These are clearly signs of progress.

Sometimes, however, the initial period of relief is followed by a period of getting worse. You find yourself becoming more anxious, especially during the hours just before each session, or you find yourself unaccountably depressed. Does this mean your therapy is making you worse? It may indeed be working in just this way, forcing you to face some truths about yourself that you would rather avoid. Or it may mean that you are not making much progress after all, that your high hopes of improvement are not being fulfilled.

When is it the fault of the therapist? Here are a few early-warning signs that you may be on the wrong course:

- You find yourself frustrated by the method of therapy being used; you don't want the therapist to turn around every question you ask with, "What do *you* think?" but to give you a straightforward answer, even if that answer is simply, "I don't know."
- You are rambling on about this and that, and the therapist is not directing you in any way; for example, you know you have some serious hangups about sex but can't find a way to bring them up and consequently avoid the subject week after week.
- You have been given antidepressant medication and it is not working at all, but the therapist refuses to consider changing the dosage, trying a different drug, etc.
- You are anxious before each session, *and* you feel dissatisfied and depressed afterward.

- The therapist has been late for three of the past four sessions and has made no offer to make up the time owed you.
- The therapist frequently interrupts your session in order to take a phone call or talk to his/her secretary.
- You are not sure if the therapist is really listening to what you say; he/she tends to forget what happened in the previous sessions, and once has clearly mixed you up with another client.
- The therapist suggests he/she can help you resolve your sexual problems by means of direct practice with the therapist. *Sex with a therapist is never therapeutic.*
- When you express some doubts about your treatment the therapist flatly says you are experiencing resistance (see below for more about this) and refuses to discuss the matter further.

You as a client are entitled to know the basic assumptions and methods of treatment undertaken, and to make sure that you and the therapist share the same goals for you. If you feel more upset during the course of therapy, it may be because you are confronting upsetting issues for the first time, or it may be because therapy is not dealing with important issues. The best way to distinguish between these is to discuss your doubts with your therapist, and without delay. Moreover, they should be fully discussed, and not dismissed with a brief, "That's resistance; you'll soon get over it," or some similar statement.

The same tack should be taken if your therapy gets into a rut. You may have heard of one or another person whose "analysis" or "therapy" drags on and on and on—for five years, ten years, even longer. There are some cases where clients must stay in therapy simply to avoid getting worse, rather than to get better, but they are not the general rule. Most of us would not even consider therapy unless we wanted it to have some more positive results than that, and in a reasonable time. Therefore if week after week you are bringing up the same material and nothing in your life is changing as a result of therapy, it's time you did something about it.

If you are truly stalled, probably the best thing to do is to ask for another opinion, that is, a *consultation*. This may involve bringing a consultant to sit in on your therapy session, or it may mean seeing a consultant separately. In either case your therapist certainly should allow the consultant to see your records (with your permission), so as to have as much information as possible on which to base an opinion.

RESISTANCE

Remember, however, that therapy is a profound and sometimes painful experience. In order to overcome neurotic symptoms one must sometimes re-experience anxiety, one must remember painful events from the past, one must give up cherished fantasies to look at the truth.

Paradoxically, you may feel worst about your therapy when it actually is working best. Though you think you want to change for the better, long-lived habits are not easily given up, even if they have caused you suffering. Most people are afraid to make major changes, and rather than understand or even acknowledge their fear, they find it easier to become angry with the therapist or complain about the treatment. Indeed, they may find it hard to express their anger at all (difficulty in expressing feelings directly is often what brings clients to therapists in the first place), and so their genuine *resistance* to change is not brought out in the open. Instead, they refuse to talk about anything important during their sessions, they arrive late or cancel appointments, or they decide abruptly to end therapy.

How can you distinguish between your own resistance and a genuine dissatisfaction with your therapist? Resistance usually comes after a period during which some good things have been accomplished, when some of your goals have begun to be attained. If you examine your dissatisfaction carefully, do you find it resembles negative feelings you have (or had) toward other important individuals in your life? Is your gut reaction one of fleeing? A "yes" to either question is a sign of resistance. If you really are not sure, the best thing is to force yourself to discuss your reluctance with your therapist. An experienced therapist has undoubtedly encountered resistance before and is likely to know ways of helping you to overcome it.

Perhaps the answer is not to look for instant or constant improvement, since therapy is likely to work in fits and starts. Instead, look for new understanding, a progressive awareness of feelings and memories, relief from distress, improved ability to deal with everyday matters. Therapy is a voyage of self-discovery, and as with other travels you must sacrifice some of the comforts of home and familiar surroundings and put up with some discomfort in order to experience new adventures. Just be sure that the journey is in the right direction for *you,* and that if your goal, for example, is a happy marriage no longer marred by your temper tantrums, it is not diverted to someone else's goal for you, such as revising your sex life or rearranging your career. If, after careful consideration, discussion with your therapist, and perhaps seeking a second opinion, you then find your therapy is not working for you, the sensible action is to terminate it.

WHEN IS THERAPY FINISHED?

Again, if your goal is a simple and objective one, such as overcoming impotence, its achievement is easily determined and your therapy can be terminated. For more subjective goals, such as having more satisfactory and comfortable relations with others, or being able to sustain an intimate relationship, the end is harder to determine. It is probably easiest to define it as the time when the effort and cost of therapy seem greater than the likelihood of further improvement.

The very process of giving up therapy and the therapist can be difficult. After all, you are giving up a person you like, and who you believe likes you. Moreover, if this person has helped you, you probably have a sense of gratitude as well, along with admiration and other warm feelings. To a large extent one's feelings of dependency on the therapist are related to the kind of therapy. In very short-term treatment and in behavior therapy, the relationship between client and therapist is less close and less emotional. Moreover, behavior therapy focuses on symptoms, not personality, and when the symptoms of illness are removed the treatment is finished. In psychoanalysis, on the other hand, the treatment is of an intense and long-term nature, and the relationship of analyst and client inevitably becomes very close. Termination of this relationship therefore is an important phase of therapy, which might take months to accomplish. In other forms of therapy it is basically the client who decides when it is time to quit, although under normal circumstances it doesn't make sense to terminate against the therapist's advice.

The time of termination often revives some of the very symptoms that brought a client to treatment. One client may experience an anxiety attack after having had none for six months; another will have nightmares; still another, whose profound depression had lifted, will again have intolerable feelings of sadness. However, the final sessions frequently can be a very useful therapeutic period during which clients, faced with the idea that this is their "last chance" to sort things out, often bring up deep concerns that they had never been able to talk about before.

Often those who find it hardest to terminate treatment are individuals who have had severe problems coping with separation and loss. The "loss" of the therapist revives the feelings of desolation and abandonment caused by earlier losses in their lives. If they can make the appropriate connections between their feelings about earlier loss and the ending of therapy, they may in the end gain a lasting sense of balance.

Even when a client is ready to end treatment, and the treatment has been successful in that his or her maladaptive behavior has ended, this does not mean that the person will never again need therapy for mental illness. New problems come up, and new difficulties arise. In the study of twenty-three psychotherapists cited above, twenty had themselves been in treatment with more than one therapist. This treatment was by no means continuous. Rather, at different times in their lives, for different reasons, they sought the help of another therapist. Further, a survey of graduates of one of the best psychoanalytic training institutes found that 55 percent of its graduates had additional therapy after completing their training analyses.

What does that signify for the much larger population of non-psychotherapists? It means simply that a "once and for all" attitude, the idea that once therapy is done one is necessarily "cured for life" is unrealistic and inappropriate. Relieved of this burden, the approach can be more practical, with the overall focus on current problems. Once those problems are solved, of course, there is no guarantee that new problems will not arise, any more than one can be sure one will never again get bronchitis or pneumonia.

If this discussion of evaluating therapy seems inconclusive, don't despair. If you genuinely like your therapist, and feel he or she likes you, chances are you are being helped. In the end, the most important factors probably are not the method used, but your faith in the therapist, your expectation of being helped, and the encouragement and supportiveness of the therapist—these ingredients are known to be effective. And, in the last analysis, some authorities point out, you may never really know what helped you. Numerous studies show that the disorders for which people generally seek psychotherapy are self-limiting, and that often as not they will improve in time (two years is the period usually quoted) *without* treatment. We are not suggesting that you put up with disabling symptoms and allow them to disrupt your life for many months in the hope that they will go away, but we are pointing out that you need not agonize unduly over whether or not your therapy is exactly right.

EVALUATING SOMATIC THERAPIES

Psychoactive drugs are used in one of two ways: on a short-term basis, to bring severe symptoms under control so that a person can benefit from psychotherapy, which will be the main form of treatment; or on a long-term basis, to control a severe chronic mental disorder, such as manic-depressive disease or schizophrenia, for which medication is the principal form of treatment. Some mental health professionals are opposed to using medication for anything but psychosis—severe mental disturbance. They maintain that medication simply removes the symptoms, not their causes, and therefore cannot be effective in the long run. Others maintain that one cannot separate symptoms from causes—the symptoms *are* the illness. Whichever point of view your mental health professional subscribes to, it is important to remember that psychoactive drugs are powerful agents, and their use should be carefully monitored. In other words, no one should continue taking the same drug for many months, or take a drug prescribed for someone else, or alter the dosage one is taking, without periodic evaluation by a competent physician. (In practice, prescriptions for such drugs frequently are for limited amounts of the drug and are non-renewable.)

How can you tell if the drug prescribed for you or your relative or friend is the right one? It would seem that if a medication modifies or eliminates the symptoms for which it is being given, and does not give rise to other undesirable symptoms you can say it is effective. Unfortunately it doesn't always work that way. Antidepressants, for example, may take as long as four or five weeks to make a person feel less depressed. If a medication does not work within that period, it still may not mean it is the wrong drug; it may mean simply that the dosage is too low. That in turn may mean you have to wait another two or three weeks, during which a higher dose is taken, to see if it works. If it does not, a different antidepressant might be tried. Obviously this is a time-consuming and cumbersome process, all the more distressing because the person taking the drug continues to suffer until it takes effect.

Another question is side effects. A drug may help the symptoms for which it is taken, but may give rise to unpleasant (or, less often, dangerous) new symptoms. The minor tranquilizers can make you feel drowsy and lethargic; the tricyclic antidepressants can cause blurred vision, constipation, and a dry mouth; the antipsychotics can cause all these symptoms and also appetite increase and weight gain; and lithium carbonate may cause stomach upsets, incessant thirst, muscular weakness, and mild tremors.

All such side effects should be reported to the physician. Some can be eliminated by lowering dosage or changing to a different drug of the same family. Others may be unavoidable. In any case, whenever there are side effects, the decision must be made as to whether the drug's benefits outweigh the undesirable effects. If you are lucky your medication will work perfectly, without side effects. If you are typical, however, you will have to make a decision as to which is the lesser evil, the illness or the drug's effects. Further, there is always a degree of uncertainty about the future, of either the illness or the drug's effects. One has to make the best possible guess, and, if one guesses wrong, one usually can change one's mind.

Why, might you ask, don't physicians who prescribe these drugs know what to expect, and if they do, why not inform their patients? The answer here is that different individuals respond very differently to psychoactive drugs. Some of the results and side effects can be readily foreseen, but many physicians believe it is foolish to warn patients of discomforts that they may never actually experience, and the fear of which may keep them from taking medication on a regular basis.

If you are truly concerned about the effects of a drug on you or your relative or friend, ask your physician. If you don't get a satisfactory answer, either ask another physician or go to your local library and look up the drug in one of the several excellent up-to-date guides that are readily available. The *Physicians' Desk Reference* (commonly called *PDR*), revised annually, lists drugs by manufacturer, generic name, and brand name, and describes dosages, precautions, and adverse reactions; a recent edition should tell you everything you want to know.

Although it is not possible to determine with certainty which, if any, of the drugs available will be most useful to a particular individual, the potential benefits should be greater than the potential side effects or risks.

ECT

There is even more disagreement regarding the use of ECT than there is about psychoactive drugs. Today it is used almost exclusively to treat severe depression, either when antidepressants do not work or for some reason are not tolerated, or to help a severely depressed person faster than drugs are likely to work.

The effectiveness of ECT usually can be judged by the end of a complete course of treatment, that is, six to eight applications over a period of two to three weeks. Concerning side effects, the most troubling of which is loss of memory, they tend to be much milder with unilateral ECT (applied only to one side of the brain; see Chapter 16 for further explanation), although unilateral ECT may be less effective than bilateral ECT.

EVALUATING A HOSPITAL

Given the high costs of hospitalization, you may not have much choice of where you, your relative, or friend can go for inpatient care. Nevertheless, you should have some criteria for differentiating good from bad care.

Good hospital care begins at the time of admission, when the patient arrives. Well-handled procedures include explaining the hospital routine from the very start, but only giving as much information as the patient is able to absorb (some patients arrive for admission in acute distress; trained personnel are sensitive to this). If papers must be signed, they should be adequately explained. Whoever accompanies the patient to the ward or room should introduce him or her to staff members there and provide a little general orientation. It should be made clear from the start which individual will be primarily responsible for the care of this patient and that information should be shared with the family member or other person accompanying the patient to the hospital.

As was pointed out in Chapter 13, the majority of hospitalized patients today—especially those who go to a general hospital rather than a psychiatric hospital—remain there for a relatively short period of time, typically ranging from one to eight weeks. In the case of serious illness—and if it is not serious, why hospitalize the patient?—intensive treatment is needed to effect a recovery in that time and prevent (or try to prevent) a recurrence of the illness. What you should look for, therefore, are signs of such intensive care, as well as ongoing preparation for being discharged from the hospital:

• What is the place of drugs in the patient's treatment?

- Will ECT be used?
- Will there be individual psychotherapy? How often for how long?
- Will there be group therapy? How often? How large a group?
- Is there milieu therapy? Regular ward meetings? Are they led by a skilled staff member?
- Is there occupational therapy? Of what does it consist?
- What facilities are there for recreation?
- How much access does the patient have to staff members? Are nurses and aides available for casual talk with patients?
- Is there a set schedule for patients' activities or are they left to their own devices?
- What, if any, preparation is made for discharge and aftercare?

For longer-term care, the same questions apply. Even if your relative or friend is in a long-term facility, typically a state or county hospital, you can assess the overall conditions and, if necessary, work for change. (Living quarters can be improved, and recreation equipment of various kinds provided; volunteer contributions, either of time or of material things, can be enlisted and encouraged.)

The basic ingredient of good hospital care, however, lies not in the facilities but in the staff. Sheer numbers alone do not ensure a good staff, although a larger staff is more apt to provide more care. It is both the amount and the quality of their contacts with patients that makes the difference. Some warning signs of poor staff:

- Staff members are not much seen. (In many hospitals psychiatric staff members wear street clothes rather than uniforms, so do not be misled, but they usually wear name tags to identify themselves.)
- Staff members are talking and interacting mostly with one another (at the nurses' stations, for example) rather than with patients.
- Staff members do not know patients by name.
- Staff members do not show proper respect for the patient (treat patient as a child—"This medicine is doctor's orders, that's all you need to know about it"; call patients by their first names but expect themselves to be addressed more formally; talk about a patient in his or her presence as though he/she was not there or could not understand).

- Staff members show impatience and try to hurry patient through routines, medication, etc.

It is not always possible, if you yourself are the patient, to evaluate hospital treatment with any objectivity. If you can, have a family member or close friend help you make such assessments. If visiting hours are too limited—to an hour or two a day—that in itself is a sign that the hospital may want to avoid such scrutiny. Another bad sign is a constantly groggy and drowsy patient. Although high doses of drugs may be necessary to give relief from acute symptoms, some hospitals routinely use them to keep patients from being troublesome and make them easier to manage. If your friend or relative seems totally "out of it" over a long period of time, that bears investigation.

EVALUATING CHILDREN'S PROGRAMS

If a particular program has been recommended for your emotionally disturbed child, either in a special class in a regular school or in a separate school for "special needs" children, you certainly should evaluate it. What should you look for?

Again, the most important factor in any such program is staff, and the single most important quality, most experts agree, is *warmth*. Do you get a sense of warmth from the teachers, a feeling of their connecting with the children? Do they know how to talk to the children in ways that bring out feelings? Do they *listen* to the children?

Other questions to ask are:

- Are classroom goals and limits clearly set and shared with the children so they understand what is considered appropriate behavior? Ideally there is a disciplined approach, but one that is not too rigid to respond to individual needs and situations.
- What happens when a child blows up? Are there experienced staff members who can work with a child whose behavior becomes unmanageable in the classroom? There should be skilled "crisis

intervention" until a child can regain enough control to rejoin the group, not just sending the child to isolation or to the principal's office for punishment.

- Is getting along with others stressed as part of the curriculum? Social relations is an important element of education, and skilled teachers can help children improve communication, develop assertiveness, handle embarrassing situations, and learn how to make friends.
- Does the program reflect an awareness of a child's need to build self-esteem?
- Is there time during the day, both formal and unplanned, for children and teachers to talk together about important questions and issues?
- Is there teamwork among the staff who work with children? Are there regular opportunities for talking things over between classroom teachers and other professionals, such as social workers, psychologists, reading specialists, art therapists, and others involved in the program?
- Is there good communication with the parents? Are they enlisted as allies in the program, or viewed as uninformed laymen or even enemies?

CHAPTER 19

The Role of the Family

Suppose you have a close relative, a sister or a husband, a parent or a child, who is being treated for mental illness. What, if anything, can you do to help? The answer depends very much on a number of factors—the severity of the illness, how it is being treated, and the nature of your relationship (parents, for example, have certain responsibilities toward a young child). Is your husband seeing a behavior therapist once a week for treatment of anxiety, for example, or is he seeing a psychoanalyst five days a week over a period of years? Is your relative's problem a mild depression, or is it schizophrenia for which he or she has been hospitalized one or more times? Is your severely depressed elderly mother receiving electroconvulsive treatment on an outpatient basis? Your role depends a great deal on the circumstances.

IF YOUR CHILD IS SEEING A PSYCHOTHERAPIST

Depending on the nature of the problem and the orientation of the therapist, your relative's therapist may or may not want to involve you in the treatment. There is only one exception: when the client is a child, the parents (or guardian) are nearly always involved to some extent.

Some child therapists see one or both parents on a frequent and regular basis, as often as once a week (in addition to the child's sessions). Others prefer to see only the child but confer with the parents on a regular basis. Still others believe therapy is a private matter between therapist and client, and that the child's feeling of trust will be violated if they share specific information with the parents, but they do keep in touch with them.

Whatever the situation for you and your child, after a few months you will no doubt have a sense of how the child is responding to treatment, and you will be able to evaluate its effectiveness to some extent. Since you in part are responsible for the decision to enter treatment at all, and presumably are paying for it as well, it makes sense to reinforce the therapist at home in whatever ways you can, and to follow whatever advice the therapist may give you in dealing with your child. Of course, if the therapist's advice seems inappropriate, you should talk it over before taking any action, and, if you continue to find yourself in disagreement, you probably will want to seek another opinion.

IF YOUR ADULT RELATIVE IS IN THERAPY

Suppose, however, that the relative seeing a therapist is an adult in your household. What, then, is your role?

Anne, 23, shared an apartment with her cousin Frances, 27, who was divorced. The cousins had grown up together in the same small town and both now worked in a distant city. Unhappy about a number of matters, Frances had been seeing Dr. Green, a psychoanalyst, three times a week for about four months. She told Anne little about her treatment except that she had been given some pills to take when she felt upset. Formerly quiet and shy, Frances now began to behave quite differently. Several nights she went out and came home extremely late. She would not tell Anne much except that she had gone by herself to "a few bars" and, from something Anne gathered, she did not remember much about what had happened. She mentioned the name of one bar, however, which Anne knew was in a very rough neighborhood, down near the docks. Extremely concerned about her cousin, Anne nevertheless did not want to alarm Frances's mother, a widow in poor health, who lived 1,000 miles away.

What should Anne do? In this case, which actually happened, Anne decided to telephone her cousin's analyst, telling him of her concern. He was not easy to get hold of, and when she finally reached him he was difficult to talk to. Anne said she was worried about her cousin's behavior. Dr. Green made no comment. Anne said she was sure Frances was drinking too much when she went out, possibly she was getting drunk and blacking out, and she was concerned for Frances's safety. Dr. Green again made no comment. Finally Anne bluntly asked him what she should do. Dr. Green suggested that she might wish to inform her cousin's mother, and then he hung up.

Anne was not sure she had done the right thing in calling. She told Frances about it afterward, and her cousin was furious, telling her to mind her own business. Nevertheless, in this situation she had done what she could. She had expressed her concern, both to her cousin and to the therapist. She also had provided the therapist with information about Frances's behavior that he otherwise might not have had, and that was relevant to the treatment (if he was prescribing medication, he should certainly know whether or not she was drinking, too).

THEY'RE GETTING WORSE

This case points out one of the common difficulties of living with a person being treated for mental illness. Whether the illness is a mild neurosis or a full-blown psychosis, the symptoms are not only unpleasant, but at times they appear to become worse during the course of treatment. The husband in therapy who is working on, and in the process, reliving some early conflicts with his mother may come home and accuse his wife of behaving "just like Mother," when in reality she has only unwittingly reminded him of a painful early conflict.

It may be even more serious. There have been instances where a spouse in treatment has, in reliving old sexual conflicts, acted them out in the present, either by seeking affairs outside marriage or by behaving differently in the marital sexual relationship. Therapy nearly always introduces tensions into family life, particularly when the treatment involves re-experiencing suffering. During these periods the family member in therapy may occasionally feel and act worse than ever, becoming increasingly moody and demanding at home.

What can family members do then? If they can tolerate the behavior, realizing that it is temporary, that may be the best solution. If they are able to respond to false accusations and displaced anger (anger directed at them when it is really aroused by someone else) with a statement such as,"That's not really true; maybe you'll see it differently one day," that also may be helpful. But if the tensions generated become intolerable, it may be wise to ask permission of the person in treatment to see his/her therapist (perhaps jointly) to discuss these problems, or even to obtain a consultation oneself from a different mental health practitioner.

At best the family's role is supportive. Listening to and sympathizing with the person in treatment, encouraging him or her to continue treatment, to keep scheduled appointments, to take medication that is prescribed—all these can be very useful. Indeed, one's family is usually a chief source of support, warmth, and love. Family members are in the best position to help one another, knowing each other more intimately than anyone else.

At the same time, the very closeness that makes it easy to help also makes it difficult, because when one is emotionally involved it is hard to be objective. Love and concern can blind one to the realities. A loving relative may be unable to see an illness for what it is. A father may make constant excuses for his daughter when the parents of other children and teachers complain about her behavior, reacting defensively rather than recognizing a real problem. The wife whose husband refuses to go out and is withdrawing from everyone may explain that he always has been quiet and shy and simply doesn't want to make an effort.

A similar problem is overprotectiveness. The woman who returns from a brief hospitalization for depression may find her family on tiptoe and whispering, as well as taking over all her normal household tasks for her. Yet most therapists would agree that the sooner one returns to normal activities, the better off one is.

A direct and open line of communication with the therapist can prevent such problems. If you don't know how to behave with an ill family member and you are afraid you may somehow make him/her get worse, ask the therapist's advice.

COMMUNICATING WITH THE THERAPIST

Anne's call to her cousin Frances's analyst was made twenty-five years ago. Today such a doctrinaire approach as Dr. Green's, who obviously wanted no contact with his patient's relative, is far less common. Most therapists, including analytically oriented ones, are willing to maintain open lines of communication with the client's family. They realize it is useful to have, from time to time, a factual account of the client's activities and behavior—what he or she did, said, undertook. However, they are apt to want a straightforward account, not the family's opinions, views, or arguments, which in effect reflect mainly their own concerns.

You certainly should be able to check on your relative's progress by calling the therapist periodically. That does not mean you should call after every appointment, or once a week, or even once a month. It makes sense to know what is happening in terms of improvement (or lack of it), but there is no reason to make a nuisance of yourself, or to violate the client's right to privacy by asking about details. If you are in doubt as to when to call, ask the therapist.

Some therapists actively involve family members, at least with some of their clients. For example, the husband of Wanda, the young woman who experienced anxiety attacks whenever she left the house, might be advised, as her therapy progresses, to accompany her halfway on a neighborhood errand and wait at the halfway point to accompany her home again. Or the sister of Jane, suffering from profound depression after her husband's death, might be told specifically to talk to Jane about her loss and to relate it to her present forgetfulness and sadness.

On the other hand, it is unwise for family members to play the role of therapist on their own. You may believe in your heart of hearts that what your teen-age son Joe really needs is to get together with the other kids at ballgames and parties and learn to have a good time, not realizing that his social withdrawal is such that it is hard for him even to eat dinner with the rest of the family. Or you may, being a person who basically disapproves of drugs and other "artificial props," sympathize with Uncle Frank when he complains that the side effects of the antipsychotic drug his psychiatrist prescribes are terrible. The reasonable course of action for you, however, is to encourage him to continue the drug.

THERAPY FOR THE FAMILY

Suppose life with your ill relative has become intolerable. You and/or the other family members are miserable. You may want to learn to cope with these stresses by considering family therapy. Some family therapists believe that when any individual is ill the entire family is necessarily involved; some even hold that it is the family that really is ill, and the "sick" person just happens to be the one who is most openly expressing that illness. Not all family therapists agree with this idea, but most will focus on understanding how the family members interact with one another. In this process they may be very helpful in indicating ways of adapting to the tensions generated in connection with the family member who is in psychiatric treatment and who is changing a formerly stable family equilibrium.

Such therapy may be conducted with or without the patient present, and with all or part of the family involved. Appropriate goals for such treatment might be learning how the family members' behavior affects the patient and vice versa, agreeing on what they may expect of the patient in terms of functioning, determining how much responsibility they should take for the patient, and deciding in advance what they should do if the patient has a severe relapse.

Suppose either you cannot find a family therapist or the other members of the family do not wish to see one. You might then consider individual counseling. Should you go to your relative's therapist or to someone else? The choice may not be yours. Some therapists, particularly those who are psychoanalytically oriented, will not treat close relatives at the same time. However, if your relative's therapist is of this persuasion and seems to be competent and effective, he or she might be able to recommend a different therapist for you to consult, one with whom he/she can cooperate. Other therapists, of course, have no objection to treating several members of the same family, individually or together.

VISITING YOUR HOSPITALIZED RELATIVE

Whether your relative is in the psychiatric unit of a general hospital or in a private or public mental hospital, you most likely will want to (or feel you should) visit him or her. Some years ago "no visitors" was a common rule in mental hospitals, particularly those treating children (whose illness often was blamed on the parents, who therefore were discouraged from visiting) and those concentrating on analytic treatment (where it was feared that visits from the real-life figures in a patient's early childhood conflicts would delay or otherwise upset the treatment). Today, the focus of most hospitals is on returning the patient to home and community as quickly as possible, and visits from family and friends are seen as a means of retaining close contact with home life. Consequently, visiting hours tend to be quite liberal, and in some hospitals, like the general hospital described above (page 198), special provisions are made for family members to share a meal with the patient and to engage in group meetings with other families and patients.

One psychiatrist has given excellent advice to families visiting hospitalized patients.* Among the points he makes are:

• Keep your visit short. A brief congenial visit is less likely to put a strain on you or the patient.
• Don't bring along your anxieties or grief over the illness, but

*Leonard Cammer, M.D., *Up From Depression* (New York: Simon & Schuster, 1969).

rather try several topics of conversation to find one of mutual interest.

- Talk about things at home but do not unnecessarily relate disturbing news; if you must, emphasize the positive aspects. (Yes, Mary did bang up the car last week, but no one got hurt, and the insurance adjuster says most of the damage is covered.)
- Bring a small gift if you wish, but make sure it is not something forbidden by hospital rules. (Usually that includes anything that is a potential weapon and any medication—even aspirin—or alcoholic drink; even if your relative is reliable, other patients there may not be.)
- Do not become too involved with other patients, bringing them gifts or gossiping with them. A friendly greeting is fine, but you are there to visit your relative, and you don't know what you are getting into if you become involved with others.
- Listen sympathetically to your relative's complaints (about the food, service, nurses, etc.) but do not act on them until you have verified their accuracy. Your relative's perceptions may be distorted.
- Do be alert for signs of physical illness in your relative. Even in the best hospitals, these are sometimes inadvertently overlooked.
- Respect your relative's privacy; don't discuss him or her with other patients or visitors.
- Encourage your relative to cooperate with his/her treatment; listen if he/she complains about it, but don't undermine it by expressing your own doubts openly.
- Don't make promises you cannot keep. Don't respond to complaints about the hospital with a promise that you'll see a change is made. And, if you're not sure when you can come again, don't promise that you'll be there again next week.
- Leave gracefully. Don't watch the clock, but give the patient something to look forward to, such as, "Let's save this topic for my next visit."

Whatever you do or say during your visits, remember that, for better or worse, you represent a part of the real world, the world to which your relative will be returning when he/she leaves the protective environment of the hospital. Therefore make his/her exposure to that real world a gentle one, but at the same time don't try to be something or someone you are not. Act yourself, and express your love and concern with warmth.

AFTER HOSPITAL DISCHARGE

Though it might seem that the brief hospital stays encouraged nowadays represent a less drastic upheaval than long-term hospitalization, remember that anyone ill enough to have been hospitalized at all has been through a traumatic experience, whatever its duration. Moreover, the end of your relative's hospitalization rarely means that he or she is "cured" and will need no further treatment. Rather, he/she is convalescent.

It is unrealistic to expect the newly discharged patient to return to normal activities and behavior immediately, but you can play an important role in speeding up that return. During the first days at home, he/she may be easily upset, and too much stress will exacerbate that situation. What is too much stress? The National Mental Health Association, in its booklet, *Helping the Mental Patient at Home,* suggests you avoid the following:

- Early mixing with too many people. It takes time to get used to crowds and social gatherings, so don't push. Go slowly.
- Constant watching. If the patient's quietly occupied, don't keep checking; it isn't necessary and may make him/her nervous.
- Threats and criticism. Don't threaten him/her with a return to the hospital, and don't nag.

You also can be of practical, positive assistance. You can help get your relative to therapy appointments and whatever other forms of aftercare (such as partial hospitalization, see Chapter 17) may have been recommended. You can help make sure he/she continues taking prescribed medication regularly. You can help intercede on his/her behalf with school authorities or employer, as well as with other family members and friends. You can help ease social commitments. You also can help with health insurance and social agency contacts. And you can continue to be a source of emotional support and encouragement, praising his/her progress toward normality and helping him/her see in perspective any failures or setbacks that may occur.

SPECIFIC PROBLEMS

The specific problems family members may encounter with a newly discharged patient vary with the seriousness of the illness. Some may be very temporary and easily dealt with. For example, the depressed person's lack of appetite may in a few weeks respond to antidepressant medication. In the meantime, you can encourage eating by offering favorite foods in small (not overwhelming) amounts and by ignoring the leftovers on his/her plate (don't nag).

Other problems also may be temporary but harder to deal with. For example, many of the antipsychotic drugs used for schizophrenia diminish one's sex drive, causing lack of desire in women and impotence in men. Sexual inadequacy not only upsets a marital relationship but is terribly detrimental to self-esteem. As the patient's sex partner, what can you do? Certainly you should bring up the problem with the patient's therapist, for both of you need a thorough explanation and reassurance in order to be patient during this period. Sometimes an adjustment in medication dosage is indicated.

Your schizophrenic relative may no longer be actively delusional or hallucinating, but may still distort reality to some extent. For example, he/she may accuse family members of causing the illness, of undermining the treatment, or otherwise making his/her life miserable and recovery impossible. This kind of accusation is hard to take, especially when family members are already bending over backwards to help their relative recover. Arguing is unlikely to help. About all you can do is point out that it is the illness that is making him/her see things in this way, and that when he/she gets better things will seem quite different.

Frequent weepiness and long crying spells also are hard to cope with. When weeping represents a normal grief reaction, of course, it is to be encouraged. Some individuals cannot cry for many months after losing a loved one and then find it a great relief to do so. But if the weepiness is inappropriate, you may want to try to stop it. One psychiatrist suggests an interesting technique for doing so: place yourself directly in front of your weeping relative and, rather than asking him/her to stop crying, insist that he/she face you and look into your eyes. If your relative complies, the tears will most likely stop, since it is virtually impossible to keep on crying while looking straight at another person. You may have to repeat the procedure several times, but it may be well worth trying to induce your relative to stop this waste of energy and instead try to talk about what is so painful.

Suppose your relative decides to make a major life change? Your son, for example, decides to move into an apartment with his girlfriend, or your wife decides she wants another baby. If your relative has been severely ill—with a major depression or with schizophrenia, for example—it is wise to persuade him or her to postpone such a change. Often, as people's emotional health changes, their views of the desirability of making a major change also alter. Moreover, seldom are major life changes necessary on an emergency basis. It is better to wait.

Any major life change represents a stress, and stress may exacerbate a mental illness, or trigger a relapse. If the proposed change is a new baby, presumably the person's mate has some voice in the matter. But suppose your grownup son insists on moving out of your house to his own place? If you cannot persuade him to wait a while, do no oppose his move but go along with his decision and help him as much as possible. Your support may minimize the stress.

Perhaps the hardest decisions to make on a day-to-day basis are those affecting your relative's independence. How much is he/she able to decide, or to do? You must try to strike the very difficult balance between over- and under-stimulation, the balance between being included in normal family activities (ranging from ordinary meals to outings and visiting) but not being forced to take part beyond his/her ability, the balance between companionship and privacy, between freedom and structure.

In the hospital most patients are on a strict schedule, and to return home to total freedom can be very difficult. Most individuals do better with some structure—meals at definite hours, waking and sleeping at certain times. Although your relative may not be able to return to work or school immediately, he/she should be encouraged to take on as many appropriate household tasks and errands as possible. In fact, a number of studies have shown that patients from less well-to-do families, in which everyone must work, recover faster than those from upper-class ones, where doing one's share is economically less important.

WHAT TO TELL THE CHILDREN?

How do you deal with the return of a hospitalized relative to a household with small children?

If the person is the children's mother, presumably the children have been told something to explain her absence. Preferably it was the truth, that Mother was ill and needed to be taken care of in a hospital to get better. On discharge, if she is well enough to take full charge of the children, she can explain again to them why she was gone. If, as may well be the case, she is not yet ready to take on her former child-care role, some kind of help will be required, ranging from a babysitter a few hours a day to a full-time mother substitute.

Whether the relative is the mother, father, or someone else, the person's behavior may for a time be different or unusual. This should be explained to the children as being part of the illness, and in fact most children are able to accept this explanation. Some of the behavior may be very frightening to a child: a father who, after ECT (shock treatment), does not remember some recent event, or an older sister, usually very gentle, who suddenly has outbursts of rage. Even if a child does not ask what's wrong—perhaps especially if the child doesn't ask—a simple explanation should be offered.

Remember, too, the great propensity of young children to assume guilt. When their parents quarrel or separate or divorce, it is common for children to believe it is their fault. When a family member, especially a parent or sibling, is mentally ill and acts peculiar, it is just as common for children to worry that it is caused by something bad they did (or thought, or wished). Other questions they may ask, or be afraid to ask, include: Is it catching? Will I get this illness, too? Can I tell anyone (my friends) about it? Can I have friends over to play?

Frankness about the symptoms and openness about unusual behavior will make it easier for everyone concerned. Children accept a great deal. Moreover, they like to be included, so call on them to help. A newly discharged relative may find it easier (less demanding and less threatening) to talk with a child than with an adult. On the other hand, don't allow a child to become too intensely involved in the relative's symptoms, a victim of aggressive outbursts or involved in a compulsive behavior pattern. Should that happen, it is up to an adult to intervene and protect the child. On the whole, however, the presence of a mentally ill person in the household, while it is hard on family members, can be a maturing experience for the children. Many families find their ability to adapt to this stress—and it is a stress—far greater than they realized.

CHAPTER 20

Paying for Mental Health Care

In 1981 an estimated $17 billion a year was being spent for mental health care in the United States, nearly 1 percent of gross national product (GNP). This amount represented only the direct cost, that is, the actual money spent for mental health services, including treatment, facilities, research, and training. It did not include the indirect cost, mostly in terms of lost productivity due to disability, which was estimated to be another $20 billion a year.

Who pays for all this? In the United States, every taxpayer pays his or her share. Of every dollar spent for mental health care, the Federal government pays about twenty cents, state and local government about thirty cents, private insurance about fifteen cents, and private noninsurance sources (mostly fees paid by clients) the remaining thirty-five cents. Even if you yourself never need mental health care services of any kind, you are paying some part of their cost. (In Canada taxpayers are responsible for a much larger share, since National Health Insurance pays not only for hospital psychiatric treatment but for unlimited outpatient psychiatric care.)

WHO CAN AFFORD TREATMENT?

Practically every American can afford some mental health care, but the kind and amount available depend to a large extent on ability to pay for it. In a true emergency it is unlikely that treatment will be denied to a person who cannot demonstrate ability to pay for it, but it can happen. A long-term mental illness can be very costly. If it afflicts a family's principal breadwinner, their savings, unemployment insurance, and other assets may be decimated. If it afflicts a parent with young children, alternate child care arrangements may need to be made. For either short-term or long-term health care, one's choices may be limited by one's funds and insurance coverage.

Approximately 60 percent of the American population have private health insurance that covers some mental health care. As a rule such policies provide far less coverage for mental illness than for physical illness, and most of that is limited to hospitalization and inpatient care. Further, such policies most often are employer-connected and are therefore lost if a person loses his or her job or is unable to work. Public insurance is available for the elderly, the poor, and the chronically disabled, but the laws governing the various benefits and the agencies administering them are extremely complicated and constantly changing.

PRIVATE INSURANCE PLANS

Private or commercial insurance policies are issued by the nonprofit organization Blue Cross and Blue Shield and by various large insurance companies. The subscribers include employers, labor unions and other groups, and individuals. The costs of these policies and the benefits they confer vary greatly and depend on many factors, including where you live (since hospital costs and practitioners' fees vary from region to region) and your own health history. As a rule group plans are more generous than individual ones.

Chances are that you or your relative has one of these policies, or possibly has coverage through the policy of a spouse or parent. Your first step should be to find out exactly what it covers. If you don't have the brochure explaining coverage, ask for it at your place of employment, from the union steward or personnel director. If they don't have it or your policy is an individually issued one, call or write the insurance company directly. When you do get it, and it may take some persistence on your part, read it carefully to see if it covers, in full or in part, the following services:

- Diagnostic consultation (evaluation or assessment)? If so, in practitioner's office or only in hospital? By a psychiatrist only? By a psychologist? Other professional? Does it include psychologic testing?
- Treatment for any nervous or mental disorder, regardless of previous illnesses?
- Office visits to a psychiatrist? Psychologist? Other professional?
- Electroconvulsive treatment (ECT) in the hospital? In doctor's office?
- Anesthesiologist assisting doctor with ECT?
- Hospitalization in psychiatric unit of general hospital? Full or partial cost of room? For how long?
- Hospitalization in mental hospital? Full or partial cost of room? How long?
- Cost of prescription drugs?
- Nursing care? In hospital? At home?
- Partial hospitalization? Day care? Night care? Halfway house?
- Transportation to and from places of treatment?
- Rehabilitation therapy after hospitalization? Physical therapy? Vocational rehabilitation?

The typical private insurance plan in 1981 allowed a total of $500 a year for outpatient psychiatric care and either sixty or ninety days for hospitalization in a general hospital and thirty days in a mental hospital, even though general hospital care was roughly twice as expensive as care in a mental hospital (as noted earlier, the latter needs less elaborate facilities and equipment). By 1981 some thirty states had adopted laws allowing licensed clinical psychologists to bill insurance companies directly for outpatient psychotherapy, but very few policies covered treatment by social workers, psychiatric nurses, rehabilitation counselors or other professionals unless it took place in a hospital or under the direct supervision of a licensed physician.

Third-party (insurance company) claims can be so complicated to handle that there actually are services that specialize in filing and monitoring claims. Individuals who have a great many medical bills to be processed may find it worth the fee to use such a service to scrutinize bills for accuracy, file and monitor claims, and do any needed followup. The increased benefits are considerable, because experienced persons file your claims and keep track of what you are owed and what the insurer actually pays. Fees for such services vary, but in 1981 most charged about $120 per year on a subscription basis for an individual (to handle all health insurance claims during that period), $220 per couple, or about $50 to handle a single hospitalization. To locate such a service, look in the yellow pages under Medical Organizations or write to Medical Claims Filing Service, 3512 South Silver Springs Road, Lafayette, CA 94549 (telephone: 415-283-1365).

In addition to health insurance, or as part of it, your employer may provide disability insurance, which pays a fixed sum per day or per week while you cannot work and which can be used to pay for treatment and/or hospitalization.

Another form of private insurance is the prepaid health plan, or health maintenance organization (HMO). All HMOs are by law required to provide mental health care, but the actual coverage and provision varies. The basic difference between HMOs and other health insurance is that here the insurer and provider are one and the same. In 1981 HMOs were among the least expensive forms of private health insurance and their number was growing rapidly. Nevertheless, they are not available everywhere. To get information about an HMO in your area, write to the Promotion Division, Office of Health Maintenance Organizations, Department of Health and Human Services, Park Building, Room 3-32, 12420 Parklawn Drive, Rockville, MD 20857, or in the city nearest you among the following: Boston, New York, Philadelphia, Atlanta, Chicago, Dallas, Kansas City, Denver, San Francisco, Seattle.

PUBLIC INSURANCE (MEDICARE AND MEDICAID)

There are two main forms of public (government) health insurance, Medicare and Medicaid, and two forms of disability insurance, Social Security and Supplemental Security Income. (In addition, armed services personnel and their dependents have special insurance, also described below.)

Medicare is a federal health insurance program run by the Social Security Administration for persons who are sixty-five or older and for some persons under sixty-five who are disabled. Medicare pays a portion of some medical expenses and has two parts, hospital insurance (Part A) and medical insurance (Part B). Hospital insurance is financed by contributions from employers, employees, and the self-employed, and is free to anyone eligible for Medicare. Medical insurance is financed through monthly premiums paid by those who wish to have it. People over sixty-five who have not worked long enough to be entitled to Medicare hospital insurance can buy this protection by paying a monthly premium, but they must then buy both hospital and medical insurance.

You may apply for Medicare three months before you turn sixty-five. If you don't apply within three months before or after that date you may not apply again until the next general enrollment period, January 1 through March 31 of each year. Also, you pay a penalty for not enrolling at sixty-five, not only in lost benefits but in the form of a higher premium.

As of January 1981, Medicare covered up to ninety days of inpatient care in any participating hospital in each benefit period. For the first sixty days it covered all costs except the first $180; for days sixty-one through ninety it covered all but $45 per day. However, there was a lifetime limit of 190 days' care in a mental hospital. In addition, Medicare covered up to 100 days in a participating skilled nursing home, and up to 100 home visits from a home health agency.

Medicare medical insurance, which in 1981 was available for a premium of less than $10 per month, covered 80 percent of covered medical costs per year (after the first $60). Included were all physician services, outpatient hospital services for diagnosis, treatment in an emergency room or hospital outpatient clinic, up to 100 home health visits per year, outpatient physical or speech therapy, and any other treatment prescribed by a physician. In addition, persons eligible for Medicare could buy *Medex* insurance, offered by Blue Cross/Blue Shield to pay the deductibles of Medicare and to lengthen the number of days of hospital coverage to 365.

Although Medicare sounds like wonderful coverage for mental health care for the elderly, there is a catch. Medicare will pay only "reasonable charges," and exactly what constitutes reasonable is decided by the carrier, that is, the organization selected by the Social Security Administration to handle claims. In 1981 that was Blue Cross/Blue Shield.

Medicaid is a medical assistance program for needy and low-income persons supported by federal, state, and county taxes. In most states the Medicaid program is administered by the state department of public welfare through local welfare offices. The program pays for doctor's fees, inpatient or outpatient hospital care, laboratory tests, X-rays, care in a skilled nursing home, and sometimes adult day care and prescription drugs. Anyone receiving Supplemental Security Income (SSI; see below) is automatically covered by Medicaid. To find out if you are eligible for Medicaid, you must contact your local welfare office. Some individuals are eligible for both Medicare and Medicaid.

How easy it is to obtain Medicaid varies widely. In some county welfare offices it is readily available to many individuals; in others one must be virtually without funds and wholly unable to work. Even if you can get Medicaid there is a catch. It covers all charges from qualified providers but it pays practitioners and facilities considerably less than their normal fees, so many will not accept Medicaid clients. (In contrast, most practitioners and facilities do accept Medicare.)

If you expect Medicare or Medicaid to pay for your hospital costs, you must tell the business office of the hospital immediately upon admission. Often the hospital must first consult with the state before filing a claim to be paid, which takes time. Therefore you may have insurance and still not be reimbursed for your hospital bill simply because you did not inform the hospital of your coverage soon enough.

SOCIAL SECURITY AND SSI

If you are a severely disabled worker of any age, with a physical or mental condition that will prevent you from working for at least one year (or that is expected to result in death), you may be entitled to disability pay from the Social Security Administration. The amount will meet most of the medical and some of the living expenses of those who qualify. In order to qualify you must have worked and had Social Security payments withheld from your paycheck for a certain period of time (usually five of the previous ten years, but the law may have changed by the time you read this). If you do not qualify under Social Security you may be able to obtain Supplemental Security Income (see below).

If you are disabled, certain members of your family also can receive benefits from Social Security: unmarried children under eighteen (under twenty-two if they are full-time students), disabled children eighteen or over if they were disabled before the age of twenty-two, or your spouse if he/she is sixty-two or older. A person disabled before he/she could work long enough to build up Social Security benefits may be eligible for benefits based on his/her parents' Social Security contributions, beginning either when they reach sixty-five or at their death. Such benefits may be applied for at any age, and they continue for the duration of the disability; they do not stop with the parent's death, and they are available for adopted children as well.

If you are divorced, you may be eligible for benefits as a dependent of your ex-spouse if you were married for ten years or longer. A divorced and disabled wife who survives a worker to whom she was married for ten years or more becomes eligible for benefits at the age of fifty.

For all these forms of disability and survivors Social Security, apply at your nearest Social Security office (see your phone book) as soon as disability or death has occurred. Go either in person or telephone and ask to have an application mailed to you. For disability benefits you need a letter from your physician and you also must give the Social Security office your physician's name, address, phone number, and a list of the dates when you saw the physician. Disability pensions may be discontinued if you return to work, even on a part-time basis, but sometimes allowances are made.

Supplemental Security Income (SSI) is a federal program that pays a monthly check to individuals in financial need who either are sixty-five or older or are, at any age, blind or disabled. Most states add to the amount that the Federal government provides. You can get SSI even if you have never worked, or if you have some assets in the form of savings accounts, stocks or bonds, or jewelry or other valuables, provided that those assets do not exceed a certain amount (in January, 1981, that amount was $1,500 for a single person and $2,250 for a married couple). A house, personal effects, or household goods usually do not count as assets, and insurance policies or a car may not either, depending on their value. You may earn some income and still get SSI; in 1981 you could earn up to $65 a month; after that you got $1 less SSI for every $2 over $65 earned in one month. You also may have unearned income (Social Security, interest on savings accounts, dividends, veterans' compensation, workers' compensation, pensions, annuities, gifts). The first $20 a month of unearned income usually does not reduce the amount of SSI awarded. However, living in the home of a relative may reduce it. SSI includes Medicaid medical insurance (see above) but does not provide survivors' benefits, that is, the children, widow or other dependents of a person receiving SSI do not continue to receive money after that person's death. In order to apply for SSI, call your local Social Security Administration office.

You need both persistence and patience in dealing with Social Security offices. If you telephone, you may have to try many times to get a free line. The best times to get through are early in the morning or early in the afternoon, and late in the month. If you decide to go in person, be prepared to wait, possibly for several hours. Bring something to read and a snack. Be sure to bring all relevant papers and documents: any correspondence you may have had with the Social Security Administration, information about your doctor (name, address, phone number, dates when you saw the doctor), and a letter from the doctor confirming your disability.

Whether you telephone or go in person, be sure to make a note of the name of the person you speak with; it may be relevant if there are misunderstandings. Do not ignore any correspondence from Social Security. If you're not sure what a letter means, telephone the person who wrote it. If you don't answer a letter, your claim may be denied on grounds of "lack of cooperation."

When people are considered disabled because of mental illness, a question arises concerning their ability to handle their own finances. If the Social Security Administration determines that they are incapable of handling their own funds (a determination usually made by a psychiatrist), someone else—usually a relative or a friend but sometimes the director of an inpatient facility, such as a hospital or halfway house—becomes the "representative payee" and the checks are made out to that person. If the ill person is hospitalized, the representative payee usually turns the check over to the hospital; if it is a state or county hospital, in some places the check may be turned over to the state office of mental health or to whatever department in that state administers hospital bills.

Bear in mind that laws and regulations governing Social Security and SSI change, and interpretations of them differ. The best source of information is the frequently updated *Social Security Manual,* which is available at some larger Social Security offices or can be obtained from the Superintendent of Documents, U.S. Government Printing Office, Washington, DC 20402.

Members of the armed forces are treated free of charge while they are in the service for any physical or mental illness, and after discharge for any service-connected conditions (see under VA clinics, Chapter 10). While they are in the service their families are covered by the most comprehensive American insurance plan in existence for both physical and mental illness. Called CHAMPUS (for Civilian Health and Medical Program of the Uniformed Services), it allowed (in 1981) 120 days of hospital care for mental illness per year, and 60 outpatient visits per year. After discharge or retirement, CHAMPUS benefits end. However, a retired member of the armed forces who is entitled to retirement pay may apply for the Survivor Benefit Plan, in order to plan for caring for a disabled child, spouse, or other family member after his/her own death.

THIRD-PARTY PAYMENTS AND CONFIDENTIALITY

According to statements made in 1981 by psychiatrists and psychologists connected with such organizations as the National Institute of Mental Health and the American Psychiatric Association's Committee on Confidentiality, thousands of men and women pay for mental health care out of their own pockets instead of applying for mental health insurance coverage provided through their employers because they fear the consequences of admitting they have an emotional problem at their place of employment. One estimate stated that 15 percent of all adults who have such insurance and are currently in therapy waive reimbursement for this reason. And, of course, countless others forego treatment entirely rather than let their employers or colleagues know they are using their mental health benefits. They feel disclosure is too high a price. The same is true in the military, especially for career officers, who fear they will not be promoted if their superiors learn they have emotional problems.

Another source of concern is the security of information that is provided to the insurance companies in the course of making claims. This information is necessarily used by the insurers and, sometimes, by outsiders for purposes of claims review or legitimate research. Yet unrestricted access to diagnoses—and one must, after all, state what a claim is for—can cause serious problems for patients if the information is widely circulated.

Some psychiatrists try to protect their patients by deliberately falsifying diagnoses on claims forms. A recent study compared several thousand actual insurance claims for psychiatric care against diagnoses recorded in psychiatrists' private files in the same geographic area during the same time period. The results revealed that when patients' names were reported (as they were in the claims), about 84 percent were diagnosed as neurotic, whereas when the patients' identities were concealed (in the information taken from the files) only about 28 percent were so diagnosed and the rest were diagnosed as having much more serious illnesses, such as schizophrenia.

One aid to greater confidentiality is for businesses offering health insurance to have claims sent direct to the insurer rather than being channeled through company personnel offices. Another, of course, is to educate the public so as to eliminate what has been called "mentalism," that is, the unreasonable fear of and prejudice against mental patients.

FINANCIAL HELP FROM OTHER AGENCIES

A variety of state and local agencies may directly and indirectly help pay some of the costs of mental health care. The trouble is that they are often hard to track down, and the services may be fragmented among several agencies. Free transportation to and from treatment and health care centers may be available, for example, as may special education courses of various kinds. The best source of such information is a knowledgeable local social worker. You may find such a social worker on the hospital staff or through the community mental health center or a social agency such as a family service agency.

Another source of valuable information and help is your state or federal *vocational rehabilitation office*. The state offices usually operate a unit in every state mental hospital; the federal unit nearest you can be found through the phone book (look in the United States government section). These offices provide a wide range of services, including a physical examination to determine fitness for employment, counseling and testing to determine vocational aptitudes, job training (a huge area, including personal adjustment training, prevocational and vocational training for specific fields, sheltered workshops, and on-the-job training), transportation to and from these services, and job placement. The evaluation, counseling, and placement all are free of charge, but there may be fees for job training and/or medical services, depending on economic need (fees are based on what clients can afford).

TYPICAL CHARGES FOR MENTAL HEALTH CARE

The fees charged for outpatient psychotherapy vary widely. In general, psychiatrists charge more than psychologists, who usually charge more than social workers and psychiatric nurses. However, this differential may be offset (or canceled out) by the fact that insurance coverage may be limited to psychiatrists, or to psychiatrists and psychologists, and not pay a penny toward therapy by a social worker or nurse.

Therapists in private practice may adjust their fees to the client's ability to pay—some do and some don't—but the reduction is rarely very great, usually no more than 15 or 20 percent. If you like the therapist but can't afford the fee, ask if it is negotiable. The worst you can get is a negative reply.

In general, clinics may charge less than private practitioners. Training institutes or the outpatient clinics of teaching hospitals, where therapists may be students (trainees or residents), may be cheaper yet. However, the name "clinic" does not guarantee a lower fee; some private clinics are very expensive. The lowest fees are those charged by community mental health centers, which are supported by local, state, and federal government funds, as well as by third-party (insurance) payments and grants and fees. They must by law consider the client's ability to pay, and they cannot refuse treatment on that ground alone.

Hospitalization in the psychiatric unit of a general hospital costs, on the average, twice as much as in a private mental hospital, but again, the difference may be offset or canceled by the fact that insurance may cover much or all of the former and little or nothing of the latter. Most private mental hospitals do not accept Medicaid inpatients. In 1982 their average charge per day was $200 (excluding professional fees).

State and county mental hospitals must accept Medicaid patients but are not, contrary to popular opinion, totally free of charge. They collect as much as they can from their patients, and also from private insurance companies and Medicaid. For patients who have no insurance but do have financial assets of one kind or another, the hospital may charge a fee based on its judgment of what the patient can afford. Moreover, in most states certain relatives of patients are legally liable for paying the costs of hospitalization, or at least for as much as they can afford. In New York State in 1981, for example, husbands or wives were legally liable for the hospital costs of their spouse, but parents and children were not. In other states, parents and adult children, as well as the spouse, were liable, and in some states the law was altogether unclear. When relatives are so liable, they must pay as long as they (or the guardians of their estate) can do so, even out of a pension or Social Security payment.

REPRESENTATIVE COSTS OF PSYCHOTHERAPY*

Kind of Therapy	Range of Cost per Session	Average Frequency and Duration	Total Cost
Psychoanalysis	$40 to $125 (less with trainees)	4 times a week for 4 years	$57,600
Insight or Analytic Therapy	$30 to $100	1.5 times a week for 2 years	$8,640
Jungian Therapy	$60 to $100 (less at training institutes)	1.5 times a week for 1 year	$5,760 (one-third that at institutes)
Adlerian Therapy	$18 to $40	Once a week for 5 years	$7,200
Client-centered (Rogerian) Therapy	$30 to $100†	Once a week for 2 years†	$6,240
Gestalt Therapy	$25 to $65 (less with trainees or in workshops)	Once a week for 1 year	$2,160 (one-fourth that with a trainee)
Bioenergetics	$25 to $100	Weekly or biweekly for 1 to 2 years	$2,880
Psychodrama	$15 to $30 per person	Once a week for 15 months	$1,200

REPRESENTATIVE COSTS OF PSYCHOTHERAPY*

Kind of Therapy	Range of Cost per Session	Average Frequency and Duration	Total Cost
Traditional Group Therapy	$20 per person (less in clinics)	Once a week for 1 year	$1,200
Family Therapy	$40 to $75 per family (less in clinics)	Once a week for 6 months	$1,300
Transactional Analysis (T.A.)	$20 per person in group (more for individual)	Once a week for 2 years	$1,920
Cognitive Therapy	$12.50 per person in group ($20 to $50, individual)	Once a week for 9 months (individual, weekly for 24 weeks)	$450 (group) ($840)
Behavior Therapy	$20 to $120 (groups, $20 to $30 per person)	1.5 times a week for 4 months	$420
Biofeedback	$130 for two initial sessions, $55 to $75 thereafter	Once a week for 12 weeks	$800

*Prices represent overall national range and may be much higher or lower in individual areas. Quoted as of October 1981.

†Most often individually negotiated, based on client needs, and therefore extremely variable.

In order to find out the law in your state, investigate at your county courthouse and also discuss your finances with the hospital business office.

The costs of partial hospitalization—day care, night care, halfway houses, etc.—are a gray area. Some private plans treat it the same as full-time hospitalization. Most do not. In general, if it is under the auspices of a community mental health center, it will be covered as outpatient care; if it is administered by a county or state hospital it is likely to be covered as inpatient care. A private facility, on the other hand, may receive little or no coverage.

Nursing homes or extended care facilities nearly always accept Medicare patients but may or may not accept Medicaid. Medicare will pay for a skilled nursing facility provided the patient meets a series of other qualifications. The charges of nursing homes vary widely, from very expensive to quite cheap, and so does the quality of care (see Chapter 17).

Some private insurance policies do cover extended care facilities.

TIPS FOR CUTTING MENTAL HEALTH CARE COSTS

Here are a few ways in which you can reduce costs for mental health care:

- For psychotherapy, consider using a teaching hospital clinic or a community mental health center.
- If psychoactive drugs are prescribed, keep a list of medications that have been effective for you in the past; make sure your prescription is labeled and write on the label the reason for taking this drug (you may be able to use it again); shop around for prescriptions (prices vary considerably); ask your doctor to prescribe by generic name instead of brand name if possible; don't buy from a hospital pharmacy unless it's an HMO pharmacy (hospital drugstore prices tend to be higher); buy in bulk—a six-month supply at a time—if your physician approves.
- If you are hospitalized, check your charges in advance so you know how much to expect; check your bill carefully to make sure your length of stay was the same as you are charged for, and to

make sure you actually received the services you are being charged for.

- If you decide to leave the hospital against medical advice, check with your insurance company to make sure they will still cover your bill.
- Deduct the cost of treatment from your federal income tax (and possibly also your state income tax). It counts as a medical expense, that is, money paid for preventing, treating, and alleviating diseases or disabilities of a taxpayer and his/her dependents. You may deduct the costs of: psychotherapy by a psychiatrist or psychologist (or others if supervised by one of these professionals); special schooling for an emotionally disturbed or otherwise handicapped child; transportation to and from such a school; sheltered workshops, a group home, partial hospitalization, or other housing if a physician orders it as a transition to normal life; diagnostic tests and evaluations; prescribed medication (in excess of 1 percent of income), including drugs, vitamins, etc.; special instruction and training; half your premium for medical insurance; a certain amount of "child care" for a disabled relative (child or adult) in your home who needs supervision while you are at work. Tax laws change frequently, and specific allowances are periodically adjusted for inflation, so be sure to check with your local Internal Revenue Service office for details. Be sure to itemize and record all such expenses, and keep with them dated and signed notes from physicians and other professionals recommending the services whose costs you may wish to deduct.

CHAPTER 21

Staying Healthy—Preventive Mental Health Care

Once the cause of a specific illness is known, there is a fairly good chance that researchers will discover not only a cure for it but a means of preventing it entirely. This, at least, has been the case with numerous infectious diseases—whooping cough, measles, diphtheria—that have been virtually wiped out by means of widespread immunization, and it may soon be the case for cancer. It may also one day be true for mental illnesses, but that time has not yet arrived. The causes of only a few disorders—mainly those involving organic brain disease—are known, and we cannot always prevent their occurrence. We do know, however, that there is increased *risk* of developing a mental illness for certain individuals or under certain conditions.

As with physical illness, the greatest risk is for those who are weakest: the very young, the very old, the convalescent (recovering from mental illness), and those who are undergoing a major life stress or who live in an unhealthy and stressful environment (the poor). Also like physical illness, the best chance of preventing serious mental illness is early detection, early intervention, and early treatment.

INHERITED DISORDERS

Some mental disorders, either the illness itself or, more often, a predisposition toward developing it, are genetically transmitted.

When one or both parents are found to carry a predisposition or an actual defective trait, *genetic counseling* can be used to determine the probability of transmitting the disorder to a child and consider the various options available. For example, if the husband carries the defect, the wife may be inseminated artificially, using a donor's sperm. For certain disorders, blood and urine tests can determine if either parent is a carrier. For others, there may be no such evidence, but the strong possibility of transmitting a very serious disorder, such as Huntington's chorea, for which no cure is known, may be a deterrent to childbearing. Similarly, when both husband and wife have (or have had) schizophrenia, there is a sizable risk (50 to 68 percent) that their children also will develop the disease.

Some disorders or defects can be detected during pregnancy by testing the amniotic fluid surrounding the fetus. With those a decision can be postponed until that procedure, called *amniocentesis,* reveals whether or not a defect actually has been transmitted. Amniocentesis can be used to detect chromosomal defects associated with mental retardation, such as Down's syndrome and fragile X chromosome, and certain inborn metabolic disorders, some of which can actually be treated *before* birth.

PRENATAL PREVENTIVE CARE

Some forms of mental disorder result from inadequate protection of the brain and nervous system during its early development in the womb. There is a clear relationship between lack of medical attention to a pregnant woman and her risk of bearing a child with a mental disorder such as retardation. Comprehensive prenatal care, with especially close attention to high-risk pregnancies (teenagers, women thirty-five or older, women with certain chronic diseases such as diabetes, and Rh blood incompatibility), can help lower the risk significantly.

The pregnant woman's diet can affect her baby. Inadequate amounts of vitamins and minerals or lack of protein can cause abnormalities in the baby's development. Her alcohol intake must be limited (some authorities say eliminated entirely). Too much can cause the baby to develop fetal alcohol syndrome, which can result in various growth deficiencies and retardation. There is definite risk to a baby whose mother has six drinks (9 ounces) of alcohol a day, and recent research indicates that even more than two drinks (3 ounces) is inadvisable.

During pregnancy certain infectious diseases can harm the baby. The best known is rubella (German measles), for which immunization (by vaccine) has been available since 1969. Any woman considering pregnancy who has not already had rubella should be immunized against it and put off conception for at least four months after vaccination (to make sure that the virus, present in the vaccine, is out of her system). Rubella can cause irreversible brain damage in the baby, as well as other serious abnormalities.

Toxoplasmosis, a flu-like illness caused by a parasite transmitted through rare or raw meat and also through the feces of domestic cats, can cause severe retardation in babies whose mothers are infected during pregnancy. A blood test before pregnancy can determine if a woman is immune; if she is not, she should avoid eating rare or raw meat and handling cat litter boxes during pregnancy.

Active genital herpes infection, a viral disease that can be sexually transmitted, may be deadly to the fetus and newborn. Some 75 percent of the babies that do survive suffer neurological damage and, often, retardation. No cure is known, but if active disease is detected in the mother before birth, a Caesarean delivery is advisable so that the baby cannot be infected during its passage through the birth canal.

PREVENTIVE CARE FOR THE VERY YOUNG

Even with careful prenatal care, some babies are at risk for conditions that can be detected only after birth. Screening at birth for one metabolic defect, phenylketonuria (PKU), now mandated by law in many localities, makes it possible to treat a baby by means of diet from infancy on, preventing brain damage. A simple blood test performed at birth for hypothyroidism (thyroid hormone deficiency) enables immediate treatment of the baby with thyroxin

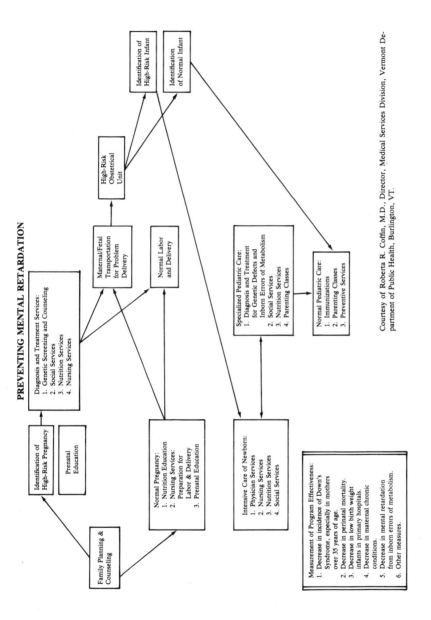

PREVENTING MENTAL RETARDATION

Courtesy of Roberta R. Coffin, M.D., Director, Medical Services Division, Vermont Department of Public Health, Burlington, VT.

and thus helps prevent cretinism, a form of retardation caused by this deficiency.

Early detection and intervention are particularly useful for babies born of diabetic mothers, who are at risk for hydrocephalus and other abnormalities that benefit from prompt treatment, as well as for babies of alcoholics and drug abusers, who may be born addicted and suffer from withdrawal symptoms.

Proper nutrition for the mother who is breast-feeding and for the baby throughout infancy and early childhood may prevent developmental abnormalities in the brain and nervous system that contribute to mental defects. The removal or avoidance of environmental hazards like lead (in lead-based paint) is also important; the consumption of lead by small children can cause brain damage. A simple blood test, the FEP (free erythrocyte proptoporphyrin) test, can be used to screen large numbers of children for lead poisoning and ensure early treatment of those who are ill.

Although all these measures may seem obvious, the President's Commission on Mental Health reported in April 1978 that nearly one-third of all pregnant women in the United States receive *no* prenatal care during the first three months of pregnancy, when the risk for the baby is highest. The Commission proposed expanded early prenatal care, as well as two other measures for preventive mental health care for youngsters: (1) more and better day care for children of working parents, with greater emphasis on children's mental and emotional development; and (2) periodic, comprehensive assessments of developmental status for every child (subject to parental consent), so that problems that might lead to emotional maladjustment or learning difficulties could be detected and treated early.

Along these lines, one community mental health center now has an Early Intervention Program to serve children under the age of thirty-six months who are lagging behind in walking, talking, or other areas; who are overly active or passive; who are born with cerebral palsy, Down's syndrome, or other developmental handicaps; who have problems with sleeping, eating, or toilet training; or who need help in learning to play with other children. After an evaluation period, the center offers a variety of services for such children and their parents. They include home visits by a specially trained teacher who brings selected materials to help a child with motor, language, and intellectual development; small groups for infants in a class setting with parent participation for learning of stimulation techniques; education and support groups for parents; small classes for toddlers to develop both individual and social skills; and help in locating and obtaining other community resources and services for special needs children under the age of three.

CHILDREN AT RISK FOR MAJOR PSYCHIATRIC ILLNESS

Schizophrenia, major depression, and manic-depressive disease all are believed to involve genetic factors, which also are suspected in antisocial personality disorders, alcoholism, and panic disorder (acute anxiety). A child with one schizophrenic parent has a 4 to 10 percent risk* of developing schizophrenia (as opposed to 1 percent for the general population). That risk can rise with stress from disease, trauma, difficulties in the family, or other factors.

Such youngsters often show early signs of poor function, in the form of deficits in fine motor development, visual and motor coordination, and other neurological development. For families known to be at risk for transmitting such a susceptibility, genetic counseling, a careful examination of each child at the time of birth, and frequent pediatric evaluation of the children allows the possibility of early intervention, such as therapeutic nursery care and special language programs (for children showing delayed language development).

PREVENTIVE CARE FOR THE ELDERLY

The mental disorders of old age are not well understood either, but definite correlations have been discovered between symptoms of

---

*Some say 10 to 15 percent. With two parents it is 50 to 68 percent.

senility and such factors as hormone deficiency, poor nutrition, depression, and social isolation. Further, minor illnesses, chronic illnesses, or even a drastic change in environment can in older persons give rise to symptoms of senile dementia. A recent study found that 35 percent of a group of patients originally believed to have irreversible senile dementia actually had a treatable and reversible medical or psychiatric disorder.

Many, if not most, older persons suffer from one or another chronic physical problem that requires medication. However, an older person's body metabolizes drugs quite differently from younger individuals. Tranquilizers, barbiturates and other sleep medications, mood-altering drugs, and diuretic-type drugs used to treat high blood pressure and heart disease are common causes of dementia symptoms that often can be eliminated simply by reducing the dosage or altering the medication.

Depression, especially in reaction to loss, is common in the elderly and sometimes takes the form of senility symptoms. Many elderly persons suffer two important kinds of loss: the death of friends and relatives, and impaired health. Often handicaps in sight or hearing and difficulty in walking prevent older people from going out much, as well as from engaging in their usual indoor activities (reading, sewing, listening to music, watching television). These constraints limit their lives. Too often such individuals end up in nursing homes or long-term care institutions where their mental health degenerates even more.

Home Care

Comprehensive health care, including nutritional and other services, often can prevent such degeneration by enabling the elderly to remain in their own homes. Traditionally such services were provided by family members, but today, with families often scattered across the country, and with more and more old people outliving many of their relatives, this is no longer feasible.

In some areas community mental health centers are able to provide needed services, and in others the slack has been taken up by a relatively recent innovation, the home care corporation, usually administered under a system established by the state department of elder affairs (known by a variety of names in different states). For example, Massachusetts had, in 1981, twenty-seven independent nonprofit home corporations, each serving its own region. Some services were provided directly by the corporation staff, and others were purchased from providers in the various communities. One home care corporation offered the following services:

- Information and referral, providing answers to most questions of concern to persons sixty years of age or older. This service included a brief interview to determine a person's need for services, referral to the appropriate resource, and followup to make sure the service was rendered.
- Home care, coordinated by a case manager assigned to each elderly client to obtain services designed to enable him/her to continue living at home, and periodically re-evaluate them as circumstances changed. Among them were homemaker service (for food shopping, personal errands, light housekeeping, laundry, and meal preparation); chore service (heavy cleaning and minor household repairs); home-delivered meals ("meals on wheels") for homebound elders unable to prepare their own meals; and companionship (regular visits by volunteers to isolated elders).
- Nutrition, providing a hot noon meal and a full schedule of activities to anyone over sixty at various central locations in the area.
- Transportation services, including rides for out-of-town medical and social service appointments (when no other means of transport were available) and to and from nutrition (noon meal) sites.
- Protective services, working with other agencies to provide immediate help for elders in crisis or those being abused or neglected, with a social worker coordinating help from medical, legal, and mental health agencies.
- Legal aid, providing counsel to elders through referral to the Senior Citizens Law Project.
- Planning, including identifying the most pressing needs of older residents in the area and creating a plan to coordinate community resources to meet those needs.

Under this excellent system, a case worker is sent to see any person over sixty who phones for help or for whom assistance is requested by the family, a hospital, or some other social agency. Most of the clients have a serious physical handicap, such as severe arthritis, but often they exhibit emotional distress as well, caused by anxiety over economic problems (rising fuel bills, for instance) and increasingly limited physical ability.

A major service provided is a day health center, which can be used by any adult (sixteen years of age or older) whose medical or psychosocial condition indicates a need for nursing care, supervision, or therapeutic services as an *alternative* to institutional placement. The day center accepts both Medicaid and private-paying participants, and requires only that a person be willing to attend a minimum of two six-hour days a week. The program, open from 9 A.M. to 3 P.M. every weekday, provides health care monitoring and supervision by a registered nurse (in collaboration with the client's own physician); personal care services; physical, occupational, and speech therapy; a hot lunch and two snacks; social, recreational, and educational activities; transport to and from the program; and referrals to and coordination of community health and social services with counseling for participants and their families.

Home care services in other states may not yet be so widespread or highly developed. With a rapidly rising elderly population, however, and the realization that institutional placement is regarded by most elderly persons and their families as a desperate last resort, home care is both less expensive and far more desirable.

PREVENTIVE CARE FOR FORMER PATIENTS

Effective aftercare for persons who were hospitalized for mental illness is a significant factor in preventing relapse and readmission to the hospital. With the emphasis today on brief hospitalization and a rapid return to the community, there has been an enormous increase in the "revolving door" syndrome—that is, patients are discharged from the hospital only to require readmittance within a few months. Estimates vary, but most studies indicate that 50 to 60 percent of patients are rehospitalized within nine months of discharge.

A coordinated transition from hospital to community is extremely important to adjustment, yet it is often the weakest link in the aftercare chain. Without vigorous efforts to familiarize patients with community treatment facilities, they often get no aftercare whatever. Personal contact appears to be vital. Aggressive planning before hospital discharge, in which the patient can see the aftercare facility (day hospital, community mental health center, etc.) and meet the new therapist in charge, as well as careful followup to make sure the patient actually carries out the agreed-on plan, are essential. (The various forms of partial hospitalization that can be used in this transition are described in Chapter 17.) In addition, most studies indicate that keeping up sufficient medication and maintaining psychotherapy of some kind after discharge significantly reduce the rate of relapse. Self-help groups such as Recovery, Inc. (see Chapter 11) also are useful, particularly when used in conjunction with other forms of aftercare.

Returning to Work

Vocational rehabilitation is an important and often underrated element in aftercare. Obtaining employment after a mental illness, particularly after hospitalization, may be very difficult. As indicated earlier, mental illness is a stigma, and some employers are unwilling to hire former patients. The help of both a vocational counselor and a therapist can be useful in advising a person about the problems of a particular job and making recommendations to particular employers. The person's own expectations also play a role. An individual who is ashamed of his/her past illness or who expects employer discrimination may back away from a promising position and drift into marginal, ill-paid work that suits his/her low self-esteem more than his/her actual abilities and training.

An excellent guide for returning to work after a mental illness is *A Bright Future: Your Guide to Work,* available free from your local Mental Health Association or from the National Association for Mental Health, 1800 North Kent Street, Arlington, VA 22209, or the President's Committee on Employment of the Handicapped, 1111 20th Street, NW, Washington, DC 20210. It answers such important questions as what to tell a prospective employer about having been treated for mental illness, where to go for job referrals, and how to behave at a job interview, as well as listing the addresses of agencies in every state that can be of assistance in finding a job.

FOR THOSE IN TROUBLE WITH THE LAW

With those forms of illness that lead to antisocial behavior of one kind or another, specifically criminal offenses and drug abuse, psychotherapy in a court clinic or correctional facility represents a kind of preventive mental health care. In some states court clinics provide evaluation and treatment for offenders, and they also may provide training in counseling for correction officers and prison guards (see also Chapter 22).

Nearly all of the states provide some form of psychiatric treatment in their prisons. However, the number of professional mental health workers in relation to the prison population is so small and their other administrative chores are so numerous that in practice very few prisoners have access to the services of a counselor.

The most promising group in terms of prevention would seem to be juvenile offenders. The findings of a recent report indicate that juvenile offenders—that is, anyone under the age of eighteen—may receive mental health services at one or more points, the most common of which are: at intake, after the filing of a delinquency petition but before a court hearing (to determine the youngster's competency to proceed with the hearing); after the hearing (to help the court determine how to settle the case); after a judicial opinion or sentence has been pronounced (in place of disposition, usually taking the form of civil commitment to a mental health facility); and following the court's disposition (for example, as a condition of parole).

Although it sounds as though juvenile offenders might receive considerable mental health services all along the line, in practice such services may consist of a single interview with a psychiatrist to determine competency rather than an extended period of individual or group therapy addressed to sorting out a youngster's emotional problems and preventing recurrence of antisocial behavior.

For young drug abusers, experience with drop-in centers for young people on drugs indicates that such facilities may attract more youngsters than hospital-based or other "establishment" clinics, even when they are staffed by the same personnel (principally social workers and physicians). For both drug and alcohol dependency, which tend to have extremely high rates of relapse, self-help groups may help prevent "backsliding" for those individuals who are willing and able to use them.

COPING WITH LIFE CRISES

Certain stressful experiences are almost universal, and it has been found that programs can be designed to teach people to cope with them more effectively. The reduction of stress associated with these experiences lowers the likelihood of serious emotional problems. Included among such experiences are a child's admission to a hospital; separation of parent from child (even for a short period); death of a family member or a close friend; a serious illness or major surgery (especially open-heart surgery); the struggles of adolescence, marriage, pregnancy, child rearing, middle age, and old age; separation and divorce; loss of a job, prolonged unemployment, and retirement. Careful preparation for effective handling of critical situations and prompt intervention when an emotional crisis does develop may prevent future problems.

Crisis Intervention

Telephone hot lines for individuals in various kinds of life crisis have sprung up all over the country in recent years. The most dramatic crisis they deal with is threats of suicide, but there also are hot lines for child abuse and other violence directed toward others.

They can be located through the phone book. (See Chapter 2 for more specific information.)

Often a telephone hot line is a strictly local service, established and staffed by concerned professionals and/or volunteers in a particular city or town. One hot line, CONTACT, is a national network (in turn a member of Life Line International, consisting of similar "teleministries" in other countries). By mid-1981 there were 104 CONTACT centers in the United States. Each is an autonomous community service linked with the national network. It provides 24-hour-a-day direct access by phone to trained lay volunteers who wait at a central location and do nothing but respond to callers.

Each CONTACT volunteer is required to have fifty hours of training in counseling, which is provided in weekly sessions over several months. Training sessions are devoted to such subjects as personality theory; empathic listening; substance abuse; crisis theory; improving listening skills; dealing with loss, dying and grief; human sexuality; and suicide prevention. Callers may remain anonymous if they wish. The service is used by more than 1.3 million persons a year, who call for a variety of reasons. At least 30 percent of the calls directly concern mental-health or emotional problems.

In 1966 the federal government created the Center for Studies of Suicide Prevention at the National Institute of Mental Health (NIMH); later it became the Section on Disaster Assistance and Emergency Mental Health. Advice for communities and groups that wish to start suicide prevention centers is available free from this agency. It strongly recommends that a center have both a 24-hour phone service and the availability of professional backup and consultation. The best centers form part of a community network, so that the ideal program, according to NIMH, includes emergency mental health services (including suicide prevention), partial hospitalization, full hospitalization, outpatient counseling, and education and consultation services available to the entire community.

Reducing Stress

A booklet published in 1980 by the National Mental Health Association, *How to Deal with Your Tensions*, recommends a number of specific steps for anyone who is unusually tense and anxious. They include:

- Talk it out (with a relative, friend, doctor, minister, anyone).
- Escape for a while (with a book, movie, brief trip).
- Work off your anger and tension in vigorous physical activity.
- Give in occasionally; if you have frequent quarrels, make allowance for the fact that you *could* be wrong.
- Do something for others.
- Take one thing at a time.
- Don't expect too much of yourself.
- Go easy with criticism of others.
- Let up on your competitive urge.
- Make yourself available to others.
- Schedule your recreation.

Not everyone has a friend or relative or doctor to confide in. For many, however, a support group made up of other individuals with the same or a similar problem can be extremely helpful. Such support groups have been organized by family service agencies, mental health clinics, churches, and numerous other organizations. Sometimes they have been formed by putting up a notice on the bulletin board of a local library or grocery store, or putting an ad in the local paper.

For example, in the spring of 1981 the Family Service Association of Greater Boston offered the following programs:

- A ten-week workshop in career planning for women, with such topics as vocational testing and job resources, locating a job (openings and training programs), applications, resumes and interviews, tips for job advancement, and child care arrangements for working mothers.
- An eight-week workshop in assertiveness training, including the difference between assertion, non-assertion, and aggression, how to feel comfortable asserting your rights, what prevents assertiveness, and special areas in which you can be more assertive.
- A six-week workshop in stress management, including how to

define stress, good and bad stress, stress on the job, and stress management techniques.
- A one-day workshop on self-esteem for women, addressing such issues as how and why women put themselves down, and ways to build self-confidence.
- A six-week workshop on preschool books as a parenting aid (with child care provided during sessions), on how to understand and communicate with your child through books, how to pick the right books for your child, and how to use books to communicate with your child about feelings.

In addition to groups for mental patients, alcoholics and drug addicts, the self-help movement has given rise to numerous support groups for individuals coping with life stresses: Reach to Recovery (after a mastectomy), Parents without Partners (with nearly 1,000 active chapters in the United States and Canada), the La Leche League for breast-feeding women, Widows Helping Widows, groups for parents of children with physical and/or emotional handicaps, as well as groups for parents whose children have died (The Foundation for Sudden Infant Death and the Society of the Compassionate Friends). See Chapter 11 for how to find a self-help group.

Divorce Mediation

With nearly one-half of all marriages now ending in divorce, the life crises of separation and divorce have become commonplace, but how they are handled has a direct bearing on the mental health of the family members concerned.

Divorce mediation is a relatively new area of counseling that offers both crisis intervention and support. Mediation by an experienced and neutral person provides the opportunity for husband and wife to work out the terms of an agreement over such issues as custody, visitation, co-parenting, the present and future needs of children, financial arrangements, and division of property. In this process, the anger and conflict associated with separation and divorce may be significantly reduced, minimizing the disruption in the lives of all family members, particularly the children. For families with children, divorce mediators tend to see a divorce not as the end of a family but as a radical restructuring, which may, if either parent remarries, eventually involve new family members as well.

Divorce mediators are counselors, lawyers, and therapists especially trained in family mediation and divorce procedures. In addition to helping a couple reach an agreement, mediators may provide individual therapy and counseling, family and children's counseling, and a variety of support groups (for separating couples, children and/or adolescents of divorcing parents, stepparents, etc.). The illustrations on pages 288 and 289 show what issues a separation agreement should include, and a sample separation/divorce agreement negotiated by a divorce mediator.

Social and Environmental Stress

While each of us has a degree of tolerance to stress, the presence of multiple sources of stress increases the likelihood of mental breakdown. For example, the combination of hunger, crowding, and racial or ethnic discrimination in our city ghettoes can become intolerable and produce unhealthy behavior in some individuals. Whereas schizophrenia afflicts approximately 1 percent of the overall population, the incidence of this disorder may be as high as 6 percent in a city ghetto. In such areas, community services potentially can play a large role in preventive mental health care.

All down the line, the poor carry the biggest risks of mental handicap. It is the poor who account for the most high-risk pregnancies and the worst levels of prenatal care. It is the poor who are likely to skip medical checkups for their children, where mental problems could be discovered and treated at early stages. It is the poor who are likely to be nourished badly and receive inadequate care for the many physical conditions associated with mental impairment.

Programs like Head Start, which enhance the physical, social and educational capacities of preschool children in economically disadvantaged areas, are a form of preventive mental health care. So are programs teaching young mothers (often still adolescents themselves) how to care for their infants, programs to help teenagers

MATTERS TO BE INCLUDED IN A SEPARATION AGREEMENT

The division of real and personal property, including its appraisal, terms of sale, and how proceeds are to be divided.

Financial obligations of one spouse to another, including support of spouse, support of children, financing of college education (sharing based on income, equally, or on savings or trusts), summer camp, medical and dental care (insurance), life insurance and retirement income, cost of living increases, reduction or other changes based on employment status.

Custody of minor children, including who has custody (one parent or shared), visitation arrangements (any time, specific times each week or month, school vacations, summer vacations, travel out of state or abroad).

Tax implications, including deductions for alimony and dependency exemptions.

Attorney's fees.

Relation of separation agreement to divorce judgment (separate from divorce terms or part of them).

Provisions for change (mediation clause, arbitration clause).

AGREEMENT OF JOHN AND MARY DOE
REGARDING THEIR SEPARATION AND DIVORCE
February 25, 1981

John and Mary, who have been married twenty-five years, have lived separately for the last ten months. They have three children, Jane, age 22, and Marjorie, age 20, who both live in the city nearby, and John, Jr., age 18, who lives at home with Mary. They have acknowledged that an irretrievable breakdown of their marriage exists, and have drawn an agreement by which to legally separate and seek a divorce.

1. Property and possessions

John and Mary have agreed that she will continue to live in the marital home on Main Street, in Ourtown until it is her decision to sell this house. The equity accrued (based on the value of the property at the time it is sold) will be shared equally by John and Mary.

John and Mary have agreed to divide their personal possessions to their mutual satisfaction by the time this agreement is presented in court.

2. Financial arrangements

In order to assume responsibility for liabilities to date, for maintenance costs, and for educational expenses, John and Mary have agreed to the following:

a. John will contribute $800 monthly to the support of Mary and son John; he will also continue to provide telephone service as possible through his employment, and to maintain Mary's car expenses.

b. Mary will find employment suitable to her skills and experience to provide income for expenses beyond those supported by John.

c. John will assume responsibility for the debts (known to both of them) incurred as of the date of the court appearance.

d. John will contribute to the college expenses of Marjorie and John, Jr., to the best of his ability, and as arranged between him and these children.

3. Insurances

John and Mary have agreed that health insurance for this family will be maintained by John's current policy as long as it is possible for Mary and the children to be covered under this plan.

They further agree to maintain their respective life insurance policies naming each other as primary beneficiaries.

4. Privacy

Pending a final divorce decree, John and Mary agree to respect each other's privacy and to allow one another to live their public and private lives as though they are unmarried individuals.

5. Mediation

In the event of any major change of circumstance, such as loss of employment, substantial increase or decrease in either of their incomes, illness or disability, John and Mary agree to discuss and negotiate any needed changes in the terms of this agreement. Should they fail to reach a suitable and workable modification of any issue, they agree to use mediation for resolution.

Courtesy: Divorce Resource & Mediation Center, Cambridge, MA.

avoid drug and alcohol dependency, programs to help the elderly. Such programs are costly, but in the long run they may cost society less than the illnesses they help prevent or mitigate, in terms of both institutional care and lost productivity.

COMMUNITY MENTAL HEALTH CARE

The basic premise of community mental health care (or community psychiatry or social psychiatry), is that the community should be the focal point for treatment and prevention of mental illness. Beginning with the establishment of community health centers, it envisions a complete range of mental health services in every neighborhood in the nation, along with the conquest of destructive social forces that contribute to mental illness—poor housing, unemployment, and prejudice. In the broadest sense, prevention includes prenatal care, nursery and school care, the development of creative skills, satisfactory job placement, and special help in emergency situations.

Community mental health care is not a new concept. Individual mental health facilities have from time to time extended their activities by going out into the community to provide services. As early as 1909 Dr. Adolph Meyer conceived an integrated program of prevention, treatment, and aftercare in which hospital psychiatrists worked with teachers, general practitioners, welfare workers, and the police. In the 1920s the child guidance clinics, ancestors of today's mental health clinics, emphasized prevention of mental illness in adults through early detection and treatment in childhood.

What is new about present-day community care is that its aims are so broad, and that it recognizes that community resources must be linked. While it is the poor who need mental health care the most, outsiders cannot barge into a ghetto community and hand down help from on high. A system of community cooperation and participation is necessary for any such measures to be truly effective.

A central role in linking community resources can be played by the local mental health association (MHA), which, despite the similarity in names, fulfills a different function from that of the community mental health center (CMHC). The MHA serves as an *advocate* for mental health, and works to prevent mental illness and help the mentally ill. The CMHC's main function is *treatment* of those who are mentally ill, have been ill, or may become ill. A major form of advocacy by the MHA chapters is to work for necessary changes in federal, state, and local laws. Another is to make sure the CMHC in the area is actually meeting the community's needs. If there is no CMHC, the MHA might work to get one started.

In addition to advocacy, the other main jobs of the MHA are information and referral. Its staff members go out into the community to run special programs in schools and businesses. One chapter, for example, operates a widow-widower support program, a Parkinsonism support group, parent-toddler and parent-preschool programs, first-time mothers support groups, a "survival course" for parents of adolescents, and separation and divorce groups. This same chapter also runs special programs on death and dying, alcohol use and abuse, child abuse and neglect, and similar issues. It conducts in-service training programs for personnel in schools and nursing homes, for the clergy and the police, probation officers, and other community members who are likely to come in contact with the mentally ill and be in a position to provide preventive mental health care and referrals. It sends speakers to churches and school, clubs and other organizations to talk about rape, wife-beating and other domestic violence, parenting, and child development. It runs a social club with weekly meetings for people who are lonely, isolated, and experiencing difficulty in everyday living situations. By educating the public about these issues and by supporting individuals who are coping with critical life situations, the MHA performs a valuable preventive service.

A POSSIBLE SOLUTION: REGULAR CHECKUPS

Preventive mental health care encompasses such a broad area of concerns that it might seem impossible to achieve, at least for a large number of people. However, one mental health professional interviewed suggested a remarkably simple remedy, which she hopes will one day be universally applied: regular mental health checkups.

Clearly this measure would cover the entire developmental gamut—from genetic counseling and prenatal care through old age. To an extent, some primary-care physicians—family doctors, obstetricians, pediatricians, internists—already perform this function, but it could be greatly expanded and legitimized. There would be no more hesitation about going for one's annual mental health checkup than there is about going for a physical checkup. Such examinations would be widely available, through school and industrial health programs and multiservice neighborhood clinics, as well as through private practitioners. This kind of program would greatly increase the chances for early detection and early treatment, if only through increasing public acceptance of mental disorders as illnesses for which effective treatment is both possible and available.

CHAPTER 22

Mental Illness and the Law

Mental illness can affect one's judgment or behavior so as to endanger oneself or others. When it does, the law may intervene to protect the individual and the community. It may judge a person incompetent and assign someone else to conduct his/her affairs. It may require him/her to enter a protective environment, that is, a mental hospital. Should a mentally ill person commit a crime, the law may shield him/her from ordinary punishment, either by finding him/her incompetent to stand trial, or, after a trial, by finding him/her "not guilty by reason of mental disease or defect (insanity)." In either case, the law usually will require the person so judged to seek treatment for the illness, most often in a hospital, which may be either an open or a "secure" (locked) facility, depending on the nature of the crime. Thus, unlike any physically ill individual, a person who has been judged to be mentally ill may be forced to be hospitalized and be deprived of control over his/her own life, at least for a time.

In practice, few mentally ill persons commit crimes against others or become involved in criminal proceedings. However, other questions involving the law may arise. Can a mentally ill person enter into a contract and be bound by it? Can he or she make a will, declaring, "I, Robert Roe, being of sound mind and body, . . .?" Can a mentally ill person sign out of the hospital? To what extent are a person's conversations with a psychotherapist confidential?

The remainder of this chapter will give an overview of the principal legal issues involved in mental illness and its treatment, in-

293

cluding such matters as responsibility for a crime, court-ordered psychiatric treatment, involuntary hospitalization (commitment), mental patients' civil rights, questions of competency (to stand trial or to conduct one's own affairs), guardianship for those who are minors or are incompetent, and a brief discussion of certain kinds of crime that are, by and large, considered mental health problems, specifically child abuse and other domestic violence, and juvenile delinquency.

A TYPICAL CASE

John B., 25, lost his job last week after getting in a fist fight with a fellow worker. It is the fourth time in less than a year that his violent behavior has gotten him in trouble. This time the other man, whose jaw he broke, is planning to sue him.

John's offense, in legal terms, is a tort, a civil wrong done to another person. Injury has occurred, but it is up to the injured person to decide whether or not he wants compensation. In this case he does. Is John liable?

John's family knows that he is unstable. How could they not, since this is his fourth violent outburst in less than a year? They tell his lawyer that he has always behaved like this, that he can't seem to help himself when his temper "takes over," and that his behavior has kept him from getting decent jobs that pay well enough for him to save some money. He doesn't have enough money now to pay damages.

Unfortunately for John, he is indeed liable. In tort cases a person may be judged to have a mental disease or defect, but that is not considered an excuse. Therefore John will have to pay as much of the damages awarded to his co-worker as he can. Luckily for his family, they are not liable for the injury he does to others (although if John were a minor, in some states they would be). Unless John can be successfully treated for what is almost certainly a mental illness and can learn to control his violent impulses, about the only thing that might help in the future is to make sure he has good personal liability insurance, in order to protect both him and others. With his past history, however, it may be difficult for him to get such an insurance policy.

Can John be forced to seek treatment? Not as a result of this case. *If* he had inflicted a fatal injury, resulting in the other man's death, and *if* his lawyer had decided to plead "not guilty by reason of mental defect," and *if* court-appointed psychiatrists had agreed that John was indeed ill and could not be held responsible for his actions, then the court might have ordered him to be placed in an institution, most likely a secure one, such as a hospital for the criminally insane.

COURT CLINICS

Treatment ordered by a court of law does not necessarily involve hospitalization.

Jimmy R., 12, small for his age, got in a street fight with a playmate and knocked the other child unconscious with a lead pipe. It was the first time he had ever appeared in court.

Jimmy lived in Massachusetts. Because it was his first court appearance, the judge handling the case requested a psychiatric evaluation, a very common practice in that state since the passage of the Briggs Act in 1921. The court-appointed psychiatrist talked with Jimmy and with his mother, a single parent of four children, and he also tested the youngster. A psychological profile emerged of a timid, nervous, frightened child, seemingly incapable of aggression.

The court granted a continuance, carrying the case for a year with no finding. Jimmy was put on probation, and part of his sentence was that he had to attend the court clinic for a year, in order to receive psychotherapy.

In 1981 Massachusetts had twenty-five court clinics staffed by 150 professionals who treated about 6,000 persons each year. Clinic clients do not come of their own accord, but on a mandatory, court-ordered basis. They are sent for evaluation, to discover whether or not they are competent to be tried (see below for more about competency), and for treatment. The clients who come for treatment are usually young (most are between the age of fifteen and twenty-five, and few are older than thirty-five), because most crimes are committed by young people. Their crimes range from arson and robbery to drug abuse, wife-beating, and child abuse. Generally they act out their personal problems by injuring the persons and property of others.

Most of the court clinics are located in district courts, which dispose of 90 percent of all criminal cases. The goal is, through proper sentencing, to make the first offense the last. It is estimated that about 70 percent of first offenders do not come before the courts again.

Massachusetts is not the only state that has court clinics, but its system in 1981 was considered the most sophisticated of its kind. However, even its twenty-five clinics were not sufficient: the state's judges declared that there was a pressing need for at least twice that number.

Jimmy's crime, like most, was an impulsive one. Law enforcement professionals maintain that the majority of offenses are not premeditated but arise out of unpredictable, volatile situations. Teaching clients the need to control their impulses is a major goal of therapy in any court clinic.

"NOT GUILTY BY REASON OF . . ."

Late in 1976 a New York City policeman named Torsney and another officer were sent in a patrol car to investigate a report of an armed man at a housing project in a tough Brooklyn neighborhood. The officers did not find the man, but as they were leaving the building six black youths appeared. One of them approached the officers, and Torsney drew his service revolver, shot the youth in the head, and continued walking back to his patrol car. He later admitted that he did not like blacks. The youth, who was fifteen, died several hours later in the hospital.

At his trial for second-degree murder, Torsney testified that he had drawn his gun and fired because he had seen the youth pull a shiny object from his waistband, which he assumed was a gun. His fellow-officer and other witnesses, however, testified they had not seen a gun, and in fact no weapon was ever found on the scene. Torsney's attorney then maintained that if there indeed was no gun, his client must be sick. A noted psychiatrist then testified for the defense that Torsney suffered from a rare organic brain disorder called psychomotor epilepsy, and that at the moment of the shooting he had been in the midst of a seizure. The prosecution also called in a psychiatrist, another eminent specialist, who said that Torsney appeared to have a neurotic character disorder that gave him a tendency to panic in situations where he thought he was being threatened, and this "emotional flaw" could have led him to mistake the boy's movement for that of pulling a gun. He could not, however, find evidence of psychomotor epilepsy or of any other psychotic disorder, and he believed that Torsney was legally sane and therefore responsible for his actions.

Competency to Stand Trial

Had the question of Torsney's sanity been raised sooner, the court would have ordered a psychiatric evaluation to determine if he was competent to stand trial at all. A defendant is found incompetent for trial if he is considered unable to understand the charge against him or unable to participate in his own defense. Such an evaluation is usually performed in a hospital, where the individual can be subjected to a variety of tests and be observed by professionals over a period of a few days.

Even then, the standard of competency is very loosely applied. Many psychiatrists believe that it is better to stand trial than to wait for a prolonged period. Moreover, those found incompetent almost invariably are committed to a state mental institution for a period of time—here, as in other specifics, the law varies from state to state—and are released only when one or more psychiatrists determines that they are no longer dangerous. (In theory, a person could be incompetent but not dangerous to others; in practice, this issue seldom arises because the question usually comes up only in cases involving a serious crime, such as murder. In Utah, in 1979, however, a court ruled that one must be *both* dangerous and incompetent in order to be committed.)

The defense used by Officer Torsney's lawyer, "not guilty by reason of mental disease or defect" at the time the crime was committed, is not invoked very often—indeed, only in an estimated 2 percent of cases, and usually only as a last resort. Most lawyers believe a jury won't be convinced by it, so they tend to use it only in cases of homicide where there is strong proof that the defendant actually did the killing. When it is invoked, each side usually gets a psychiatrist (or several psychiatrists) to testify in its behalf, and very frequently the two sets of psychiatrists present conflicting opinions, as they did in Torsney's case.

Until Officer Torsney killed the young black, his eight-year record on the police force had been untarnished. The jury in this case chose to believe the defendant's psychiatrist and acquitted Torsney "by reason of mental disease or defect." (In the case of Jack Ruby, who killed President John F. Kennedy's assassin, Lee Harvey Oswald, the jury did not believe the defense experts who maintained that Ruby had shot Oswald during a psychomotor epileptic seizure. In the case of John Hinckley, who tried to kill President Ronald Reagan, they voted for acquittal.)

Sanity Is a Legal Term

Sanity is a purely legal concept. It refers to an individual's capacity for assessing reality, making choices, and taking responsibility for his/her actions.

The rules for "not guilty by reason of insanity" vary among different jurisdictions. One of the oldest, long in use in American state and Federal courts, is the M'Naghten Rule. In 1843 a man named Daniel M'Naghten shot to death British Prime Minister Robert Peel's secretary, whom he mistook for the Prime Minister. Peel, he believed, had been pursuing him because he had voted against him, and Peel had devised the Corn Laws to ruin him. M'Naghten was found not guilty of the crime by reason of insanity, which, it was determined, meant that he did not know that his action was wrong. The problem with this rule lies in the words "know" and "wrong"— how not know? Not understand the consequences? Wrong in the sense of the law or according to prevailing moral standards? In a number of states and in the federal courts, therefore, the very restrictive M'Naghten Rule was broadened by a rule called "irresistible impulse," which stated that even though a person might know that an action was wrong, he or she was not responsible if unable to resist the impulse to commit it anyhow.

In 1954 Judge David L. Bazelon of the United States Court of Appeals for the District of Columbia handed down still another standard, called the Durham Rule. It said "an accused person is not criminally responsible if his unlawful act was the product of mental disease or defect." At first it was hailed as a huge improvement, since "mental disease" could now be interpreted according to the most recent medical knowledge. Later many lawyers and judges (including Bazelon himself) decided it was too ambiguous, since it now could be argued that merely commiting a crime was evidence of mental illness, and in practice psychiatrists who testified in court generally could not satisfactorily explain their reasoning to juries.

In 1972 the American Law Institute proposed still another definition, the Model Penal Code, whereby a person should not be held responsible for a criminal act if, as a result of mental disease or defect, he lacks substantial capacity either to appreciate the wrongfulness of his conduct or to conform his conduct to the law.

All these rules represent attempts to answer once and for all the question of responsibility for crime. None is totally satisfactory, and indeed, some authorities believe this question can have no single answer but must be resolved in every specific instance.*

In any case, acquittal on grounds of mental illness generally leads to another form of imprisonment, confinement in a mental institution.

---

*In April, 1982, Idaho enacted a law eliminating the plea of mental illness as a defense in criminal cases, although such illness would be considered by the judge in sentencing. Taking effect July 1, 1982, the new law was expected to be tested in the courts.

Involuntary Hospitalization for a Crime

The law in New York State says that a person acquitted on grounds of insanity must be committed to a mental hospital until it can be determined that he or she is no longer a danger to self or others. The individual can then be released if a judge accepts this determination by a psychiatrist at a court hearing.

As it happened, Torsney remained hospitalized for a year and a half, even though the psychiatrists at both hospitals where he was confined could find no indication of either psychosis or psychomotor epilepsy. (A report by the state department of mental health indicated that the median hospital stay of one-fourth of the murder defendants in New York who had been so acquitted during a five-year period had been less than one year.) When Torsney finally left the hospital, he tried to retire from the police department with a $14,000-a-year medical disability pension, on the ground that a psychiatrist and a jury had declared him subject to a mental disease or defect and he therefore was unfit for duty. However, a departmental trial found no evidence of the psychomotor epilepsy on which Torsney's acquittal was based; his request for a pension was turned down, and he was dismissed from the force on the ground that he had without provocation shot and killed a young man.*

VOLUNTARY AND INVOLUNTARY CIVIL ADMISSION

There are several forms of voluntary and involuntary civil (noncriminal) admission to a mental hospital. Bear in mind, however, that each state has its own laws governing this matter. In order to learn about the law in your state (or your relative's state), you may have to consult a local lawyer, or the legal department of your state department of mental health. You can read the relevant statutes in your state at the library in your county courthouse. Another useful source of information is *The Rights of Mental Patients* by Bruce J. Ennis and Richard D. Emery, the revised edition of a basic Amer-

---

*The details about Torsney's case are based on an article by Susan Sheehan in *The New Yorker*, May 25, 1981.

ican Civil Liberties Union guide (New York: Avon Books, 1978). If you or your relative want a lawyer to represent you, you may need one who is expert in mental health law; you can find one either through your state bar association or by contacting the American Civil Liberties Union.

The least restrictive form of voluntary admission in practice is *informal admission,* but few mental hospitals allow it, although it may be used for admission to some general hospitals with a psychiatric unit. Informal admission consists simply of signing into the hospital, exactly as though for medical or surgical treatment. The patient then can request a discharge or leave at will, without giving advance notice. However, he/she will usually be required to sign a form releasing the hospital and its staff from all responsibility if the discharge is against "medical advice."

For *voluntary admission* a person comes to a mental hospital and signs a paper indicating that he/she seeks admission and treatment of his/her own free will. Such a patient may leave the hospital at any time, although in some states he/she may have to give a few days' notice. The precise period varies from three to ten days. It allows the hospital to petition a court for commitment of any patient it believes should not be released because he/she represents a danger to self or others. (This is an uncommon practice, but instances of it have occurred.) However, a discharge order can be written at any time by the patient's attending doctor, and then no waiting period (or advance notice) is required.

As indicated above, each state has its own laws. In Massachusetts it is not up to a patient to prove that he or she should not be hospitalized. Rather, it is up to the party seeking to prolong hospitalization and treatment (the hospital or, more often, family members) to prove in a court of law that the patient should be retained against his/her own will. Further, in such cases, actual behavior that demonstrates the patient's dangerousness or incompetence must be established. Once it has been established, however, a patient's voluntary admission can, in effect, be converted into an involuntary admission. Hospitalization by court order is likely to be for a much longer period than most voluntary admissions—in Massachusetts for a period up to six months for a first court order and for a period up to twelve months for second and subsequent court orders.

Involuntary admission, also called *commitment* or *certification,* was at one time fairly easy to obtain. Often a family simply got two physicians to certify that one of its members was mentally ill and in need of treatment, and then that person could be hospitalized for an indefinite period. As a result, thousands of individuals were unreasonably and unjustly confined in mental hospitals and deprived of their liberty and basic civil rights, often under conditions far worse than those found in penal institutions.

THE MENTAL PATIENTS LIBERATION MOVEMENT

In the 1960s the civil rights movement that swept the country was extended to mental patients as well, assisted by a small but vocal group of mental health professionals who insist there is no such thing as mental illness. Among them was Thomas Szasz, a well-known American psychiatrist who maintained that it is only our intolerance to those who are different from ourselves that leads us to label them as "mentally ill." Mental illness, according to Szasz and others, is a social definition imposed on individuals who either represent a threat to the community (the criminal and the deviant), or who disturb or frighten those around them (a person who hears "voices" or claims to be Jesus Christ), or who represent a burden (old people). Consequently, they oppose involuntary psychiatric treatment of any kind, including involuntary hospitalization. Hospitals for the criminally insane, civil liberties lawyer Bruce Ennis pointed out in his *Prisoners of Psychiatry* (1972), contain only a very few patients who actually have been convicted of a crime; most of the inmates have merely been accused of a crime and then judged mentally incompetent to stand trial. Moreover, said Ennis, for those confined because they represent a danger to others, the judgment often is interpreted as "potentially dangerous"; no one can predict accurately which person will actually be dangerous.

In response to these ideas, in the early 1970s mental patients began to organize liberation groups that stressed not treatment but political action. One of the first groups formed was the Mental

Patients Liberation Project in New York (a similar group was formed about the same time in Vancouver, Canada). Among other things, it formulated a mental patients' bill of rights, consisting of basic rights that its members believed were frequently denied to mental patients. Some of the groups, which still exist in various localities, publish newsletters and make available information concerning local statutes affecting mental patients. If they exist in your area, they may be listed in the telephone book under such names as Mental Patients Liberation, Network against Psychiatric Assault, or Patients Rights Organization.

NEW LAWS CONCERNING INVOLUNTARY HOSPITALIZATION

In response to pressure both from civil liberties advocates and from the deinstitutionalization movement, new laws and court decisions have radically changed concepts and practices concerning the rights of mental patients. Today involuntary hospitalization beyond a brief emergency period, rarely exceeding fourteen days, involves numerous guarantees of the individual's rights.

In 1972 a Federal district court in Wisconsin ruled that involuntary commitment must involve the following:

- Timely notice of the charges justifying confinement.
- Notice of the right to a jury trial.
- An initial hearing on probable cause for detention beyond a period of 48 hours.
- A full hearing on the necessity of detention beyond a period of two weeks.
- Legal counsel to represent the detained person at the hearing.
- No admission of hearsay evidence at the hearing.
- Protection of the detained person against self-incrimination under the Fifth Amendment.
- Proof of mental illness and dangerousness to self or others "beyond a reasonable doubt."
- Inquiry into less restrictive alternatives than involuntary hospitalization.

• No treatment until the detained person has had a probable cause hearing.

This ruling was hailed by civil rights advocates as the "Ten Commandments" for the mentally ill. Virtually all the procedural questions (concerning the right to a hearing) have been further litigated, and many of the court's decisions have been incorporated into state law (all of them in Wisconsin and various ones in other states). The substantive proof of mental illness "beyond a reasonable doubt," however, has been interpreted in a variety of ways, and in 1979 the Supreme Court ruled that only "clear and convincing proof" was needed. Further, numerous states now mandate periodic review of patients who have been committed to see if they really must remain hospitalized. Despite the changes in law, however, in practice the decision to hospitalize a person against his/her will tends to remain in the hands of the court-appointed review officer, and in the end a decision to commit is usually made by a judge, attorney, or physician, rarely by the law or by a patient.

The bulk of involuntary commitments are made on a temporary, emergency basis. For this, too, each state has its own laws. In Massachusetts, a physician or police officer may apply for involuntary hospitalization at a mental hospital for a period of up to ten days. If the person is unwilling to go to the hospital, he/she may be transported by medical or police personnel, who may use restraints if necessary. However, no person may be admitted involuntarily unless he or she (or his/her parent or guardian) has been given the right to apply for a voluntary admission.

Once the person arrives at the hospital, a psychiatric examination must be conducted within two hours to determine if failure to hospitalize this person would create a likelihood of serious harm by reason of mental illness. Finally, the ten-day period of involuntary hospitalization can be extended only by court order.

RIGHTS IN THE HOSPITAL

Even when a person is hospitalized involuntarily, his/her civil rights cannot be curtailed. In many states a bill of rights for mental patients must be posted in the patient areas of all hospitals. Among the rights protected are the right to send and receive mail, to keep and use personal possessions, to communicate with an attorney, to vote, and to hold a driver's license. Further, in all states mental patients have two other basic rights: *the right to refuse treatment*—in practice this usually refers to drug treatment, electroconvulsive (shock) treatment, or surgery—except in emergency situations when there is immediate risk of physical injury; and *the right to receive treatment* for their illness. In other words, no one can be forced to take drugs or undergo shock treatment,* nor can one be held in a mental hospital without receiving treatment. By extension, therefore, any involuntarily confined patient who is not dangerous must receive treatment or be released.

Before the development of psychoactive drugs, violent mental patients frequently had to be restrained for long periods, or confined in padded cells, or both. Today, however, *restraint* and *seclusion* may be used only under highly controlled conditions, if at all, and informed consent must be secured for various forms of specific treatment.

Each state has its own statutes and regulations establishing procedures for and limitations on the use of restraints and seclusion. In New York, for example, a patient may be put in a seclusion room for two hours only; if further seclusion is believed necessary, a physician must renew the order for it, again for only two hours. Also, most states require hospitals to keep detailed records of their use of seclusion, which they must submit to the state department of mental health.

PRACTICAL PROBLEMS RAISED BY CIVIL RIGHTS SAFEGUARDS

Although the new laws and regulations do protect patients from abuse of their rights as citizens, they sometimes impose constraints that raise both clinical and ethical questions.

*In some cases a guardian can authorize treatment (see guardianship, below).

The legal process for obtaining involuntary hospitalization is cumbersome, and while it protects against unnecessary confinement it does not always serve the severely psychotic patient who is not dangerous but badly in need of treatment. For example, when does the homeless "bag lady" who wanders the city streets in icy weather and sleeps in doorways under cardboard coverings represent a "danger" to self?

Then, hospitals sometimes find themselves in a double bind: they must by law provide treatment, but patients may by law refuse any or all treatment. The right to refuse treatment and the application of the rule of informed consent for accepting treatment may be fine for those patients rational enough to make a considered judgment. That may not be the case for some acute schizophrenics, for example, who are not lucid enough to realize they need antipsychotic medication and whose behavior without such treatment has a detrimental effect on fellow patients.

This issue has become the focus of a number of legal battles, some of which have not, at this writing, yet been resolved. Prolonged use of antipsychotic drugs, as indicated in Chapter 15, sometimes leads to serious and irreversible side effects. In one court case a former aircraft pilot who had been hospitalized for seven years in a New Jersey state hospital insisted that involuntarily hospitalized patients who have not been legally declared incompetent have a constitutional right to refuse antipsychotic drugs regardless of doctor's orders (under New Jersey law at that time, only voluntarily committed patients could refuse medication). Hospital psychiatrists countered that lawyers and judges should not interfere with their professional decisions about what is best for a hospitalized mental patient. Nevertheless, the Federal district court judge who heard this case in 1978 ordered the state of New Jersey to provide "informed consent" forms, listing all the adverse effects of any drug, which had to be signed by all patients in state mental hospitals (or by their guardians if they had been declared incompetent) before medication could be administered. He also directed the state to establish a system of autonomous patient advocates to serve as informal counsel to patients who wished to refuse medication, and to provide a panel of independent psychiatrists to review all decisions to medicate a patient against his/her will. The state appealed to a highter court to overturn this ruling, calling the restrictions it imposed complex, highly intrusive, unprecedented, and unsound. The state's director of mental health and hospitals testified that the order had caused an increase in patient violence because medication had not been taken or had to be delayed, and this had led to morale problems among the staff and deterioration in the condition of some patients who had refused their medication.

A similar question arises with respect to suicidal patients. Should one honor such a patient's right to forego treatment or to be discharged? Should a man who says he wants to die be permitted to end his life? Or should his expressed desire be considered a symptom of illness that will presumably disappear when the illness has been effectively treated? In California, a person who is suicidal may be committed for fourteen days to a mental hospital for intensive treatment, and, if still suicidal after that period, may be required to remain another fourteen days. At the end of that period, however, even if the patient is still suicidal but is not shown to be dangerous to others, he/she must be released.

Even the riht to treatment, which has given rise to court actions setting standards for staff-patient ratios and treatment programs, among other things, has created problems in some hospitals. For example, as a result of such action, treatment teams in one large mental hospital were required to review and revise each patient's treatment plan once a month. One large ward in this hospital housed both acutely ill young adults and a group of older, chronically ill patients. The treatment team for this ward, which formerly met for two hours a week, now needed an extra ten hours a week in order to interview each patient once a month to review his/her treatment plan, including even chronic patients whose mental status had not changed in years. As a result, the time available for treating the acutely ill younger patients, who were far more likely to benefit from intensive treatment, was sharply curtailed.

Finally, the principle of placing a person in the least restrictive environment consistent with proper care means, for many, discharge from the hospital because such care costs money that the states do not have. For those who lack family and community supports, such discharge poses grave problems; in effect they are cast adrift.

THE RIGHT TO CONFIDENTIALITY

State laws differ concerning protection of the privacy of psychiatric patients. As indicated in Chapter 20, the very fact of making an insurance claim can jeopardize confidentiality, depending on who has access to this information. When seeing a private practitioner there usually is no danger that a client's revelations will be disclosed. This privacy is necessarily less exclusive in a clinic, however, where details of treatment are discussed at staff meetings. Most clinics keep records for all their clients, and they vary in the extent to which they limit access to their records. In some the records may be used for research, training, or demonstration purposes.

Should clients and patients be allowed to examine their own records? Laws and opinions concerning this issue differ considerably. The federal government and consumer rights advocates hold that people should be able to find out what is written about them; many of the states as well as many hospitals and individual practitioners disagree. In Massachusetts the current law states that psychiatric records are to be private and not open to public inspection except upon a judicial order, whether or not there are pending judicial proceedings, or upon the written request of a patient's attorney when accompanied by an authorization from the patient, or when determined by a hospital's medical director to be in the patient's best interest.

The confidentiality of conversations with a therapist is not protected by law in the same way that conversations with either a priest or a lawyer are. Most states consider it "privileged" communication, which protects patients from disclosure unless they waive that privilege, but there are still exceptions. A therapist who is subpoenaed by a court may be required to reveal confidential information about a client, especially in a criminal case but sometimes also in civil matters, such as child custody.

INCOMPETENCY AND GUARDIANSHIP

For a person who is judged incompetent (some states call it "gravely disabled"), a court may appoint a guardian (also called *conservator*) who then exercises that person's rights and handles their personal and/or financial affairs. When such a person, called the *ward,* is hospitalized—and many if not most individuals who are judged incompetent need the extensive supervision or care available only in an institution of some kind—the guardian acts on the patient's behalf, accepting or refusing medication, applying for hospital discharge, and so on. A guardianship may be temporary, commonly lasting for ninety days or less, or it may be permanent, unlimited in duration.

The person who is judged incompetent usually loses a number of rights, among them the right to vote, to enter into a valid contract, to practice a profession, to hold a driver's license, to adopt children or to prevent the adoption of one's own children, and to sell (or give away) property. Incompetency also is considered evidence of inability to execute a valid will, although in practice this question usually does not arise until after a person has died (when a dissatisfied family member sues to have a will set aside on the ground that the testator was incompetent). Although marriage is also a contract, a person who is judged incompetent and then marries usually is considered to be legally married unless such a marriage is set aside (by annulment). As far as divorce is concerned, a person judged incompetent may have trouble initiating divorce proceedings, and, similarly, his/her spouse may have trouble suing for divorce.

Persons who have been judged incompetent remain so until a court certifies them to be competent. Only then can they regain control over their affairs and property.

One can contest being placed under guardianship. In an emergency a temporary guardianship sometimes is ordered without giving the person prior notice. However, in this instance notice usually must be given within a specified time, such as three days. At the time the notice is received, a person may request a court hearing to object either to the guardianship itself or to the specific individual nominated as guardian. Again, state laws vary. In Massachusetts when a person seeking guardianship applies for authority to admit his/her ward to a mental health facility, a hearing must be held with the ward in attendance (or, if this is impossible, in the presence of the ward's attorney).

For minors, the parents are usually considered the guardians, but according to a recent Supreme Court ruling, their request to hospitalize their child against his/her will need only be reviewed by a neutral and independent physician.

DOMESTIC VIOLENCE

Certain mental health problems frequently entangle a person with the law. Antisocial personality disorder, the name given to the illness of John B. (see above) and others whose violent behavior gets them in trouble, is one example. Domestic violence—child neglect and abuse, spouse abuse, abuse of elderly parents—is another, as is juvenile delinquency.

Child neglect and abuse is a growing problem in America, found among all social classes. Legally a child is any person under the age of sixteen. A neglected child is one deprived of adequate food, clothing, shelter, education, or medical care by parents who either can afford to provide them or who have been offered help to do so. An abused child is one whose parents or guardians have inflicted physical injury or sexual abuse on him or her, or have allowed such injury to be inflicted by others.

Most states have laws requiring teachers, physicians, nurses, and social workers to report child abuse and neglect, but once a situation has been reported the solution is not easy. Mental health professionals believe that it requires the cooperation of a mental health professional, pediatrician, social worker, and the court if violence is not to recur, and that both parents—not just the abusing one—should receive counseling. Because many parents who maltreat their children were themselves maltreated by their parents, it is believed they need extensive support and therapy to improve their poor self-image and to learn to control their violent impulses, as well as education in the proper care of children and in child development.

A national self-help organization, Parents Anonymous, has an extensive network of local chapters where parents can turn for help, remaining anonymous if they wish. The national headquarters is at 22330 Hawthorne Boulevard, Suite 208, Torrance, CA 90505 (telephone toll-free 800-421-0353 from outside California; 800-352-0386 within California).

The abuse of wives by their husbands (and, less common but occasionally found, of husbands by wives) also is an increasing problem, as is abuse of the elderly by their children or other family members. In October 1981, New York established a 24-hour toll-free hot line for victims of domestic violence, who could call for crisis counseling and referrals to shelters and service programs in their localities. The service is operated by the New York State Coalition against Domestic Violence, a group composed of thirty-five service and advocacy programs for victims of domestic violence. The hot line team handles complaints from all classes of victims, including nonmarried cohabitants, the elderly, and minors. In New York alone, it was found, figures from family courts indicated that more than 20,000 wives each year were applying for orders of protection against violent husbands, and the number of violent incidents resulting in injuries to all classes of family members was estimated to be ten times that.

New York is by no means unique in this respect, and hot lines and shelters are springing up all over the country. Although the courts may stop individual instances of wife-beating, for example, by temporarily restraining a husband from access to his wife and children, legal action alone is rarely enough to resolve such cases. Extensive counseling for all the members of the family—abuser, victim, and children—are needed if the family are to remain together without a repetition of violence.

JUVENILE DELINQUENCY

Juvenile delinquency is essentially a legal term. A juvenile delinquent or juvenile offender is basically a child who comes to the attention of a juvenile court for having committed acts that would be considered crimes if they were committed by an adult, or for certain statutory offenses that pertain only to children, such as truancy, running away from home, and, in some jurisdictions, disobedience to parents or teachers.

The term "juvenile delinquent" thus covers a broad range, lumping together youngsters who have committed armed robbery with those who have merely played hooky from school. Richard Bush, a child psychologist, suggests that it should be applied only to adolescents who exhibit a recurring pattern of antisocial behavior, who show little or no regard for the rights or feelings of others, who have little concern for their own safety or for the consequences of their acts, and who tend to associate in groups or gangs with other young people who share similar values and behavior patterns.* Before adolescence these youngsters are called "predelinquent."

Traditional insight psychotherapy is generally not very successful with such youngsters. Behavioral therapy tends to work better (see Chapter 13). For the younger ones whom family courts are likely to leave in the charge of their parents, a coordinated effort among teachers, parents, social worker, and mental health specialist to provide a firm, structured environment with close supervision may help. For older teenagers, an out-of-home placement of some kind often is indicated.

Some juvenile delinquents have other, identifiable mental disorders, such as brain damage or retardation. Indeed, some authorities believe there is a definite link between learning disabilities and juvenile delinquency. Certain kinds of learning disability, they feel, are associated with behavior patterns that tend toward delinquency, specifically impulsiveness, limited ability to learn from experience, and limited ability to decipher social cues (understand what is considered acceptable behavior). The child with learning problems develops little self-esteem and may feel the need to compensate for school failure through absenteeism, suspension (for disciplinary reasons), or dropping out altogether. Although these theories may seem speculative and many others believe that the underlying causes of juvenile delinquency are more readily found in poverty, broken homes, cultural alienation, and social disadvantages—in other

---

*Richard Bush, *A Parents' Guide to Child Therapy* (Delacorte Press, 1980).

words, an environment such as an urban ghetto—studies of high delinquency areas indicate some differences between those youths who get in trouble with the law and those who do not.

One major problem for juvenile delinquents is the lack of facilities where adequate treatment is provided. The families of these youngsters often cannot afford private treatment, and state hospitals, as indicated above, have little room for children or adolescents. Some communities have established halfway houses for adolescents, but to date the need for such facilities far exceeds the supply. As a result, juvenile offenders may end up in a highly inappropriate setting, such as a state hospital for the criminally insane; that is, a maximum security facility for the mentally ill who represent a grave danger to the community. One man in his mid-twenties, for example, who has been in trouble since his teens, in and out of state hospitals and police lockups, recently spent six months in a hospital for the criminally insane after he was arrested for trespassing on his parents' property. Though originally scheduled for only twenty days of pretrial observation, a legal mixup kept him living among murderers, rapists, and assaulters—those considered the most deranged and violent criminals—for half a year. His case is unfortunate but not unusual.

A Pennsylvania state task force on juvenile offenders recently made the following recommendations to improve the delivery of mental health services to this group:

- The juvenile court system should have available to it preadjudication and predisposition mental health services for diagnosis, evaluation, and consultation.
- Ambulatory (outpatient) mental health services should be provided in youth development centers, youth forestry camps, and state-supervised juvenile facilities.
- A total of 180 to 210 decentralized maximum-security beds should be provided in the youth services system for violent juvenile offenders, with specialized mental health treatment and research services available.

The task force also recommended additional secure beds in mental hospitals for mentally ill juvenile offenders, aftercare services, liaison between mental health and social service offices, and review of the laws relating to the mentally ill juvenile offender.

Few if any states today offer this range of facilities and services, yet without adequate intervention juvenile offenders almost invariably become adult offenders.

CHAPTER 23

The Future—Avenues of Research

The field of mental health care has undergone rapid change in the past two decades. Sophisticated new technological equipment has spurred research into possible biochemical factors in mental illness, and though the final answers are still elusive considerable progress has been made. At the same time, there have been improvements in methods of evaluating or assessing mental illness, in determining what individuals are at greater-than-average risk for developing mental disorders, and in actual treatment methods.

POSSIBLE BIOCHEMICAL FACTORS

Unlike the ancients, we no longer attribute mania or depression or schizophrenia to a brain that is too hot or too cold or too dry or too wet. However, modern researchers strongly suspect that the answers to at least some disorders lie in the brain and central nervous systems, particularly in the chemistry of those areas. It is, after all, the brain that controls all of the body's vital functions: breathing, heart activity, circulation, muscular movement, digestion, body temperature. And it is the brain that enables us to perceive the world outside our bodies, through sight, sound, smell, taste, and touch.

The Brain

Our knowledge of the brain is relatively recent and still rudimentary. The fact that the nerves in the brain emit electrical signals was discovered only in 1924. When large numbers of brain cells are engaged in coordinated activity, they cause measurable currents to flow through the brain, the membranes surrounding it, the bony skull that encases it, and the scalp (skin) that covers it. These currents can be detected by means of electrodes placed on the skin, along with suitable amplifiers. A record of the currents is called an electroencephalogram (EEG).

The crude picture of brain function yielded by an EEG is useful for some diagnostic purposes—for diagnosing epilepsy, for example—but it is not refined enough to diagnose learning disability or mental retardation with any certainty. One line of research now being pursued is a battery of tests that measure the EEG from a score of electrodes under a large variety of test conditions. The enormous amount of data so generated is then analyzed with the aid of a computer. Such analysis, it is hoped, will eventually enable differentiation between normal and learning-disabled children, and perhaps also between different kinds of learning disability.

Another promising approach involves the measurement and analysis of infinitesimally small pulses of electricity in the brain that are called *evoked potentials* (EPs) because they are generated (evoked) by stimulation of different sensory nerves. This new tool reveals a good deal about the brain's workings in brain-injured patients, even when they are in coma, and may help to predict how much brain damage has occurred and how much dysfunction can be expected. The technique already is used to assess the brain status of stroke victims and multiple sclerosis patients, as well as patients before, during, and after brain surgery.

The computer also has been useful in producing very sophisticated X-rays of the brain. Among the newest instruments is the PET scanner, a cousin of the CAT (for *c*omputerized *a*xial *t*omography) scanner which was introduced in the early 1970s. The CAT gives cross-sectional views of soft-tissue structures in the body. The newer PET (for *p*ositron *e*mission *t*omography) can make what are, in effect, metabolic portraits of the brain, which reveal the rate at which sick and healthy tissues consume various chemicals. Computerized scans have been used to determine treatment for persons who have had strokes or epileptic seizures, and some researchers are using PET scans to explore the brains of victims of schizophrenia, manic-depressive disorder, and senile dementia, in hopes of uncovering distinctive patterns of biochemical activity that will reveal the biochemical nature of these diseases.

Nerves and Neurotransmitters

The brain is often described as a complex message center, receiving signals from outside the body and from different organs within the body, and sending messages to other organs. Within the brain these messages are transmitted from nerve cell to nerve cell (neuron to neuron), a process that occurs in fractions of a second. The brain contains perhaps 100 billion neurons (or even ten times that number). Each message must pass over miniscule gaps between the neurons, called *synapses*. There are far more synapses than neurons: each neuron has 1,000 to 10,000 synapses over which it may transmit messages, and it may receive messages from some 1,000 other neurons.

The message transmitted by a neuron is actually an electrical signal; it is this activity that is measured by the EEG. In order to cross a synapse, the electric signal must be momentarily turned into a chemical one. To accomplish this, a special chemical substance called a *neurotransmitter* is released at the synapse by the transmitting cell. The neurotransmitter chemical comes in contact with the receiver cell across the synapse and activates or stimulates the receiver cell. Having done this, the neurotransmitter chemical either is broken down or returns to the transmitting cell.

About thirty neurotransmitters have been identified so far. They are vital in the transmission of messages, and at least some of them are believed to be central to regulating mood, perception, thought, and behavior. The effect on behavior of many drugs, ranging from the caffeine in coffee and hallucinogens like mescaline and LSD to the medications used to control mania and depression, arises from their ability to disrupt or change the chemical transmission of messages between neurons.

Among the neurotransmitters known to be affected by psychoactive drugs are norepinephrine, serotonin, and dopamine. Dopamine is related to arousal, alertness, and euphoria. Serotonin, on the other hand, appears to be related to states of drowsiness. Both substances are believed to be central to depression and manic-depressive disease, which respond to drugs that change their concentration. The tricyclic antidepressants (see Chapter 15) work by making more norepinephrine available (by blocking its reabsorption); the MAO inhibitors work by blocking the metabolic breakdown of neurotransmitters by the enzyme monoamine oxidase and therefore increase their concentration. Lithium, used to control manic-depressive disease, is believed to promote the synthesis of serotonin, which may in turn regulate norepinephrine levels.

In the early 1970s it was discovered that a compound called MHPG (for 3-methoxy-4-hydroxyphenylglycol), which is derived from norepinephrine, is present in the urine and spinal fluid of human beings (and other animals). Since then researchers have been working to establish standards for different MHPG levels in urine in hopes of thereby being able to distinguish between different kinds of depression and also to help predict how individual patients would respond to different antidepressant drugs.

The neurotransmitter dopamine is believed to be connected also with the development of schizophrenia. The phenothiazines, the most effective of the antipsychotic drugs developed so far, act by blocking the effects of what seems to be an excess of dopamine. Amphetamine, on the other hand, which is a powerful stimulant, triggers the release of dopamine; a large dose of amphetamine can disrupt a person's thought processes and give rise to hallucinations and delusions of persecution like those found in acute schizophrenia.

The symptoms of Parkinsonism, a disease of the central nervous system of unknown cause, are related to a deficiency of dopamine, and since the late 1960s this formerly untreatable disease has been treated with L-dopa, a chemical precursor of dopamine. (An overdose of L-dopa also leads to schizophrenia-like symptoms.) Because L-dopa is not effective for all Parkinsonism patients, neurosurgeons have been pursuing a new approach, the transplantation directly into the brain of tissue from the adrenal glands, which produce dopamine as a chemical step in synthesizing certain hormones. As of this writing, animal experiments showed this procedure might well be feasible but it had not yet been attempted in human patients.

Another class of neurotransmitter are the peptides, some of which appear to act not only in the brain but also as pituitary, adrenal, and gastrointestinal hormones. Research in peptides in the 1970s revealed that two kinds, the endorphins and enkephalins, are involved in pain perception, the control of respiration, thirst, memory, and sexual behavior. A synthetic peptide, beta-endorphin, has been used to treat both schizophrenia and manic-depressive disease, with mixed success.

The Blood-Brain Barrier

Where do the neurotransmitters come from? Their precursors (chemical forerunners) are nutrient substances that modify their release. Unlike other organs, which can use a variety of food substances (sugars, fats, amino acids), the brain can use only blood glucose. Moreover, much of the brain is protected by a selective filter system called the blood-brain barrier, which isolates it from the rest of the body's circulatory system. Through this barrier only small molecules, such as those of oxygen, can pass very readily. Most of the larger ones required by brain cells, like those of glucose, must be actively taken up by special transporting mechanisms. This phenomenon has particular significance for medications intended to affect the neurotransmitters: in order to be effective they must penetrate the blood-brain barrier.

Since the neurotransmitters are in effect converted food substances, it seems reasonable to presume they can be affected by food intake. In fact it has been found that the consumption of carbohydrate foods, for example, triggers the release of serotonin, which increases sleepiness, decreases sensitivity to pain, and also decreases the craving for carbohydrates. The rate at which serotonin forms depends on how much of its chemical precursor, the amino acid tryptophan, gets into the brain. When one eats meat or another protein-containing food, the protein is broken down by digestion into its constituent amino acids, which then enter the bloodstream. Six of the amino acids, including tryptophan, are carried into the brain. Although tryptophan is found in many foods, it is outnumbered by the five other amino acids that compete with it for entry into the brain. Therefore, eating lots of protein does not increase tryptophan (or serotonin) levels in the brain. However, consuming carbohydrates triggers the pancreas to produce insulin to process these foods. Insulin lowers the blood levels of the five amino acids that compete with tryptophan and therefore allows more tryptophan to reach the brain, so that more serotonin can be formed.

Other neurotransmitters are influenced by diet. For example, choline, which is consumed in foods like soybeans and egg yolks, is a precursor to acetylcholine, and increases the level of that neurotransmitter in the brain. Since acetylcholine plays a role in memory, researchers are now trying to determine if treatments that increase choline levels in the brain can counter memory loss in patients with Alzheimer's disease and other forms of senile dementia.

Weather and Mood

Wind and light appear to affect people's moods. Certain weather conditions, notably such warm dry winds as the foehn in Europe, the sharav of Israel, the sirocco of Italy, and the Santa Ana in southern California, have long been suspected of affecting mood to the point where they trigger accidents, crimes, and suicides. A recent experiment on human volunteers showed that weather changes caused by such winds (and also by other factors, such as pollutants, radioactivity, and high-voltage electric lines) generate a large number of positive ions in the atmosphere, which in susceptible individuals appear to increase tension and irritability as well as slow down reaction times. These results are supported by experiments with mice, in whom exposure to high levels of positive ions raises the blood levels of serotonin and depletes brain levels of this neurotransmitter.

Sunlight also appears to affect both fertility and mood. In Finland, for example, the conception rate peaks in June and July, when Finns are exposed to about twenty hours of sunlight a day, and dips in the dark winter months. In the temperate and polar zones, there are seasonal patterns in depression, mania, and suicide attempts.

Our bodies have daily and annual rhythms as well as seasonal ones. A number of events take place in the course of every 24-hour day, biological events that are endogenous (arise within the body). The sleep-waking cycle is the most familiar, but there are others, some of which can be determined or measured only by means of special techniques. For example, body temperature regularly rises every day, from its lowest point at dawn to its highest point in the evening. At night the pineal gland secretes the hormone melatonin, which reaches its peak levels in the body sometime between 11 at night and 7 in the morning. The secretion of melatonin appears to be directly related to a person's exposure to light.

Although these body rhythms are largely self-sustained, they can be influenced by the environment. Sunlight, drugs, and hormones—particularly the sex hormones estrogen and testosterone—can change the timing. This may, some researchers suspect, help account for the high incidence of affective disorders (depression and mania) at certain times of life when hormone levels are very high or very low—during puberty, pregnancy, in association with the menstrual cycle, and during menopause. The female body experiences these endocrine variations more than the male, and women suffer far more frequently from affective disorders than men do.

A classic symptom of major depression, as was noted in Chapter 4, is early morning wakening; depression is at its worst at that time, and a gradual improvement of mood occurs during the course of the day. It is suspected that this may be due to some upset in the body's regular circadian (daily) rhythms. (Similarly, in temperate climates depression has a seasonal peak, in April, and a secondary peak, in fall. Mania also appears to recur seasonally, but results of research are still inconclusive as to when and how.) Some researchers believe that depression involves what they call a *phase advance* of circadian rhythm, that is, everything occurs a little sooner than it should, and hence the whole 24-hour cycle is shortened; thus, instead of waking up at the normal time, one wakes up several hours earlier. The cause of this advance is not known. It may be that some individuals have intrinsically shorter cycles owing to genetic factors, hormonal factors, or exceptional light sensitivity. In mania, on the other hand, the cycle appears to be lengthened, or delayed. During an acute manic episode it is common to experience one or more alternate nights of total sleeplessness. Some of the antidepressants may work, it is suggested, by lengthening the circadian period, whereas lithium mitigates mania by shortening the period. Practical applications suggested by studies of melatonin secretion and its effects have led to such treatment as exposing victims of seasonal (winter) depression to high-intensity light for several hours a day, but considerably more work in this area is needed before it can be widely applied.

ADVANCES IN DIAGNOSIS

More accurate determination of just what is wrong with someone is important to effective treatment. During the past decade a number of new tools have been developed to improve diagnosis.

One of the first steps is a personal interview with an experienced mental health professional. It has been found, however, that interviews conducted with three different professionals, for example, can result in three quite different diagnoses. At least one reason for this is the simple fact that three such interviews can be—and often are—conducted differently. To avoid this, some researchers have concentrated on developing a standardized interview—that is, a series of specific questions to be asked in a fixed sequence—as well as a rating scale that would help analyze the answers. One such scale, the brief psychiatric rating scale (BPRS), consists of eighteen scales scored from ratings made following an interview, for such symptoms as concern about one's body (or physical symptoms), guilt feelings, hostility, suspiciousness, anxiety, emotional withdrawal, etc.

For observation, a step particularly important in assessing children, the use of one-way mirrors has become more widespread, enabling clinicians to observe behavior without influencing it (people who know they are being watched often act differently).

Computers are being used more and more in clinical assessment, both to gather information from individuals and to put together all the information gathered by means of interviews, tests, and other assessment procedures.

Blood Tests for Mental Illness

The secretion of the adrenal hormone cortisol rises markedly in many patients with a major depression, particularly during the afternoon, evening, and early morning hours, and then returns to normal levels. In normal persons a dose of an adrenal corticosteroid, dexamethasone, given by mouth in the evening, signals the hypothalamus and pituitary to suppress cortisol production for about twenty-four hours. Patients with a major depression, however, do not respond in this way; their cortisol production is not suppressed. By means of a simple blood test, the dexamethasone suppression test (DST), researchers hope to be able to diagnose psychotic depression accurately, differentiating it from schizophrenia and other disorders whose symptoms may appear similar.

Another hormonal abnormality found in depression is a changed response to thyroid-stimulating hormone. Research indicates that in manic-depressive disease the amount of thyroid-stimulating hormone released in response to injection of thyrotropin-releasing hormone is markedly increased, whereas in depression without mania it is decreased. Since the depressive phase of manic-depressive disease has symptoms identical to those of depression without mania, this test may enable a psychiatrist to distinguish between the two and give the appropriate medication sooner.

Another blood test being developed both to diagnose clinical depression and to predict which individuals are most likely to develop it involves examination of the platelets, small blood cells that control clotting. The surface of platelets apparently contains receptor sites through which the neurotransmitter serotonin enters the cells. Depressed patients have 30 to 40 percent fewer serotonin receptor sites both on their platelets and in the brain. By measuring the receptor sites on platelets, it is hypothesized, one can determine if brain cells show a lack of sites, too. Drugs that increase serotonin levels then might be useful not only in patients already suffering from depression but in those who are found to have a high risk for developing it.

Platelets also are used to measure monoamine oxidase (MAO) levels, which may rise with depression. When they do, it is likely that MAO inhibitors will help relieve the symptoms.

Blood tests of the kind associated with regular physical examinations or with hospital admission may be useful in diagnosing alcoholism, a recent study has shown. In order to identify alcoholism, twenty-five test values are analyzed as part of three separate test batteries, which all are commonly ordered by physicians to screen for potential problems or to identify nonspecific complaints. Abnormal values in some of the individual tests have been noted among alcoholics for years, but the study was the first to use a special statistical technique, quadrant discriminant analysis, to examine all twenty-five values for distinctive changes in their relationship to one another. When this is done, significantly different patterns emerge for alcoholic and nonalcoholic subjects. It is hoped that this test will help identify the early problem drinker.

HIGH RISK AND EARLY INTERVENTION

Another important avenue of research is epidemiology, the study of what kinds of population suffer from what kinds of disorder, and to what extent, and how these data are related to events in the environment, social phenomena, hereditary factors, etc.

Genetic Research

Long-term studies of mental illness among natural and adoptive families of schizophrenic patients, as well as studies of identical twins, point to the strong probability of a hereditary component in this illness. Similar findings exist for alcoholism, manic-depressive disease, and depression. The evidence indicates that it is a genetic *tendency* to develop these disorders that is passed on, and that only those who are exposed to certain experiences in life—a stressful life or work situation, physical trauma at work, abrupt changes in diet, infection with a virus, and so on—are the ones who become ill.

When one identical twin suffers from depression, there is a 57 percent likelihood that the other twin will also be affected, and only a 14 percent chance if the twins are fraternal. (Identical twins have the same genes; fraternal twins are no more alike than ordinary siblings.) For schizophrenia the chances are about 63 percent for identical twins and only 21 percent for fraternal twins; for alcoholism it is about 50 percent for identical twins and 30 percent for fraternal twins. Twin studies are not yet extensive, since for the ideal study the twins are subjected to quite different environments from birth on, which happens only when they are separated by adoption or some similar occurrence.

The implications of an inherited vulnerability to mental illness have numerous potential clinical applications. A chronic inborn susceptibility suggests that there may be need for long-term treatment even in the absence of symptoms. Genetic counseling may be required, since family members are vulnerable to the same disorder as they enter the age of highest risk—for example, late adolescence and early adulthood for the depressive disorders.

Although it is not known exactly how genetic transmission of mental susceptibility takes place, it appeared from a study published late in 1981 that genes on chromosome number 6 are associated with at least some cases of depressive disease. If and when this preliminary evidence is confirmed, it may enable very early detection of persons at risk, possibly even before birth (by analyzing the fetal chromosomes). It also may eventually enable molecular biologists to identify the substance(s) produced by the genes that is responsible for susceptibility.

Stress and Risk

In the late 1970s formal studies confirmed what had long been suspected—that people in particular life situations are more likely to develop mental illnesses. Among the groups so identified were individuals who had recently been divorced, individuals who were physically disabled, and elderly persons who live alone. By pinpointing such groups it is possible to take preventive measures as well as plan early intervention. For example, the establishment of community youth centers (some of them consisting of mobile vans) in poverty areas has made available such vital services as drug and alcohol programs conducted by former addicts, discussion groups for personal problems, job counseling, and the like to teenagers who otherwise would be unwilling or unable to seek out such services.

For individuals who have undergone some terrible experience, such as being taken hostage or abducted by terrorists, research indicates that various kinds of short-term crisis-oriented therapy begun as soon as possible after their ordeal can prevent the development of serious long-term emotional difficulties.

DEVELOPMENTS IN TREATMENT

During the past decade there has been increasing emphasis on briefer forms of treatment that address themselves more to specific problems than to changing a client's overall personality. Rather than taking a single doctrinaire approach to one or another form of therapy, clinicians have been increasingly inclined to borrow from various disciplines and adapt the treatment to the client. In some cases this has been an informal process (see the description of eclectic therapy at the end of Chapter 14), but in others there have been formal amalgamations of formerly separate schools, as, for example, with cognitive behavior therapy. No doubt this is in part a reflection of the current consensus regarding the causes of mental illness; that is, it results from a multitude of factors, including hereditary predisposition, childhood experiences, social environment, stress, and so on, rather than *only* from learned maladaptive behavior or *only* from unresolved inner conflict.

One promising development in psychotherapy involves the use of biofeedback to control symptoms, an area greatly aided by the development of more sophisticated technical equipment to monitor blood pressure and other physical phenomena affected by one's emotional state. Biofeedback has been useful in controlling migraine headache and high blood pressure, two physical conditions affected very much by mental states, as well as physical symptoms of acute anxiety.

One of the fastest-growing fields in psychotherapy in the past decade has been family therapy, today used by more than one million American families a year. An innovative form of family therapy developed by Dr. Mara Selvini Palazzoli and her colleagues at the Center for Family Studies in Milan, Italy, has come to be called *Milan-style therapy.* Although short in terms of sessions required— a total of ten, on the average—the course of therapy is extended over a long period, since sessions usually take place once a month. The format requires that two therapists sit in a room with the family while two more therapists observe from behind a one-way mirror in an adjacent room. After each hour-long session, the family wait while the four therapists meet alone to develop a prescription suitable for the family's problem. This prescription is then presented to the family; it usually involves a particular task or ritual to perform during the course of the next month. The focus of the task is frequently paradoxical, that is, the family's situation is described and they are urged not to change it, thus putting the family into a double bind: if they don't change they are obeying the therapists' very peculiar orders; if they wish to resist the therapists, they must change. In fact many of the families do change, regrouping in healthier ways. The theory underlying this seemingly odd technique is what Palazzoli calls *paradox.* The paradox, she maintains, is the unhealthy situation or repetitive pattern that may have trapped the family members in a situation that is bad but that is necessary for family cohesiveness (without it the family would fall apart). The therapists' interventions she calls *counterparadox.* Unlike many (if not most) modes of psychotherapy, this approach keeps the therapists strictly neutral toward all the family members—the relatively large number of four therapists prevents them from being drawn into the family's unhealthy situation and unwittingly perpetuating it—so no close, supportive relationship between therapist and client can develop.

Another growing trend has been the movement of mental health professionals into the community and cooperation among different disciplines, seen in a variety of ways. The team approach to mental health is most evident, perhaps, in the evaluation of a child suspected of learning disability, mental retardation, emotional disorder, or some combination of these. However, it operates in other spheres as well. One is the field of *liaison psychiatry,* in which mental health professionals work with medical and surgical specialists to help patients being treated for cancer, heart disease, and other serious medical problems. Another is the work of psychiatrists and psychologists with teachers, social workers, and police officers, in teaching these professionals from other disciplines to identify individuals at high risk for mental disorders and deal with them more effectively. Mental health professionals thus provide guidance for dealing with such situations as rape victims, domestic violence, and alcoholism, among others.

Sometimes mental health professionals teach others how to carry out psychotherapy. For example, several years ago one community mental health center set up a behavioral program for chronically disruptive junior high school students. Run by the school administrators and the teachers, who also enlisted the cooperation of the youngsters' parents, it involved the use of a token economy, in which students could earn early dismissal, extra recess time, and other rewards at school, as well as a system of home incentives offered by parents on the basis of good school reports. The results over a number of years were excellent, in terms of reducing both grade failures and disciplinary suspension and expulsions.

Some researchers are trying to test and compare the effectiveness of various psychotherapies. A critical question for any treatment is how many patients will get better by themselves, without treatment. (Unless more get better with treatment than without it, a treatment is probably useless.) One difficulty with testing any form of psychotherapy is the lack of uniformity of treatment. Because most forms of therapy involve two individuals talking together and there is no way to specify precisely what a therapist should say at any given time, it is virtually impossible to know whether method A practiced by Therapist Smith is the same as method A practiced by

Therapist Jones. Consequently the most practical approach to testing psychotherapies has been to take large groups of clients who are treated by many different therapists using various methods and record the outcomes of treatment, which, it is hoped, will yield at least an approximate idea of the effectiveness of therapy.

Still other areas of research include seeking body correlates of psychiatric disorders (for example, what body chemistry changes consistently occur with given disorders? can changes in brain waves, or perceptual habits, or liver functions, etc., be related to kinds of disorder, progress in therapy, the families of patients, etc. ?), and basic studies in behavior (how do emotions influence thoughts? how do thoughts influence emotions? why are some things important to some individuals and not to others, or at some times and not other times?).

Human behavior, the human brain, the human body, the human being in relation to the environment—all these are topics of a complexity that will probably never be wholly understood, at least not in the sense of enabling precise and accurate prediction of how people will feel and act. Nevertheless, the research currently underway in many different areas has already shown progress in improving prevention, diagnosis, and treatment of mental illnesses.

APPENDIX A

Useful Addresses and Phone Numbers

American Group Psychotherapy Association
1865 Broadway, 12th Floor
New York, NY 10023

American Psychiatric Association
1700 Eighteenth St., NW
Washington, DC 20009

American Psychological Association
1200 Seventeenth St., NW
Washington, DC 20036

Association for Advancement of Behavior Therapy
420 Lexington Ave.
New York, NY 10017

Canadian Mental Health Association
52 St. Clair Avenue East
Toronto, Ontario, Canada

Canadian Psychiatric Association
Suite 103, 225 Lisgar St.
Ottawa, Ontario K2P OC6, Canada

Canadian Psychological Association
Suite 46, 1390 Sherbrooke St., West
Montreal 109, Quebec, Canada

Family Service Association of America
44 East 23rd St.
New York, NY 10010

National Association for Mental Health
1800 North Kent St.
Arlington, VA 22209

National Association of Social Work
1425 H Street, NW, Suite 600
Washington, DC 20005

National Clearinghouse for Alcohol Information
(301) 468-2600

National Clearinghouse for Drug Abuse Information
(301) 443-6500

National Clearinghouse for Mental Health Information
(301) 443-4514

National Council of Community Mental Health Centers
2233 Wisconsin Ave., NW
Washington, DC 20007

National Register of Health Service Providers in Psychology
1200 Seventeenth St., NW
Washington, DC 20036

Public Citizens Health Research Group
Ralph Nader
2000 P St., NW
Washington, DC 20005

Veterans Administration Information Service
(202) 389-2443

FOR SPECIFIC PROBLEMS

Alcoholism
Al-Anon Family Groups
1 Park Ave. at 32nd St.
New York, NY 10016

Alcohol and Drug Problems Association of North America
1101 Fifteenth St., NW
Washington, DC 20005
(provides list of major state agencies for alcoholism)

Alcoholics Anonymous
P.O. Box 459
Grand Central Station
New York, NY 10017

National Council on Alcoholism
733 Third Ave.
New York, NY 10017
(lists nonprofit agencies in many cities making referrals to private physicians and public and private agencies that provide treatment)

Autism

National Society for Autistic Children
Suite 1017
1234 Massachusetts Ave., NW
Washington, DC 20005

Learning Disabilities

Association for Children with Learning Disabilities
4156 Library Rd.
Pittsburgh, PA 15234
(412) 341-1515

Self-Help Groups

National Self-Help Clearinghouse
Graduate Center of City University of New York
33 West 42nd St.
New York, NY 10036

Self-Help Institute
Center for Urban Affairs
Northwestern University
Evanston, IL 60201

Nursing Homes

American Association of Homes for the Aging
1050 17th St., NW, Suite 770
Washington, DC 20036
(nonprofit homes)

American Health Care Association
1200 15th St., NW
Washington, DC 20005
(proprietary homes)

Legal Questions

American Bar Association Commission on the Mentally Disabled
Washington, DC
(202) 331-2240

Mental Health Law Project
2021 L St., NW
Washington, DC 20036
(202) 467-5730

Child Abuse

Parents Anonymous
22330 Hawthorne Blvd., Suite 208
Torrance, CA 90505
(from outside California: 800-421-0353; in California: 800-352-0386)

INDEX

amitriptylene, 162
amniocentesis, 273
analysis, analyst. *See* psychoanalysis; psychoanalyst.
analytic psychotherapy. *See* insight therapy.
amobarbital, 162, 165
amphetamine, 25, 171, 318
Amytal, 162
anal stage, 115
analysand, 117
anesthesia, 141, 176
anger, 18
animal magnetism, 141
animal phobias, 24
anorexia nervosa, 3 (case), 40–41, 51
Antabuse, 169, 172
antialcoholism drugs, 169, 172–173
antianxiety drugs, 162, 164–165, 169
antibiotics, 32
anticonvulsants, 164, 165
antidepressants, 25, 31, 139, 161, 162, 166–168, 169, 318
antihistamine, 162, 165
antimanic drugs, 162, 168–170
antipsychotic drugs, 34, 38, 161, 163, 169, 170–171
    right to refuse, 306
antisocial behavior, in children, 52, 58 (*see also* juvenile delinquency)
antisocial personality disorder 2 (case), 46, 294, 310
anxiety, 21–25, 130, 136
    castration, 115
    chronic, 24
    free-floating, 24
    generalized, 24
    in children, 51
    recurrent, 23–24
    separation, 51, 55
    symptoms of, 22–23
    treatment of (*see also* antianxiety drugs), 25
anxiety attack, 11, 22–23, 168
anxiolytics. *See* antianxiety drugs.
appetite, changes in, 16, 28
Arlene H. (case), 61
arson, 52
Arthur S. (case), 17
artificial insemination, 273
art therapy, 82
assault, 11
assertiveness training, 131–132, 285

assessment. *See* evaluation; also, diagnosis.
Association for the Advancement of Behavior Therapy, 134, 330
Association for Children with Learning Disabilities, 59, 332
Association of Private Psychiatric Hospitals, 214
asylum (*see also* hospital, mental), 185–187
Atarax, 162, 165
Ativan, 162
attendant, 81
attentional deficit disorder, 57
audiotaping, in therapy, 154
auditory hallucinations, 34, 37
autism, 53–55, 134
autogenic training, 130
Aventyl, 162
aversive conditioning, 132
Azene, 162

BA (degree), 80
back pain, 31
barbiturates, 25, 162, 165
Bayley Scales of Infant Development, 64
Bazelon, David L., 299
Beck, Aaron T., 136
behavioral psychology, 134
behavioral therapy. *See* behavior therapy.
behavioral contracting, 133
behavior control, 133
behavior modification, 129
behavior rehearsal, 131
behavior therapy, 25, 78, 129–137, 269, 328
    and juvenile delinquency, 312
    and obesity, 42
    cognitive, 134–137
    cost of, 269
    for families, 153, 154
    in institutions, 133, 328
Bender Visual Motor Gestalt Test, 65
Bender Visual Retention Test, 65
Benzedrine, 171
benzodiazepine, 162, 164
Berne, Eric, 156
beta-adrenergic antagonist, 162
Betty A. (case), 2, 39
Bicêtre, 186
bilateral treatment (ECT), 177
bill of rights for mental patients, 304
Bini, Lucio, 176
Binswanger, Ludwig, 127
bioenergetic therapy, 142, 147, 268

family planning, 275
family sculpture, 154
family service agency, 71-72, 100-102
Family Service Association of America, 100, 331
family tasks, 153
family therapy, 102-103, 146, 151-156, 269, 275, 327-328
  communications, 153
  contraindications to, 156
  conjoint, 155
  cost of, 269
  experiential-existential, 153
  insight-awareness, 153
  multiple, 155
  multiple family group, 154
  multiple impact, 155
  strategic-behavioral, 153
  structural, 153
  systems, 153
fatigue (symptom), 16, 28, 29, 31, 52
fear (*see also* phobia), 18, 22, 23, 24
  in children, 56
fees. *See under* cost.
Feingold, Benjamin E., 181
feminist therapy, 144-145
fetal alcohol syndrome, 274
Fifth Amendment, 303
flattened affect, 27, 37
flight of ideas, 33
flooding, 131
fluphenazine, 163, 171
flurazepam, 162, 164
flurothyl, 175
foehn, 320
food/allergy, 180
foster care, 101
foster home, 220
Foundation for Sudden Infant Death, 286
Fountain House, 221
fragile X chromosome, 273
free association, 116, 119
free erythrocyte proptoporphyrin, 276
free-floating anxiety, 24
Freud, Sigmund, 38, 113-118, 141, 145, 156
Fromm, Erich, 123
frontal lobotomy, 183
Frostig Developmental Test of Visual Perception, 65
functional mental illness, 8
funding, community mental health centers, 98, 99

family service agencies, 102
self-help groups, 110

gambling, 19, 141
gastritis, 44
Gattell Infant Development Scale, 64
genetic counseling, 273, 324
genetics and mental illness. *See under* mental illness.
genital herpes, 274
geriatric psychiatrist, 49
German measles. *See* rubella.
gerontologist, 49
Gestalt therapy, 128-129, 147, 153, 268
Gheel, 220
ghetto, for mental patients, 287
Glasser, William, 125-126
goals of treatment, 223-228
grandfather clause, 76n
grand mal epilepsy, 175, 176
group encounter, 157-158
group home, 207, 219
group practice, 94
group shelter, 207
group therapy, 128, 132, 144, 147-159, 205
  candidates for, 148-150
  contraindications, 148-149
  cost of, 147, 268
  evaluating, 228-230
  for couples, 150
  insight, 150
  multiple family, 154
guardianship, 309-310
guidance center, 95
guidance counselor, 87
guided fantasy, 143, 154, 159-160
guilt, 16, 28

habit abuse (*see also* alcoholism; drug abuse), 141
hair-pulling, 51
Haldol, 163, 171
halfway house, 218
hallucinations, 35, 144, 161, 171
  auditory, 34, 37
  visual, 48
haloperidol, 163, 171
handicapped, education of, 86
hand-washing, 26
headache, 31, 52, 61-62
head-banging, 51
Head Start, 287
Health and Welfare Canada, 111

nerve cell. *See* neuron.
nervous breakdown, 7
network therapy, 154
neural surgery, 75
neurolepsy, 170
neuroleptics. *See* antipsychotic drugs.
neurologist, 75–76
neuron, 317–318
neurosis, 9, 28–29, 31
neurosurgeon, 75
neurotic disorder. *See* neurosis.
neurotransmitters, 166, 170, 317–19
New Haven-Boston Collaborative Depression Projects, 139
New York Psychoanalytic Institute, 105
night care, 215
nightmare, 52
night terrors, 51
nondirective therapy. *See* client-centered therapy.
nonprofit hospital, 200
nonprojective tests, 65
norepinephrine, 166, 168, 318
Norpramin, 162
nortriptylene, 162
nurse, psychiatric, 76, 80–81
  licensed practical, 80
  registered, 80
nursing home, 207–10, 270
nutritional therapy, 179–181

obesity, 41–42
obsession, 25
obsessive-compulsive disorder, 25–26, 134, 136–137
occupational therapist, 82
occupational therapy, 198
Oedipal conflict, 115–116
old age. *See under* elderly.
one-way mirror, 154
open staff, 199
operant conditioning, 130, 132–134, 198
oral contraceptive, 32
oral stage, 115
orderly, 81
organic mental illness (*see also under* brain) 8, 9, 47–49, 61–63, 182–183
organic therapy. *See* somatic therapy.
orgasm, 140
orgone therapy, 121–122, 142
orientation, test for, 66
orthomolecular psychiatry, 180

Oswald, Lee Harvey, 298
OT, OTR, 82
outpatient clinic. *See under* clinic.
overeating (*see also* obesity), 19, 51, 141
oxazepam, 162
oxygen, 176

pain relief, 141
Palazzoli, Mara Selvini, 327
palpitations, 22, 24, 31
Pamelor, 162
panic. *See* anxiety attack.
paradoxical prescription/intention, 153, 326
paranoia, 35, 36, 45, 136
parent (ego state), 156
parenting, 286, 291
parent-preschool program, 291
Parents Anonymous, 311, 333
Parents without Partners, 286
pargyline, 162
Parkinsonism, 318
Parkinsonism support group, 291
Parnate, 162
partial hospitalization, 97, 105, 216, 215–218, 258, 270
passive–aggressive personality disorder, 46
pastoral counselor, 87–89
patient representative, 195
patients' rights (*see also under* right), 194–195, 302, 303–304, 305
Pauling, Linus, 180
Pavlov, Ivan, 129
Peel, Robert, 298
peer review, 95
pemoline, 162, 171–172
penis envy, 116
pentobarbital, 162, 165
pentylenetetrazol, 175
peptides, 319
perception, tests for, 65
Perls, Frederick S. (Fritz), 128
perphenazine, 163
personality disorder, 10, 44–46
  antisocial 2 (case), 46
  paranoid, 45
  passive-aggressive, 45–46
  schizoid, 46
  schizotypal, 36
personality tests, projective, 64–65
personnel officer, 70
Pertofrane, 162
PET scan, 316